THE GOTHIC LINE

DOUGLAS ORGILL

The Gothic Line

The Italian Campaign, Autumn, 1944

W · W · NORTON & COMPANY · INC ·
New York

Copyright © 1967, by Douglas Orgill

Library of Congress Catalog Card No. 67–15816

PRINTED IN THE UNITED STATES OF AMERICA

1 2 3 4 5 6 7 8 9 0

To my Mother and Father

CONTENTS

ILLUSTRATIONS
(Imperial War Museum)

Between pages 114-115

MAPS

ACKNOWLEDGMENTS

I have been very greatly helped in writing this account by discussing the campaign with several of the British senior commanders who took part. They are, with their Gothic Line commands in brackets:

Lieutenant-General Sir Oliver Leese (Eighth Army)
Field-Marshal Lord Harding (Chief of Staff to General Alexander)
General Sir Charles Keightley (V Corps)
General Sir Sidney Kirkman (XIII Corps)
Field-Marshal Sir Richard Hull (1st Armoured Div.)
Major-General Arthur Holworthy (4th Indian Div.)
Major-General John Whitfield (56th Div.)
General Sir Richard Goodbody (2nd Armoured Brigade)
Brigadier Allen Block (139th Infantry Brigade)

It would not have been possible to write the book without the help extended by these officers, and I am very grateful to them. They provided me with a great deal of the background of the campaign, and where they are specifically quoted they are referred to in the reference section. The views expressed in this account, however, are my own, as is the responsibility for errors or omissions. In particular, the opinions about British armour given in Chapter Eight are my own, and were not discussed with Field-Marshal Hull.

More than 100 other former members of Fifth and Eighth Armies have given me help, supplying diaries, letters, private papers, maps, and personal reminiscences. My thanks are due to them all, but I should especially like to name Mr Herbert Ball, Mrs Margaret Carey (widow of Brigadier O. R. C. Carey), Mr Paul Carr, Lieut.-Col. A. de Chimay, Lieut.-Col. S. J. Linden Kelly, Major R. Mangles, Mr I. G. Mansell, Mr P. L. Neild, Lieut.-Col. A. Noble, Mr Stephen Owen, Major-General Sir Peter St Clair-Ford, Dr James Speer, Mr John Strudwick, Major D. S. Tee, Mr James Thomson, and Squadron Leader J. F. Wallace.

I should like to express my appreciation of the patient and courteous help extended by the librarians and staff of the Ministry of Defence Library, the Imperial War Museum, and the *Daily Express* Reference Library.

I am also grateful to the following authors and publishers for permission to quote from books in their copyright: Maj.-Gen. C. H. Beddington's *The Queen's Bays*; William Kimber and Co., Ltd., Kesselring's *Memoirs*; Longmans, Green and Co., Ltd., Wynford Vaughan-Thomas's *Anzio*; Cassell and Co., Ltd., Winston Churchill's *Second World War*, Vols. IV, V, and VI; Capt. B. H. Liddell Hart's *The Tanks*; Gen. Siegfried Westphal's *The German Army in the West*; Macdonald and Co., Ltd., General Frido von Senger's *Neither Fear Nor Hope*; Hamish Hamilton, Ltd., *The Goebbels Diaries* (ed. Louis Lochner); George G. Harrap, General Mark Clark's *Calculated Risk*; The Queen's Printer, Ottawa, Col. G. W. Nicholson's *The Canadians in Italy*; Her Majesty's Stationery Office, John Ehrman's *Grand Strategy*, Field-Marshal Alexander's *Dispatch*, and Eric Linklater's *The Campaign in Italy*.

Maps 4, 5, and 6 are based, by kind permission of Col. Chester G. Starr, upon those in his *From Salerno to the Alps*.

Finally, I want to thank my wife, who translated Italian material for me, and clambered willingly over the Gemmano and Coriano Ridges on a number of hot afternoons.

THE GOTHIC LINE

'Before we embark on major operations on the mainland of Europe, we must have a master plan and know how we propose to develop those operations. I have not been told of any master plan and I must therefore assume there was none.'

Field-Marshal Montgomery, diary
entry on landing in Italy, 5 Sept 1943.

I

The Battleground

Dividing the plain of Lombardy from the hill towns of Tuscany, the towering mass of the northern Apennines stretches diagonally across the upper part of the Italian peninsula, from northwest to south-east, until the mountains turn more truly south to become the backbone of Italy. In the north, however, they form an unbroken barrier, 140 miles long and 50 deep, from the Mediterranean almost to the Adriatic. The peaks are high, rising in some cases to 7,000 feet; the crest line of the northern Apennines is the highest in all the great Apennine system, though there are taller individual peaks farther south, in the Abruzzi.

At the Mediterranean end of this northern range, near the great naval base of La Spezia, the mountains reach nearly to the seashore. In the east, on the Adriatic, the edge of the Apennine barrier falls away in a line of ridges until it reaches Route 16, the coastal road which runs up the side of Italy to the seaside resort of Rimini, and thence north to Ravenna and Ferrara. Before the modern Autostrada del Sol was built, eleven principal roads twisted through the mountains, cut and blasted by the skill of Italian engineers through the rocky sides of valleys to link the centre of Italy with the industrial north.

At its lower levels, especially to the north of Florence where the foothills shade into the blue line of the mountains proper, the Apennine landscape is still idyllic, a world of cypresses and poplars, small villages, graceful bridges over clear streams, and castle-crowned hills which have changed little since Renaissance painters showed them through the windows behind fifteenth-century Madonnas. Higher in the mountains, however, there is a harder, harsher world, of bare stone and jagged razor-backed slopes, where the big stands of oak and chestnut thin out into scrub, and finally into nothing but rock. In the autumn, the mist and fog cling wetly round the dripping stone of these peaks; in the winter the snow lies in deep, undulating drifts; in the summer all is dry and arid. Few people other than goatherds live this high, except where an occasional huddle of cottages shows that peasants still manage to scratch a living from the flinty soil. This is not the golden world painted by Piero della Francesca, but the inhospitable, even grotesque, one of Cosimo Tura, where both men and rocks seem contorted in unending, meaningless battle.

It was in terms of battle that the mountain mass of the northern Apennines came under the scrutiny of the planners of the *Oberkommando der Wehrmacht* – the German Armed Forces High Command – in the summer of 1943. Nowhere in Italy, probably nowhere in Europe, was there a better position from which to defend the Reich, and it was with the defence of the Reich that the OKW planners were now concerned.

The year 1943 saw Hitler's strategic world contracting. It was no longer open to him to choose which great venture the Reich would undertake. Stretched beyond its limit of effectiveness, the German system was forced to wait to deal with each attack of its enemies as and where it was made. Hitler could not now dictate events; he could only respond to them.

On the other side of the Atlantic, American factories were turning out war material on an increasingly prodigious scale: in the Atlantic itself the U-boats had been forced by unacceptable losses to retreat. Stalingrad had lost the Führer one army, and at Kursk and Orel the Russian front was sucking up German divisions like blotting paper. In North Africa another great German army had laid down its arms, and Sicily was being seized by the Allies. Hitler knew, too, that his Axis partner Italy was near the end of her will to fight, and that from treachery, or incompetence, or both, the Italians might soon afford to the Allies a foothold on the Continent from which they had been driven in 1940. The invasion of Italy was near.

Nevertheless, when Mussolini was arrested on 25 July, and Badoglio took over the Italian Government, the Führer's vanity took a hard knock. Mussolini's régime, superficially at least, bore some resemblance to his own, and to see it fall into ruin was a deeply disturbing experience. Dr Joseph Goebbels, the shrewish little propaganda minister, noted Hitler's fury in his diary:

'The Führer regards the whole Italian problem as a gigantic example of swinishness. . . . The Italians simply don't want to fight, they are happy when they can lay down their arms and even happier if they can sell them.'[1]

Hitler had little faith in Badoglio's perfunctory protestations that Italy would continue to fight on Germany's side, and he saw at once that Italy's defection would open the back door of southern Europe to the Allies. He was never slow to react to a new situation, however. At the beginning of August German troops were moving south through the Brenner Pass, many of them without consultation with the Italian *Comando Supremo*. By the time Badoglio announced the Italian armistice early in September, there were sixteen German divisions in Italy. They were split between two field-marshals. Eight were in Army Group B in the north, under command of Field-Marshal Erwin Rommel, who had led Germany's defeated forces in North Africa. The remaining half, the Tenth Army (including one panzer grenadier division in Sardinia), were stationed near Rome or in the south. They were commanded by Field-Marshal Albert Kesselring, who had just completed the successful evacuation of the German units from Sicily.[2]

Hitler did not, at first, care much about central and southern Italy. His first appreciation of the situation calculated that these areas could not be held without the help of the Italian army.[3] But the valley of the River Po and the plain of Lombardy, with their sprawling complex of industrial and agricultural wealth, were a different matter. He could not yield these to his enemies – especially since with them went the use of air bases excellently situated for attacking the vital industrial centres of southern Germany.

The Führer made his thinking clear to his subordinates on 10 September, a few hours after the Italian surrender was announced to the world. Goebbels was summoned to Führer Headquarters at Rastenburg in East Prussia.

'It poured with rain . . . in keeping with this critical day,' he noted.[4] But his talk with Hitler made him more cheerful.

'The Führer believes that he will master this situation, albeit with some difficulty. Naturally, we shall not be able to hold southern Italy. We must withdraw northwards beyond Rome. *We shall now establish ourselves on the defence line that the Führer always envisaged; namely, the line of the Apennine mountains.* The Führer hopes we can withdraw and build up a first line of defence at that point. It would, of course, be a good thing if we could remain in Rome. But in Rome our flanks would be too long and too vulnerable. We would always be in danger there. Of course, if we permit the English and Americans to go into Italy as far as the Apennines, this will constitute a steady threat to the Balkans, for Italy is the best springboard for the south-east. . . .'[5]

Hitler's first intention was to hand over command of the Italian theatre of war to Rommel. Kesselring was to withdraw as best he could to the northern Apennines, where his forces would be absorbed into Rommel's. Rommel would make his stand there, where the ground was pre-eminently in his favour, and where his forces should be adequate to deal with any Allied attack. Kesselring, whose somewhat independent conduct of operations had always caused him to be regarded coolly by the OKW, was to be given a remoter command. Norway was suggested.[6]

Kesselring claimed after the war that the OKW – and Hitler himself – had privately written off the eight divisions in the south as being in a hopeless situation.[7] These German troops certainly had a formidable task ahead of them, since they had at the same time to disarm the defecting Italian troops all around them, fight off the advancing Allies, and make their way north. Their retreat, moreover, would be made especially difficult if the Allies made their expected parachute invasion of Rome, through which Kesselring's supply lines ran. It seems unlikely, however, that the OKW would readily have sacrificed eight good divisions, and, indeed, the Operations Staff War Diary for 8 September notes that 'the most urgent problem is to get Tenth Army and the Luftwaffe out of southern Italy'.[8]

As the autumn advanced, two considerations began to make

Hitler think again. Most important, he was worried about the Balkans, the danger of losing their oil, bauxite, and copper supplies to the Allies, and the threat that the Allies might be able to establish some line of communication with the Russians through the area. To yield southern Italy, he reasoned, would be to give the Allies a springboard for a Balkan invasion.[9]

The second consideration was Kesselring himself. Fighting brilliantly, and improving desperately, Kesselring began to confound those who thought he had little chance in the south. He did manage to disarm the co-operative Italians, and the Allies did not drop on Rome. The German troops, far from being trapped, were soon formed into a continuous front from the Mediterranean to the Adriatic.

Hitler's two commanders pulled him different ways. Rommel, now depressed and defensive-minded, warned him that to defend Italy south of the Apennines was to risk his armies being trapped by an Allied landing up the coast at their rear.[10] Kesselring disagreed. He wanted to fight at the narrowest point of the Italian peninsula, south of Rome. He believed that he could delay the Allies there for up to nine months. During that time, an impregnable defensive position could be constructed in the Apennines north of Florence.

Kesselring had two things in his favour with Hitler. First, he was an air force general, and a general in the uniform of the Luftwaffe was always more acceptable to the Führer than were some of the professional army officers whom he regarded with impatience and distrust. Second, Kesselring was by nature a hopeful, idealistic, and sanguine man. Nothing could have pleased Hitler more than this combination of qualities at this stage of the war.

For weeks, the Führer hesitated. At last, he chose Rommel, and the message giving the order was actually in transmission when he changed his mind again, and on 6 November gave the command to Kesselring.[11] A year later, in conversation with a group of senior officers, he revealed his reasoning:

'. . . I have been justified in my decision to leave Field-Marshal Kesselring down there (in Italy). I reckoned that politically he was an incredible idealist, but that militarily he was an optimist, and I don't believe you can be a military commander unless you're an optimist. Within certain limits I think Rommel is an extraordinarily brave and able commander. I don't regard him as a stayer. . . .'[12]

Hitler's decision meant that Kesselring became *Oberbefehl-shaber Südwest*, or Commander-in-Chief South-West, and his forces – the Tenth and Fourteenth Armies – were designated Army Group C. Rommel was withdrawn to the western front, to prepare for the expected Allied landing in north-west Europe.

The cancellation of the Rommel telegram by Hitler changed the course of the war. Italy now entered upon what Churchill called 'the most tragic period of her history'. Both Germany and the Allies were committed to an arduous and bloody campaign for eighteen months over difficult terrain, often in appalling climatic conditions. Ninety thousand men of the Allied forces would find their graves on the Italian peninsula, and 110,000 Germans would lie beside them.

* * *

For the Allies, the Italian campaign opened in an atmosphere strangely compounded of hope, suspicion, and doubt. The reasons for this were buried deep in the history and traditions of Britain and the United States, and in the personalities and training of their leaders. The Allied dispute over the Italian campaign has provided the most significant strategic argument of the war.

To Winston Churchill and Britain's military leaders, the North African victory of 1943 and the Allied success in Sicily offered glittering opportunities to destroy Hitler by hitting at him in southern Europe, where he would be forced to dissipate his strength in order to guard against the many strategic options available to an enemy who commanded both the sea and the air.

After the battle of Alamein, in a memorandum dated 25 November 1942, Churchill had written:

'The paramount task before us is, first, to conquer the African shores of the Mediterranean and there set up the naval and air installations which are necessary to open an effective passage through it for military traffic; and, secondly, using the bases on the African shore, to strike at the under-belly of the Axis in effective strength and in the shortest time.'[13]

The American Chiefs of Staff, led by the formidable General George Marshall, differed from this view. Marshall had been brought up in a military tradition which was intensely suspicious of British imperialism; he was not interested when, as he thought, Churchill and his generals seemed to be trying to use United States soldiers and equipment to further British designs in the Mediterranean, an area of which he had little military understanding, and which held no strategic interest for him.

Marshall was not a mean or petty man; he had already demonstrated a far-sighted generosity after the fall of Tobruk, when he took the first three hundred new Sherman tanks from American armoured divisions and sent them at once round Africa to fight under British crews in the desert.

The British Chief of the Imperial General Staff, General Sir Alan Brooke, hit near to the truth when he confided to his diary in early 1943:

'Marshall's thoughts revolve round the creation of forces, and not on their employment.'[14]

He had raised, trained, and equipped the greatest field army in the history of the United States; he had assigned a great proportion of it to the European theatre in loyal support of Roosevelt's pledge to destroy Hitler's Germany before turning with full strength upon Japan; and now he wished to use those troops, with his Allies, in the one operation which seemed to him to be a clear, forceful, uncomplicated blow to Germany's heart . . . Operation Overlord, the great Channel crossing into France. He had served under Pershing in the First World War, and his experiences had convinced him of the rightness of concentrating all efforts on a Western Front. He had, too, a characteristic American belief in a massive confrontation with the enemy; the operations which Churchill supported, biting and stinging round the periphery of Hitler's ramshackle empire in the Dodecanese, the Balkans, and Italy, seemed to him to be a foolish dispersal of strength. Finally, he was an American and not a British general, and the war with Japan occupied a much larger proportion of his mind than it did of Sir Alan Brooke's. In common with many other American commanders, he wanted to clear up the war in Europe in what seemed to him the quickest way, so that he could turn the full attention of the United States to Japan.

His most powerful supporter and admirer was Henry Stimson, the old and dour Secretary for War, who ceaselessly struggled to guard his President from the insidious siren song that Churchill sang.

'The water barrier of the Channel under the support of Britain-based air power is far easier than either the Mediterranean or the Atlantic,' he warned Roosevelt as early as June 1942. 'The subsequent overland route into Germany is easier than any alternate. Over the Low Countries has run the historic path of armies between Germany and France.'[15]

By August 1943, his distrust of British evasiveness had grown. At the Quebec Conference, he wrote to the President:

'We cannot now rationally hope to be able to cross the Channel and come to grips with our German army under a British commander. His Prime Minister and his Chief of the Imperial Staff are frankly at variance with such a proposal. The shadows of Passchendaele and Dunkirk still hang too heavily over the imagination of these leaders of his Government . . . their hearts are not in it. . . .'[16]

Throughout 1943 the dispute went on, coming to the surface at any conference where future operations were discussed. Much of the time the British got their way – the cross-Channel operation was pushed back to spring 1943, then to autumn, then to the following spring. Meanwhile the Mediterranean campaign, in spite of initial over-optimism as to the speed with which it could successfully be fought, burst into full strategic flower.

In 1942 came the invasion of North Africa, followed next year by the conquest of Sicily. Sicily seemed to lead inevitably to the invasion of Italy. The American Admiral Ernest King noted that in spite of British assurances that the Mediterranean operations would be limited, 'they nevertheless as time went on and succeeding conferences took place, continued to press more and more for operations in the Mediterranean and to oppose final and firm commitments for the cross-Channel operation.'[17]

The invasion of Italy went ahead, more because it seemed the best way to knock Mussolini out of the war than for any more distant strategic object. But the American Chiefs of Staff, like their country, were now mobilizing their strength, and just as the preponderance of war effort began now to be America's, so did the preponderance of strategic choice. Thousands of American soldiers were to fight and die in the Italian campaign, but from the moment of its inception the American planners saw it as a sideshow, little more than a holding operation.

The rights and wrongs of this strategic argument will not be discussed here, in the history of one part of the Italian campaign. But the argument itself, and the way it was resolved, vitally affected each of the separate stages of the war in Italy, and most of all the stage that was fought in the autumn of 1944 – the Battle of the Gothic Line.

For it was the Gothic Line that waited for the Allies at the end of their long and bloody climb up the Italian peninsula.

'The defence line the Führer always envisaged . . . the line of the Apennine mountains,' Goebbels had noted in his diary after that wet autumn morning in 1943. It was not, at that time, called the Gothic Line, receiving that romantic name much later, when Hitler was trying to impress on his soldiers its importance as a door into the Nazis' Fortress Europe.

In September 1943 the Gothic Line lay a year ahead. Yet the uncertainty in which the battle for it was to be fought, and the lack of any clear conviction as to why it should be fought, had cast their shadows ahead.

On 3 September, General Sir Bernard Montgomery, commander of the Eighth Army and victor of Alamein, wrote to Sir Alan Brooke:

'I attacked across the Straits of Messina this morning at 0430 hours. And at 1030 hours I stepped ashore myself on the mainland of Europe just north of Reggio. It was a great thrill once more to set foot on the continent from which we were pushed off three years ago at Dunkirk. It is a great day.'[18]

To his diary he was less optimistic. He had made his usual clear-headed appreciation, and he knew there should be a master-plan for the Italian campaign. But he had been told of no plan, and therefore there was none.[19] Montgomery had, in fact, already seen the flaw in Allied thinking which, in almost exactly one year's time, was to cost the Allies thousands of lives in exchange for a few muddy miles of the Apennine mountains.

2
The Contestants

In August 1944 the Allies stood before the Gothic Line. Since Montgomery entered his doubts in his diary at Reggio, Allied troops had advanced nearly 500 miles up the Italian peninsula, and were confronted now with the last great military obstacle between them and the Alps.

It had been, on the whole, a bitter year – a year of blood and disappointment, lightened only by the triumph of the fall of Rome. The hopes of 1943 had withered in the face of the fighting on the Sangro, the stalemate at Cassino and Anzio, and Kesselring's success in extricating his battered armies from their retreat north of Rome safely behind the line of the Apennines.

A year ago it had seemed simpler. In a war paper dated 17 August 1943, Churchill wrote:

'If by November our front can be established as far north as the Leghorn-Ancona line, the landing craft in the Mediterranean will have played their part. . . . Although I have frequently spoken of the line of the Po or of the Alps as being desirable objectives for us this year in Italy, it is not possible to see so far at present. A very great advantage will have been gained if we stop at the Leghorn-Ancona line. . . .'[1]

But in spite of optimism in London, Ancona did not fall until 18 July of the following year, and Leghorn on 19 July. Slogging up the calf of Italy, the Allied troops broke their way through line after line of defences, crossed mountain after mountain and river after river, to find waiting north of Florence the same German armies who had defied them for so long. These armies had been severely manhandled during their long retreat, but they had never been broken, either in spirit or material, and they were now esconced in what German propaganda confidently proclaimed to be the strongest line of all.

Only once, at Anzio, had the Allies held in their hand the strategic ace which would have beaten Kesselring. But ineptitude and delay in breaking out of their beach-head had destroyed that chance, and the card was not one which could be played again. There would be no more large-scale landings in Italy, because the American Chiefs of Staff controlled the landing craft, and, as will be seen, they had other uses for them. In August 1944 Kesselring could look south from the Apennines in reasonable confidence, and with satisfaction in a job well done. The Allied frustration was due to him, and to the remarkable fighting qualities of the German soldiers in Italy.

Kesselring had fought one of the best defensive campaigns of any German commander during the war, and, from the point of view of a soldier who might wish to win the accolade of history, it was his misfortune that he fought it on a secondary front.

In 1944 he was fifty-eight. He came from a good Bavarian middle-class background, his family being farmers and brewers. He entered the German Army in 1904.

'I wanted to be a soldier,' he wrote later, 'indeed, I was set on it, and looking back I can say that I was always a soldier heart and soul.'[2]

The young Kesselring served on the Western Front for two years and then joined the General Staff. During the 1930's he was transferred to the Luftwaffe, and became Chief of Air Staff under Goering. In 1940 he became a Field-Marshal, commanding German arms in the battles for Britain, Malta, and now Italy. By 1944, indeed, he was used to retreat and defeat. But as we have seen, he was a man of cheerful and optimistic temperament. Defeat, which destroyed Rommel, was a spur to Kesselring.

To anyone studying the Italian campaign, Kesselring's outstanding qualities were the strong will-power with which he managed to rally his staff and his armies at successive desperate moments, and the swiftness of reaction and adaptability with which he greeted an unexpected threat. Mixed with this, however, was a curious sentimentality, amounting at times to a refusal to face unpalatable facts. He was, for instance, a passionate Italophile, who in the face of repeated warnings from his superiors, and also of mounting personal evidence, refused to believe in the possibility of Italian defection from the Axis until it actually happened.[3]

Even during the campaign his affection for Italy led him to decisions which appear strangely uncharacteristic of the conventional image of a German general. During the retreat north of Rome, German troops complained that they were put to risk and difficulty because of the Field-Marshal's insistence that the city must be spared from damage, and the bridges over the Tiber were not blown because of their historical value, and because they carried pipes and cables vital to the city's life.[4]

This capacity for seeing the world through rose-coloured spectacles served Kesselring well in Italy, where a glance over his shoulder at the reeling Reich behind him might have daunted a more realistic mind. But it raises doubts about whether he can really be considered among the great commanders. On other fronts, at other times, optimism of Kesselring's kind might well have led to disaster.

If Kesselring did not conform to the expected blueprint of a German general, the man who faced him on the other side of the hill was certainly all that a British general would wish to be. General Sir Harold Alexander was fifty-two years old. He had impeccable family connections by birth and marriage – he was the son of one earl, married to the daughter of another. Harrow and Sandhurst lay behind him, together with a brilliant fighting record in the First World War, where he won the Distinguished Service Order and the Military Cross, was mentioned in dispatches five times, and wounded three.

In 1943, he had been Montgomery's superior during the victories in North Africa. He was brave, handsome, charming, highly-intelligent and widely-read. No one could possibly have been more acceptable to the British military establishment. He had caught the eye of Sir Alan Brooke when he commanded the 1st Division in Brooke's corps during the retreat to Dunkirk.

'What an admirable commander he was in a tight place,' Brooke said of him later, '. . . completely composed and appeared never to have the slightest doubt that everything would come right in the end.'[5]

He was liked, too, by the Americans. 'If the British would give him to me, I would like to have Alexander,' wrote Eisenhower to Marshall, asking for a commander of the British forces for the cross-Channel invasion.[6] The choice eventually fell on Montgomery, but Churchill still expected great things of Alexander. He described him in dazzling words:

'Nothing ever disturbed or rattled him, and duty was a full satisfaction in itself, especially if it seemed perilous and hard. But all this was combined with so gay and easy a manner that the pleasure and honour of his friendship were prized by all those who enjoyed it, among whom I could count myself. . . .'[7]

Few British generals have been as well-liked by their troops. To British soldiers, with their knack of summing up the salient points of personality of a commander, Kesselring was known as 'Smiling Albert'. But from the C.I.G.S. to the private in a slit trench, Alexander was always 'Alex'.

However, Alexander's charm, like Kesselring's optimism, was his strength at one end of the scale and his weakness at the other. It helped him to run the polyglot armies which he commanded in Italy with a success that probably no other Allied commander could have achieved. But it could also infect him with a disconcerting diffidence about getting his own way, even when convinced that he was right.

At Anzio, when the American commander General Lucas dallied laboriously inside his beachhead instead of striking out beyond it, Alexander knew clearly what should be done. When Churchill asked angry questions from London about why Lucas was so slow, General Sir Henry Maitland Wilson, Supreme Commander Mediterranean, replied on Alexander's behalf that 'there was no lack of urging from above, and . . . both Alexander and Clark went to the beachhead during the first forty-eight hours to hasten the offensive.'

Churchill's comment was tart.

'Senior commanders,' he said, 'should not "urge" but "order".'[8]

In August 1944, Alexander commanded the Allied Armies in Italy, which were made up of the British Eighth Army and the United States Fifth Army. Neither army, however, was correctly described under its national name. The Fifth, though predominantly American, included at this time a British corps and a Brazilian expeditionary force, while the Eighth, in addition to its British and Indian divisions, included a Greek brigade, a Canadian corps, a Polish corps, an Italian brigade, and a New Zealand division.[9]

Two decades of military interdependence in Europe have made the idea of an army of mixed nationalities on this scale relatively commonplace, but in 1944 it seemed like a vast experiment taking place under the guns of the enemy. After the war Alexander listed twenty-six nationalities who had served, more or less simultaneously, under his command in the Italian peninsula.[10] This vast body of men, eating different food, worshipping in different ways, speaking different languages, had to be forged into a weapon with which the Allies could strike some of the finest divisions in the German Army, waiting in positions which they had planned and prepared for months.

Alexander's two army commanders were men of a vastly different kind. The Eighth Army was led by Lieutenant-General Sir Oliver Leese, a big, good-humoured careful soldier who had won a D.S.O. in France in 1916. He had caught Montgomery's eye early in the war, and had left the command of the Guards Armoured Division at Montgomery's request to take over XXX Corps just before Alamein.

'I never regretted that choice,' Montgomery wrote afterwards. 'He was quite first class at Alamein and all through the campaign to Tunis, and later in Sicily.'[11]

Tall and deceptively languid, Leese had a studied casual approach. No one talked shop during the evening meal at his headquarters: 'I never could have lived with a lot of serious-minded brigadiers and major-generals,' he said. Behind this façade, however, he was a thorough and capable commander, always careful of the lives of his men. He believed, he said, that 'a general who has a lot of casualties is an inartistic general'.[12]

If Leese was in many ways a typical Englishman as seen through foreign, and especially American, eyes, his opposite number in Fifth Army was equally an Englishman's idea of an American.

General Mark Clark, like Leese, had served in the First World War. In 1942 he was a colonel. Two years later he was commanding an army, and he was still in a hurry. Tall and thin, with a narrow, intelligent face, Clark was not a man who would allow himself to be sold short by any superior on either side of the Atlantic. He believed in publicity and he had a knack of getting it. But he had other qualities, too. 'His planning, training, and organizing ability,' said Eisenhower, 'I have not seen excelled in any other officer.'

To British eyes, there was always something of a larger-than-life, Hollywood quality about Clark. His relations with his British colleagues were not always cordial, and to be assigned to Fifth Army was not a popular move for some British generals. With Alexander, Clark maintained a rather prickly friendliness, but one feels that Alexander's considerable abilities in handling men accounted for a good deal of the success of this relationship.

Other British generals found him less compatible. No doubt there were faults on both sides; the patient air of superior experience which emanated from some British commanders could be very galling to an American general. These failures of relationship were natural enough in an army group made up mainly of British and American troops, but they were more important than just a subject for headquarters gossip. Military politics, as well as strict military considerations, would decide the shape of the campaign for the Gothic Line.

The Allied troops themselves had recovered well from the slump in their status caused by the battle in France and the Low Countries. Six months before, they had been the only Allied troops fighting on the Continent of Europe, earning the headlines and the praise. Now, suddenly, they were a subsidiary front, far, apparently, from where the decisive battle was being fought. Even the capture of Rome in June had been obliterated in the public memory within forty-eight hours by the drama of the D–Day invasion.

There was, however, surprisingly little bitterness, and a good deal of wry humour. The troops called themselves the 'D-Day Dodgers', basing this on a remark said to have been made by a lady Member of Parliament, though this was swiftly denied by the lady herself in the Eighth Army newspaper. Jon, the Eighth Army cartoonist, published a cartoon showing his famous Two Types, complete with luxuriant moustaches and

neck-scarves, gazing puzzledly at each other and asking:
'Which D-Day do you think they mean?'

A little song caught on, and began to be heard everywhere.
Sung to the tune of Lili Marlene, each ribald verse ended with
the refrain:

> 'We are the D-Day Dodgers,
> In Sunny Italy.'

With the same sort of pride with which the Old Contemp-
tibles of the First World War had seized on another apocryphal
remark, the veteran troops in Italy began to take a perverse
satisfaction in being overlooked.

For the enemy, they had the soldier's usual wary respect.
They called the Germans 'the Teds' – an expression derived
from *tedesco*, the Italian word for German. Sometimes, half-
affectionately, the German soldier became 'Old Ted'.

★ ★ ★

It was not just in the headlines of the British and American
newspapers that the status of the Allied Armies in Italy had
slumped. Churchill and Alexander dreamed of a landing at the
head of the Adriatic to threaten the German flank and rear, and
an advance through the Ljubljana Gap in the mountains of
northern Yugoslavia to Vienna and the plains of Hungary.
But now came the full harvest of American distrust of British
motives in the Italian campaign, and of the lack of geographical
objectives with which the campaign had begun.

The blow did not fall at once. As late as 13 June, the Combined Chiefs of Staff sent Wilson a vaguely worded directive
which told him:

'When we have reached the Pisa-Rimini line,* three possible
courses of action will be open to us:

(*a*) an amphibious operation against the south of France,

(*b*) an amphibious operation against the west of France,

(*c*) an amphibious operation against the head of the
Adriatic.[13]

* The earlier name for the Gothic Line.

The directive went on to say that no final choice between these three operations could yet be made. But in fact the Americans had already chosen. They meant to have the invasion of the south of France, then code-named Anvil, later changed to Dragoon. On 17 June, Marshall went to the Mediterranean to discuss the future with the Allied commanders, and found that Wilson, the Supreme Commander, now favoured the Adriatic operation. At once Marshall's suspicions of Britain's 'Balkan' policy flared again. He pointed firmly to France as the decisive front, insisting that the forty or fifty divisions now waiting in America to sail to Europe must have the ports in the south of France for their unloading.[14]

Six days later came the *coup de grâce*. Eisenhower told the Combined Chiefs of Staff that he wanted Anvil to be undertaken, even at the expense of the Allied Armies in Italy.

'In my view,' he warned, 'the resources of Great Britain and the United States will not permit us to maintain two major theatres in the European war, each with decisive missions.'

This was the end, though a final effort to make the Italian campaign meaningful came from the British. The British Chiefs of Staff warned that the mounting of Anvil on a scale large enough for success would so hamstring Alexander's forces that 'any further activity would be limited to something very modest.'[15]

On 28 June, Churchill cabled to Roosevelt a last, almost desperate appeal. He said:

'The deadlock between our Chiefs of Staff raises most serious issues. Our first wish is to help General Eisenhower in the most speedy and effective manner. But we do not think this necessarily involves the complete ruin of all our great affairs in the Mediterranean and we take it hard that this should be demanded of us. . . . I most earnestly beg you to examine this matter in detail for yourself.'

Roosevelt's reply was uncompromising:

'My interest and hopes centre on defeating the Germans in front of Eisenhower and driving on into Germany, rather than limiting this action for the purposes of staging a full major effort in Italy. I am convinced that we will have sufficient forces in Italy, with Anvil forces withdrawn, to chase Kesselring north of Pisa-Rimini, and maintain heavy pressure against his army at the very least to the extent necessary to contain his present force. I cannot conceive of the Germans paying the price of ten additional divisions, estimated by General Wilson, in order to keep us out of northern Italy.

'We can – and Wilson confirms this – immediately withdraw five divisions (three United States and two French) from Italy for Anvil. The remaining twenty-one divisions, plus numerous separate brigades, will certainly provide Alexander with adequate ground superiority. With our air superiority there is obviously sufficient air in the Mediterranean to furnish support both for operations in Italy and for Anvil, and to provide overwhelming air support during the critical moments of either operation. . . . I cannot agree to the employment of United States troops against Istria and into the Balkans, nor can I see the French agreeing to such use of French troops. . . . Since the agreement was made at Teheran to mount Anvil, I cannot accept, without consultation with Stalin, any course of action which abandons this operation. . . . Finally, for purely political considerations over here, I should never survive even a slight setback in Overlord if it were known that fairly large forces had been diverted to the Balkans.'[16]

Later Churchill commented, perhaps somewhat disingenuously, that 'no one involved in these discussions had ever thought of moving armies into the Balkans, but Istria and Trieste were strategic and political positions which . . . might exercise profound and widespread reactions, especially after the Russian advances'.[17]

However, the dream was over. There was a dying flurry of cables, but by 8 August Churchill told the President resignedly:

'I pray God you may be right. We shall of course do everything in our power to help you achieve success.'

The effect of these decisions on the post-war face of Europe, and the free hand which the Allies thus gave to the Russians in central Europe, has been exhaustively argued since the war. But in 1944 the future after victory was still far away. What the Allies were taking was basically a military decision – and as a military decision the mounting of Anvil was to have a profound effect upon the Gothic Line campaign.

At first sight, it seemed to render it virtually meaningless. The British Chiefs of Staff had already received a sombre warning from Alexander, who told them on 28 June:

'The ghost of Anvil hangs heavily over the battlefront. For example the Americans have been ordered to send back 517 Regimental Combat Team* and 117 Cavalry Reconnaissance Squadron, which are actually engaged in contact with the enemy. They are also required to release now an engineer regiment and other service units required for the conduct of the battle. . . . Eighth Army are not directly concerned with Anvil but as long as there is doubt and uncertainty about the future, so long will there be a moral weakening. Armies have a very delicate sense and they are beginning to look over their shoulders. . . .'[18]

Operation Anvil began now to eat into Alexander's forces in a way which Kesselring had never achieved. He lost four French and three United States divisions, considerably more than Roosevelt had estimated to Churchill. The French troops included the mountain warfare units who would have been invaluable in the storming of the Gothic Line. Between June and August the strength of Fifth Army fell from 249,000 to 153,000 men.[19] Alexander was told, too, that his air strength would be sharply reduced – probably by about 70 per cent.

The reactions of the American Chiefs of Staff to these reductions in the striking force in Italy were curiously sanguine. Marshall, indeed, who seemed to understand little of Hitler's almost pathological dislike of giving up a yard of ground, had already aired a strange theory that Alexander might find his forces 'beating at the air' if Kesselring retired quickly behind the Alps.[20] In fact, although a great United States army was still engaged there, the American commanders had decided that what happened now in Italy mattered little.

On the British side there was still hope, though it was muted. It became clear that Alexander was not content to sit south of the Gothic Line until the war was won. At the end of June he told Wilson that although his forces were reduced and unbalanced, he still felt that an advance into north-eastern Italy was possible and should be attempted.

* Roughly equivalent to a British brigade.

His problem was formidable. He estimated Kesselring's strength at the beginning of July as equal to about fourteen full-strength divisions, with likely reinforcements bringing it up to between eighteen and twenty-one divisions. The Allied armies now totalled fourteen infantry and four armoured divisions, with seven independent armoured brigades.

'For a successful assault on the Gothic Line,' he reported later, 'carried to the Po, a total of eighteen divisions would be required, of which not more than two or three should be armoured; to follow this up as far as the Piave again required eighteen divisions, and to force the Piave and exploit to the Ljubljana Gap also eighteen divisions. It would obviously be impossible, although the Allied strength just equalled eighteen divisions, to use the same divisions for all these assaults, even if the roles of offence and defence were rotated; a reserve of at least a third, or six additional divisions, would be required.'[21]

Yet though his troops were too thin on the ground for comfort, Alexander always held in his hand in Italy the card which, even if it could not give him certain victory, was enough to protect him against anything more than a local, tactical reverse. The card was air power. The Allied Air Forces ruled the Italian skies so completely that British and American soldiers could serve for months in the peninsula without ever seeing or hearing a Luftwaffe plane. For the Germans, on the other hand, constant interdiction of their activities by enemy air action became part of daily life. A war correspondent who flew with the Allied Air Forces remembered later:

'Nothing was more striking, to anyone who flew on a daylight sortie in Italy, than the complete contrast between the two sides of the front line. As your aircraft flew north to bomb, you could look down on a busy countryside. Great columns of lorries moved on the roads, traffic jams formed on the outskirts of the towns, and jeeps raced everywhere, even on the narrow tracks in the mountains.

'You crossed the line of smoke that always marked the front line and looked down on another world. On the German side the roads were deserted, the railway lines empty. Nothing moved in a dead and lonely landscape. The shadow of air power lay over it all.'[22]

The Germans, however, had learned to make limited but effective movements inside the straitjacket which the Allied bombers imposed upon them. They became adept at making large-scale troops movements by night, and their camouflage experts were masters of deception. In Italy pilots would sometimes return triumphantly with air photographs of shattered bridges over important rivers. There, crumpled in the middle of the stream, would be the wreckage of the centre span, and subsequent photographs would show that the bridge remained broken for weeks. Yet within a night or two, German troops would be crossing that river by bridge, because German engineers had constructed a pontoon near by which was moored to the bank by day, camouflaged to look like part of the river's edge, and only swung across under the cover of night. Thus in defence, at least, the German command was able to do something to offset its disadvantage; but Kesselring was well aware that his lack of air power made a counter-offensive against the Allies unthinkable. 'Ground once lost,' he said later, 'could never be regained.'[23]

Secure, then, in the air, but stretched to his limit on the ground, Alexander now began to comb both Allied and ex-enemy sources for troops. First, however, on 5 July came a directive from Allied Force Headquarters in Algiers. After warning Alexander that Anvil now took priority, and that he was to make sure that the troops which Anvil needed were ready in the right place at the right time, it defined his task as:

(1) To advance over the Apennines and to close to the line of the River Po, securing the area Ravenna–Bologna–Modena to the coast north of Leghorn, and if possible to seize the road centre of Piacenza.

(2) Subsequently to cross the Po to the line Venice–Padua–Verona–Brescia.

(3) He would receive further instructions after reaching this second line.[24]

So far from operations being limited to something 'modest' as the British Chiefs of Staff had so recently envisaged, it now seemed that what was proposed was little, if at all, short of what Alexander might have hoped to achieve in Italy *before* he lost the seven vital divisions.

In his dispatch, he dryly described the 5 July directive as 'somewhat optimistic'. Yet in spite of his previous warnings, he accepted it. The vagueness of the third paragraph still held out, though distantly, the hope of the Ljubljana Gap and the plains of Hungary. A great success might still be achieved. All at once, the atmosphere at Allied Headquarters turned from gloom to hope.

The acceptance of the challenge was in its way admirable. The next few weeks would also prove it to be over-sanguine. The battle of the Gothic Line was no longer a military operation planned for, progressively insured against, and ruthlessly executed. It was now a hopeful venture. In many ways this suited Alexander's gay, cool, imperturbable temperament. But it was a battle which Field-Marshal Montgomery would never have fought.

3
The Plans

The name of the Gothic Line was first revealed to Allied Intelligence on a map captured at Kesselring's former headquarters at Monte Soratte, north of Rome.[1] The Apennine position had been called this since April 1944, though on 16 June it was renamed 'the Green Line' by the Germans. In subsequent Allied appreciations and accounts, it continued to be called 'the Gothic Line', and this practice will be followed here.

In spite of the pressing demands of the Allied invasion of northern France, the Italian front received a good deal of attention from the OKW during June. On 7 June, the day after the D-Day landing in Normandy, the deputy chief of the OKW Operations Staff, General Walter Warlimont, set out for Italy to look at the situation for himself.

'Even before I left,' he said later, 'I had been convinced that in the existing situation it was more necessary than ever to turn the naturally strong Apennines position into the main defensive line in the Italian theatre, and that only an eventual withdrawal to this prepared position would allow us to free forces from Italy for the west.'

His visit reinforced these conclusions, and after a three-day tour through the northern Apennines he reported as much to the Operations Chief, Colonel-General Alfred Jodl.* Jodl, however, was better acquainted with the atmosphere at Führer Headquarters, and with the mood that Hitler was in.

'I can only advise you most emphatically,' he told Warlimont on the telephone, 'to be most careful when you get back here and make your report.'[2]

* Hanged at Nuremberg, 16 October 1946.

Hitler, in fact, did not now wish to hear anything about a quick withdrawal to the Gothic Line. His thinking was its usual mixture of realistic military assessments and grandiose dreams. He was under no illusion that victory in the conventional military sense was any longer a possibility for Germany. He hoped however to stave off defeat until the V-weapons then being used on England would make the Allies re-appraise their policy of unconditional surrender. He dreamed also, fantastically in the circumstances of 1944, of a great clash between Russia and the Western Allies, so that the latter might at least stand aside while he defeated Bolshevism. Every retreat by his troops seemed to him to bring Germany's defeat nearer, and to push his dream farther away. Running through all his thinking was his characteristic doom-laden Wagnerian sense of history.

'If the German people cannot win the war,' he told Rommel in 1943, 'then they can rot.' But first they would fight to the end – for every house, every hill, every position. It was an historical necessity, said the Führer, for a great people to die heroically.[3]

By June 1944, Hitler's unwillingness to yield a yard of ground to his enemies had become obsessive. When Warlimont, in spite of Jodl's advice, tried to put his case at a briefing conference, he was ignored. Hitler waved away Warlimont's maps and tables without a glance at them, saying that it was obvious that it would be at least seven months before the Gothic Line was ready.

A peremptory order, of a kind ominously familiar to other German generals on other fronts, arrived at Kesselring's headquarters. The retreat was to stop. The defensive was to be resumed and stabilised on an unyielding line, 'at least on the latitude of Lake Trasimene', *south* of Florence and the shelter of the northern Apennines. Meanwhile, the name of the Gothic Line was changed to Green Line – presumably to disabuse the German troops of any notion that it represented some sort of romantic fortress into which they could safely withdraw.

Kesselring was an optimist, but he was not a sycophant. He was a Hitler man all the way, and he did not often question the Führer's *strategic* judgement. But when it was a question of handling his two armies, Kesselring knew who knew best, and also who knew most. On 3 July, accompanied by his operations chief, Colonel Dietrich Beelitz, he flew to Führer Headquarters, then situated at Hitler's Bavarian mountain home at the Obersalzberg. A German officer who visited the Obersalzberg a few weeks before Kesselring arrived has described Hitler at this desperate point of his career:

'He wore a yellow military blouse with a yellow tie, white collar, and black trousers. . . . His complexion was sickly, colourless and flabby. His large blue eyes, which evidently fascinated many people, were watery, possibly due to his constant use of stimulating drugs. His handshake was soft, his left arm hung limp and trembling by his side. Yet a striking feature, contrasting with his notorious screaming during speeches or fits of rage, was the quiet and modulated voice that almost inspired compassion since it barely concealed his despondency and weakness.'[4]

Kesselring and Beelitz listened while Hitler lectured them for nearly an hour on the need to halt the retreat. 'The only area which offers protection against the enemy's superiority and restricts his freedom of movement,' the Führer told them, 'is the lower gut of Italy.'

Noting this approvingly in his diary, Jodl – who was present at the conference – added:

'A graphic description of the situation by the Führer, and insistence on the necessity of fighting for every square mile of ground and every week of time.'[5]

When Hitler had finished, Kesselring spoke. His reply, according to his own account, was short and heated. He told the Führer:

'The point is not whether my armies are fighting or running away. They will fight and die if I ask it of them. We are talking about something entirely different, a question much more vital: whether after Stalingrad and Tunis you can afford the loss of yet two more armies. . . . If I change my plans to meet your ideas, sooner or later the way into Germany will be opened to the Allies. On the other hand, I guarantee, unless my hands are tied, to delay the Allied advance appreciably, *to halt it at latest in the Apennines*, and thereby to create conditions for the prosecution of the war in 1945 which can be dovetailed into your general strategic scheme.'

This somewhat vague pledge seems to have satisfied the Führer. According to Kesselring's account, 'Hitler said no more – or rather, he muttered a few words which, according to Beelitz, were not uncomplimentary. Anyhow, I had won my point.'[6]

* * *

Kesselring, however, had made Hitler a promise, and he now began to work desperately to keep it. To give himself time to finish the Gothic Line, he fought a series of delaying actions on temporary defence lines north of Rome. For Hitler had been right about one thing. After nearly a year of planning and construction, the Gothic Line was not ready. Its weaknesses worried some German commanders. On 18 June, Colonel Karl Heinrich, Count von Klinckowstroem, Chief of Staff of 51st Mountain Corps, anxiously informed General Fritz Wentzell, Tenth Army Chief of Staff, that the Line was not yet suitable for defence, and asked to be told what sector his corps would occupy at the end of the long retreat north. He requested also that he might detail construction officers to oversee the building of the defensive works.

Wentzell's reply was cold. He told von Klinckowstroem:

'The construction of the . . . Line is not the affair of the Corps. The present task is to hold the Frieda Line. The Corps should keep its eyes to the front.'[7]

Wentzell's rebuke was exactly in line with the thinking of his Führer, but nevertheless no one knew better than the Tenth Army Chief of Staff of the feverish efforts that were being made. The Gothic Line's completion had been delayed earlier in the year by the diversion of labour and materials to the Gustav and Hitler Lines in the south, but in June work was resumed once more in the Apennines, and the OKW issued the Gothic Order.[8]

The defences enumerated in this document were formidable. It called for thirty 88-mm. Panther gun turrets embedded in steel and concrete bases, a hundred Todt steel shelters, rock-tunnelling of defence positions, the carving out of fire embrasures, deep minefields, and the creation of an obstacle zone some ten miles wide. The whole of the Italian populace was to be evacuated from the construction area, which was to be a belt between twelve and fourteen miles deep. Fifteen thousand Italian labourers were conscripted for the work, aided by a Slovak technical brigade of 2,000 men.[9] The whole operation was supervised by the engineers of the Todt Organization – founded by Dr Fritz Todt, the man who built the pre-war German autobahns and the Siegfried Line.

The defences were about two hundred miles long. They began in the valley of the River Magra, a few miles south of La Spezia, and then stretched south-east through the Apuan mountains to a series of strongpoints blocking the various passes through the Apennines, being especially formidable at the Vernio Pass north of Prato and at the Futa Pass north of Florence. The eastern end of the line ran along the valley of the River Foglia to the cliffs between Pesaro and Cattolica on the Adriatic. The Adriatic corridor, where the mountains thinned out as they approached the sea, was thick with defences, and excellent use was made of the successive lines of hills and ridges which lay cross-grained to the Allied line of advance.

Not all the construction, however, was of good quality. The hearts of the Italian labourers were not as strongly in the work as those of their German masters, and wherever the growing partisan movement was powerful, there was a certain amount of subtle sabotage and delay.

Nevertheless, Kesselring was told at the beginning of September that considerable progress had been made. Listed to him as complete were 2,376 machine-gun posts, 479 anti-tank gun, mortar, and assault gun positions, 120,000 metres of wire, and many miles of anti-tank ditch.

Thus the minor defences were ready on an impressive scale, but only four of the Panther turrets were in position. Work was being frantically pushed forward on a further eighteen. Kesselring himself looked over the greater part of the mountain defences during August, and declared himself satisfied with the work done, especially with that on the Adriatic side.

'I contemplated,' he said, 'an assault on the left wing, violent as it was sure to be, with a certain confidence.'[10]

★ ★ ★

At this time, however, Alexander had no intention of assaulting Kesselring's left wing. Instead, he proposed to storm the Gothic Line in the centre, in spite of the loss of his seven divisions to Operation Anvil. This plan had much to recommend it. It was the shortest route to the plains of Lombardy. Little regrouping of forces would be necessary for the attack, since both Fifth and Eighth Armies were already approximately in their assault positions. It was, also, the heaviest blow which Alexander could strike, since he proposed to attack with both Armies simultaneously. Finally, and most important of all, it gave him the opportunity of using to the full the one military factor which might quickly bring Kesselring to his knees. That factor was speed. Alexander was well aware of its importance.

'In the days when I still had my full forces,' he reported, 'I expected to be able to rush the Apennines almost without stopping; in my present situation some slight pause would be necessary, but I was determined to reduce it to the minimum.'

With these things in his mind, he sent to Clark and Leese on 26 July a four-phase plan for the Gothic operation. This embraced an assault on the centre of the line between Dicomano and Pistoia; a thrust over the Apennines; the destruction of the enemy south of the Po by swift exploitation across the Po valley; and a bridgehead over the Po north of Ferrara.[11]

As we have seen, Alexander realized that by the time they reached the Po, his tired and thinning forces would be too weak to exploit their success by pursuing a beaten enemy. To defeat Kesselring, he must bring the Germans to a decisive battle south of the river. In the middle of July, therefore, he launched an air operation, codenamed Mallory Major, designed to destroy all the nineteen Po bridges between Piacenza and the Adriatic. This, he hoped, would at the same time prevent Kesselring from receiving reinforcements, and also cut his line of retreat. The air attacks began on 12 July, and fifteen days later it was reported to him that all the bridges were cut.

Meanwhile, an elaborate deception operation, meant to convince the Germans that the attack was coming on the Adriatic side instead of in the centre, was begun by the intelligence staffs. Wireless signal traffic in the coastal area was increased to give the impression of the presence of large formations, and soldiers wearing the identifying flashes of the Canadian Corps were allowed to be seen there.[12] The presence of these men was duly reported to Kesselring by enemy agents behind the British lines. By the beginning of August, it seemed that the moment for Alexander's *real* attack, in the centre of the Gothic Line, was near. But it was not to be.

On 4 August, Alexander and his Chief of Staff, General Harding, met Leese at the latter's request on the airfield at Orvieto. Leese was worried. He did not like the plan. The sun was hot, and the three generals sheltered beneath the wing of a Dakota while he set out his objections.

First, the mountains. The centre attack would mean mountain warfare, and the loss of the French expeditionary force to Operation Anvil had stripped Leese of his most experienced mountain troops. Eighth Army was not, said Leese, experienced in this kind of fighting. The combination of tanks and guns had been the basis of its previous successes; in the Apennines the chances of using such a technique effectively were small. Leese suggested instead a 'surprise' attack along the Adriatic coast, where the mountains had dwindled to ridges, and where there seemed to be more chances for the set-piece artillery-armour assaults with which Eighth Army was familiar.[13]

Leese's second objection was psychological. He thought that if Fifth and Eighth Armies were to fight side by side, there might be invidious comparisons, and a spirit of rivalry of quite the wrong kind.[14] The influence of military politics was making itself felt.

The third man at this informal conference, General Harding, Alexander's Chief of Staff, did not share Leese's view. Harding believed that a massive single blow by both armies in the central mountains was the best and quickest way to break the German armies, though, of course, as Alexander's Chief of

Staff, his job would be to put all his weight behind whatever decision was finally taken.[15] Leese, too, though he wound up by saying that he was not confident of his ability to break through on the central front, assured Alexander that whatever strategy was finally adopted, he would try his best to make it succeed. If Alexander insisted on the central attack, Leese would, of course, comply.

Alexander did not insist. Once more, his essential reasonableness and his predilection for not interfering with the man on the spot, took over. In the words of an official account:

'Realizing how impolitic it would be to persuade an Army Commander to fight a battle against his inclination and judgement, General Alexander acceded to General Leese's new proposal.'[16]

Alexander said after the war that, like Leese, he himself had doubts about the now-abandoned centre attack. 'It was,' he wrote, 'anything but certain that our heavy blow in the mountains of the centre would take us through to our objective, and if the first attack there fell short of our expectations, the advantage would be all with the defenders.' The Germans had much easier communications in the shape of the main highway of Route 9 – the Via Emilia – which ran north-west across the rear of their position, from Rimini to Milan. It would thus not be difficult for them to build up a counter-concentration.[17]

Looking back in the comfort of hindsight, twenty years after the airfield meeting at Orvieto, it is difficult to find these arguments convincing. It is certain, of course, that *no* operation against the Gothic Line, whether in the centre or on the Adriatic, was anything other than hazardous, in view of the depleted state of Alexander's armies, and of their serious imbalance, with too much armour and too little infantry. But the Eighth Army planning staff had already rejected the Adriatic offensive,[18] on the grounds that it would be difficult to bring the necessary concentration of forces to bear; that there would be poor opportunities for exploitation; and that Eighth Army was likely to get enmeshed and cut about in a series of river-crossing operations over the many smallish streams which emptied themselves transversely across the Adriatic 'corridor' into the sea.

The cogency of these last two objections was to be demonstrated in the next few weeks. Alexander himself, in originally
deciding on the centre attack, must have taken these considerations into account. His sudden abandonment of his previous
thinking – and, incidentally, of his deception plan – seems ex-
plicable only as another instance of the readiness to see the
other man's point of view that inhibited Alexander as a commander.

For, unknown to Alexander, or Clark, or Leese, there *was*
a weakness in the Apennine defences, and it was in the centre, at
Firenzuola. The question now was whether this weakness could
be discovered before it was too late.

★ ★ ★

Meanwhile, however, a great burst of energy swept through the
Allied armies. Operation Olive, as the new Adriatic offensive
was christened, meant that the bulk of Eighth Army – V Corps,
the Canadian Corps, and Army Headquarters – had to be
transferred from the Foligno area in the centre of Italy and
concentrated behind the Polish Corps, north of Ancona on the
east coast. This move had to be conducted at speed and in
secret. Soon the mountain roads were thick with traffic. A war
correspondent remembered:

'Trucks and armoured cars and tanks and weapons carriers
and guns and jeeps and motorcycles and ambulances packed
the roads, and it was not at all unusual to spend four hours
going twenty miles. The roads were ground to powder by this
traffic and the dust lay in drifts a foot thick . . . whenever you
could get up a little speed the dust boiled like water under the
wheels. Everyone's face was greenish white with dust, and it
rose in a blinding fog around the moving army and lay high
over the land in a brown solid haze.'[19]

Thousands of vehicles climbed across the spine of the Apennines from the central province of Umbria to the Adriatic
Marches. The inadequate roads were buttressed and reinforced
at high speed in a vast operation by the army engineers, who
also opened a one-way tank route, 120 miles long, in order to

preserve as far as possible the surfaces of the existing roads for the soft transport vehicles. This complicated move of tons of thousands of men and vehicles was successfully completed by 20 August.

At the same time, a new deception plan was devised. The situation was grotesque, in that the earlier deception plan had been devised to convince Kesselring that the attack was coming on the east coast – and that was exactly what was now going to happen. Allied Intelligence attempted a double bluff, which aimed at making the Germans believe that the real attack was coming in the centre, and that the earlier 'evidence' of a large Allied presence on the east coast had been intended to deceive.

A new and complicated programme of wireless deception was begun; wireless sets continued to operate at their previous signal intensity on their old sites, busily exchanging orders for formations which at the moment were pouring east over the dusty mountain roads.[20]

The success of these plans is hard to measure. The headquarters of the German Tenth Army, holding the sector which was going to be attacked, noted with interest the noise and dust of the Allied convoys winding through the mountains, but was half-inclined to believe the opinion of General Traugott Herr, commander of 76th Panzer Corps, that the movement might be connected with some big unloading of war material at newly-captured Ancona.[21] The relative impotence of the Luftwaffe in relation to the great power of the Allied Air Forces made effective air reconnaissance highly difficult, if not impossible, and the German command was reduced, as usual, to guessing.

Ironically enough, however, Kesselring – partly convinced by Alexander's earlier deception plan – had already agreed to reinforce Tenth Army with the formidable 1st Parachute Division commanded by General Richard Heidrich. This – one of the best divisions in the German Army – was lying behind 278th Division on the coast, and Kesselring intended that Heidrich's men should shortly relieve 278th Division, which had been seriously mauled by the Poles north of Ancona.[22]

Kesselring was also hedging his bets by keeping two divisions in reserve near Bologna, so that to this extent the Allies had succeeded in keeping him wondering. But no one knew better than Alexander that the excellence of the German lateral communications behind their mountain defences would make it possible for Kesselring to wait and see whether Eighth Army's coming advance was a feint or the real thing, and then to move swiftly to respond to it. No deception plan, however successful, would give Alexander more than a brief advantage.

★ ★ ★

Nevertheless, there was one further important factor in the military situation favouring Alexander – a factor of which British commanders now take little account, but which to German commanders in the autumn of 1944 was a matter of desperate urgency. The north of Italy, the sector occupied by the Germans, was in a state of intermittent civil war.

After Mussolini's rescue from exile on the Gran Sasso in the Abruzzi by German glider troops in September 1943, the Duce set up a new Fascist republic with its seat of government at Salo on Lake Garda, where he lived with his staff under German supervision. Over the next year, Italian resistance to the so-called Salo Republic grew steadily. It began with small bands of fighters in the Alps led by royalist army officers, or by escaped prisoners of war. Then it was taken up by the loose but widespread Communist organization, sprouting from strikes in Turin to armed groups of partisans operating in central Italy and along the lines of communication through the Po Valley.

By April 1944, partisan activity was causing Hitler serious concern. When he met Mussolini at Kressheim, he told him:

'In Italy there are two bottlenecks for the Germans: one is the Apennines. If the roads crossing the Apennines were dominated by the partisans, it would be impossible for us to hold a position to the south. The second bottleneck is the Alpine roads. If we are to go on fighting in Italy against overwhelming superiority, we will have to dominate and make secure the Alpine passes so as to be sure that no partisans would be able to threaten those narrow supply routes.'[23]

After some initial German reluctance, it was now proposed to use the Italian troops still loyal to Mussolini to fight the partisans. The task of organizing them was given to Marshal Graziani, the Italian soldier who had been so comprehensively defeated by Wavell in North Africa in 1941.

Only four Italian divisions training in Germany could be considered to be viable military formations, and in August 1944 two of these divisions – the Monte Rosa and the San Marco – arrived in Italy. With three German divisions they were formed into Army Liguria and stationed around the St Bernard Pass and the coastal region of La Spezia. Although Army Liguria was formed partly with the intention of safeguarding the north-west of Italy against either an Allied landing or an attack through the Alpine passes, in practice its role became almost entirely anti-partisan, if only to protect its lines of communication.[24] Thus even as the Gothic Line campaign began, Kesselring's potential reserves were becoming more and more deeply embroiled in a subsidiary battle with the armed bands of the partisans.

There had been formed meanwhile the special anti-partisan units known as the Black Brigades. These were made up of armed Fascist Party members. Their venal brutality made them the most hated military units in Italy, and probably did more than any other factor to strengthen sentiment in favour of the partisans.

For this sentiment was growing rapidly, and the effect on the German command was considerable. By now, the sheer weight of German casualties was assuming mounting importance. According to Kesselring:

'With German soldiers scattered over a deep zone, exact statistics of our considerable losses cannot be obtained because every kind of disappearance was simply listed as "missing". In the period June–August my intelligence officer reported to me some 5,000 killed and 25,000–30,000 wounded or kidnapped. These figures seem to me too high. According to my estimate, based on oral reports, a more probable minimum figure for those three months would be 5,000 killed and 7,000–8,000 killed or kidnapped, to which should be added a maximum total of the same number of wounded. In any case, the proportion of casualties on the German side alone greatly exceeded the total partisan losses.'[25]

These figures seem astonishingly vague for an army run with German efficiency, and possibly too much credence should not be placed in them. Kesselring was writing after the war, and after he himself had been found guilty of responsibility for the murder of hostages. But if his figures are even half accurate, they give some indication of the gigantic problem which was posed for the German command.

In spite of savage German repressive measures, with hostages shot and hanged, and villages burned, the partisans grew stronger. By September 1944 their daring and courage brought about a situation in which, even in the area immediately behind the main German battleline in the Apennines, German generals were unable to move freely without danger.

'Every time I drove to the front now, I had to pass through a guerrilla-infested district,' wrote von Senger, commander of 14th Panzer Corps. 'Normally I drove in the little Volkswagen and displayed no general's insignia of rank – no peaked cap, no gold or red flags. . . .'[26]

One German general who was not so cautious did not get a second chance. The partisans caught and killed the commander of the 20th Luftwaffe Field Division, General Crisolli, as he returned from a conference at corps headquarters. It was an anxious background against which to defend the Gothic Line.

4
Leese Attacks

The date selected for the launching of the new offensive was 25 August. The orders went out on 16 August. Alexander gave his intention as 'to drive the enemy out of the Apennine positions and to exploit to the general lower line of the Po, inflicting the maximum losses on the enemy in the process.'[1]

The early – and what then seemed to be the vital – burden was to be borne by Eighth Army, which was ordered to break through into the Po Valley and seize Bologna and Ferrara. Fifth Army was meanwhile to make threatening motions on the centre front, in an effort to draw the German reserves from the east coast. General Clark was ordered to be ready to launch his own offensive five days after Eighth Army's attack. His object then would be to break through the centre of the Gothic Line on the Florence–Bologna axis. The powerful British XIII Corps was transferred to Clark's command, to bring him up to the strength needed for this operation.

The new plan embodied the principle of what Alexander called 'the two-handed punch' – that is, it aimed at attacking the enemy in two vital areas either simultaneously or alternately, so that Kesselring's reserves would be split. Its defect, as Alexander recognized, was that the Allies had all their goods in the shop window, and themselves had no central reserve with which to influence the battle.

'In a sense,' Alexander said, 'Fifth Army might be regarded as the Army Group Reserve, for in the two-handed strategy which I planned, its blow would be held back until the moment I judged right.'[2]

He was, of course, making the best of a shortage of troops

which was not his fault; Fifth Army could be regarded as a reserve only in a very restricted sense of the word, since its influence could be imposed only on the front immediately before it, and in a pre-determined attack which it would not be possible to change. If the Germans could hang on long enough on the Adriatic front, Fifth Army's influence as a reserve would be very limited indeed.

Two days before Eighth Army's offensive began, Leese gave his own briefing to an audience of senior officers in the glittering interior of the theatre at Iesi. To those who watched him, he seemed superbly confident, and his vigorous and informal style was in the best tradition of British leadership. The country over which the troops had to advance was not easy, he warned. But Eighth Army was stronger than ever before, and for this attack it had available 1,200 tanks, 1,000 guns, and ten divisions. This might well, said Leese, be the last big battle in Eighth Army's history.[3]

Sir Oliver's audience already knew his plan, which had been issued a few days before. It was simple, but it appeared none the less effective for that.

Three army corps – the Polish Corps, the Canadian Corps, and the British V Corps – would attack simultaneously in line along a thirty-mile front stretching inland from the Adriatic coast north of Ancona. The Poles, no longer at full strength because of their losses and lack of reinforcements, would seize the high ground north of the coastal town of Pesaro. The Canadians, in the centre of the advancing line, would attack on the left of the Poles, and then swing across to the sea to take over from them at Cattolica, and advance to Rimini. The British V Corps, on the left, was to advance on Bologna and Ferrara.

When the Eighth Army officers left the theatre at Iesi, Leese's confidence had infected them. At last, it seemed, the final push in Italy was near. 'Non-stop to the Po' was a phrase increasingly heard during the next few days. If they could crack the Gothic Line – and they had surprisingly few doubts about that – the soldiers of Eighth Army could see on the map the plains stretching away to the north. Men who had fought at Alamein remembered the speed and exhilaration of armoured pursuit, and rubbed their hands.

In the New Zealand Division, lying now in reserve as Eighth
Army's *corps de chasse*, the men were given lectures on Venice,
which was still more than 100 miles behind the enemy lines.[4]
Few armies are lighthearted before a great offensive, but
Eighth Army was confident and hopeful as it waited among the
sunlit valleys of peach orchards and grapes for the last few hours
to pass before 25 August. Some Eighth Army men recalled this
optimism ruefully later.

'We were soon told the army plan and intention for the great
armoured breakthrough to kingdom come, all over the Po
Valley and beyond, and we were promised a good sure-thing
gallop,' wrote an officer of the King's Royal Rifle Corps.
'Everyone was excited, and we were addressed by the army
commander and the brigadier, and visited by our new corps and
divisional commanders. We spent a very pleasant fortnight in
this way, and then . . . we drove out of our easy life into the
battle of the Gothic Line.'[5]

As much as possible was done both to train and relax officers
and men before the assault. The British 4th Division, for instance, while it waited at Foligno before moving over to the
Adriatic coast, spent more than three weeks overhauling and
repairing weapons and equipment, and held exercises designed
to familiarize the troops with the kind of operations that the
planners envisaged in the weeks ahead.

The lighter side was not neglected. There were short leave
trips to Naples and Rome; the Ensa show 'Eve on Leave' had a
run of a week at the theatre at Foligno; the Black Watch won
the divisional football competition in the town stadium; and on
the shores of Lake Piediluco the division made an empty school
into a rest camp, with its own boathouse and boats, gift shops,
barber's and post office. There were even three 'pubs' – the Jeep
and Trailer, Peter's Corner, and the Red Lion. Only the death
of two soldiers of the Royal Hampshire Regiment, killed by a
German booby-trap in the rest-camp boiler room, was a reminder that the war was still only a very short distance away.[6]

Leese issued a last message to his troops.

'Now,' he said, 'we begin the last lap. Swiftly and secretly,
once again, we have moved right across Italy an army of immense strength and striking power – to break the Gothic Line.

'Victory in the coming battles means the beginning of the end for the German armies in Italy. Let every man do his utmost and again success will be ours.

'Good luck to you all.'

This message, while doubtless encouraging to those who were waiting for the advance, was unusually explicit. This was to have unforeseen and serious consequences in the next few days.

★ ★ ★

After a hot, sunny day the night of 25 August was cool. The moon was down before midnight, and above the steep green hills of the Marches the sky was sprinkled with thousands of stars. Between the two armies lay the narrow stream of the Metauro, and on both sides of the line there was silence after the movement and disturbance as the Allied troops shuffled into position in the past two days.

South of the river, the three attacking army corps were lined up along their thirty-mile front. On the Adriatic coast, the Polish Corps, with the Kresowa and Carpathian infantry divisions and the 2nd Polish Armoured Brigade, covered the first seven miles stretching inland from the sea.

In the centre, the Canadian Corps, commanded by Major-General Eedson Burns, had a narrow front of just over two miles. Under command, Burns had the 1st Canadian Infantry Division, the 5th Canadian Armoured Division, the 21st British Tank Brigade and the Household Cavalry Regiment.

On the left of the line, farthest west in Eighth Army, was Lieutenant-General Charles Keightley's giant V Corps, which had been entrusted with the major role in the offensive. Keightley planned to advance in the first phase of the attack with two infantry divisions leading – the British 46th Division on the right and the 4th Indian Division on the left. *(Map 1.)*

In the second phase, the British 56th Division, which was to be held back until 46th Division was heavily involved, would be brought in on either left or right as necessary.

The third phase was the crux of the plan. In this, the 1st British Armoured Division was to pass through either 46th or

56th Divisions, and then exploit northwards or north-west-wards as ordered. The 4th British Infantry Division would follow 1st Armoured, to harden up the punch of the anticipated breakthrough.

This phase was to consist of the most deep and rapid advance possible, with the aim of encircling and destroying the whole left wing of the German Tenth Army, thrusting at its eastern flank and rear.[7]

In addition to his one armoured and four infantry divisions, Keightley had available the six tank regiments of the 7th British Armoured Brigade and the 25th British Tank Brigade. These he parcelled out to act as support for the attacking infantry divisions.

His artillery support was impressive. He had 472 guns under corps command for the battle, out of a total of 1,052 guns in the Adriatic sector for all three corps. In addition to the field artillery regiments, with their self-propelled or jeep-drawn 25-pounder guns, one medium regiment, equipped with 5·5-inch guns, was allotted to each of the leading infantry divisions, so that they could move forward with the battle, giving heavier support.

Far to the west of V Corps lay Fifth Army, waiting for its own moment still some days ahead. Between the two armies was spread lightly the British X Corps, made up of the 10th Indian Division and the 9th British Armoured Brigade. It was to take no part in the initial attack, but would be used as flank protection. In the rear of Eighth Army, the 2nd New Zealand Division and the Greek Mountain Brigade – then newly arriving from the Middle East, were in Eighth Army reserve.

Over the Metauro waited the German Tenth Army, though the great bulk of its forces lay behind the main works of the Gothic Line, which followed the course of the River Foglia, twelve miles farther north. The eastern half of the line – the German left – was held by 76th Panzer Corps, commanded by the redoubtable General Herr. He had five divisions – three in the line, two in reserve, and all of them infantry.

The right of the German line was occupied by 51st Mountain Corps, commanded by General Valentin Feuerstein. He also disposed of five infantry divisions. General von Vietinghoff, the able and experienced Prussian Guardsman who commanded

Tenth Army, held another infantry division – the 98th – in reserve near Bologna. The eight divisions of the German Fourteenth Army were farther west, opposite Fifth Army.

The Germans, too, in spite of a year of retreat, were in good heart. They were well aware that they had acquitted themselves creditably during the campaign, and they included some of the best units and commanders in the German Army.

Kesselring's Chief of Staff, General Siegfried Westphal, has described the successful transition from offence, to delaying action, to defence in the mind of the German soldier:

'For almost a year, the German troops had been engaged in one retreat after another. These had begun at Alamein in the first November days of 1942, and had by no means ended at Cape Bon on the north-east tip of Tunisia. In the last resort the fighting in Sicily and southern Italy had been nothing better than a series of rearguard actions. Now, however . . . the troops were told that the time of delaying actions was over, and that rocklike defence was needed. But would they take these exhortations seriously after retreating for about three thousand miles in all? That was anybody's guess. In the event, it was astounding to see how quickly the German soldier adjusted himself to the new requirements. After all, quite apart from the difference of psychological attitude, defence demanded from all arms . . . an entirely different mode of warfare.'[8]

Westphal was writing of the time of Cassino, but even now, many months and thousands of lives later, German troops were still aggressively confident. A letter written two days before the Eighth Army offensive by an N.C.O. in the German 211th Grenadier Regiment, while fanciful enough in some respects, gives no impression that the prospect of inevitable defeat for Germany was yet taken seriously by German soldiers:

'At the moment it is fairly quiet, though Tommy is pushing forward with strong armed forces. We are in the hills near Pesaro. But we shall soon sort them out. The English have threatened every member of our regiment with twenty-five years' forced labour, and you can see how they hate us. But then, we are acknowledged to be the best regiment in the southern theatre of operations. . . .'[9]

German confidence, in fact, was at this time being carried to

a fault. Incredibly, in view of the situation, both von Vietinghoff, the Tenth Army commander, and Heidrich, the paratroop
general, were on leave on 25 August. At the same time a general
regrouping was taking place, involving the relief of the German
71st and 278th Infantry Divisions and their retirement closer to
the Gothic Line proper.[10] Into this situation of military confusion, the three attacking Allied corps advanced at one hour
before midnight.

In order to achieve the maximum surprise, the five divisions
in the first wave across the Metauro went in without preliminary
artillery support. There was virtually no opposition as the infantrymen waded through water no more than three feet deep
and pushed forward through the olive groves and up the slopes
on the other side. At a minute before midnight, the ground
trembled and the sky was lit by flashes as the artillery began to
rain shells down in a creeping barrage 400 yards ahead of the
advancing troops, moving forward 100 yards every six minutes –
the estimated rate of advance. By dawn five divisions were
across, well embedded into the stretch of hills between them and
the Foglia.

On the left of the Allied line, the advance of V Corps was led
by the 46th Infantry Division, commanded by Major-General
Sir J. Hawkesworth, one of the most competent and skil-
ful divisional commanders in the British Army. General
Sir Richard McCreery – who later in the campaign was
to command Eighth Army – called Hawkesworth 'a master
of infantry tactics . . . he varied his methods and was always
ready to encourage surprise, a silent night approach, and
fieldcraft.'[11]

These were virtues which were now to give the Allies a flying
start in the battle of the Gothic Line.

Hawkesworth's statement of intention in his orders was brief:
'46th Division will BUST the Gothic Line.' The divisional
advance was led by 128th Brigade, which was made up of three
battalions of the Royal Hampshire Regiment, and commanded
by Brigadier Douglas Kendrew, a celebrated international
Rugby player before the war. At first, they were delayed more
by craters and demolitions than by the sporadic resistance
of enemy outposts. As the sun rose, they took the small town

of Montefelcino, and pushed on a further two or three miles.

The next objective was the chain of three peaks – Monte Bartolo, Monte Tomba, and Monte Grosso. The last of these, a considerable feature 1,400 feet high, gave the British infantry a chance to show in what good heart they had started the offensive. It was attacked by a company of 5th Hampshires, and a platoon commander, Lieutenant J. F. Wallace, remembers:

'Two platoons were going up the slopes, when I heard some firing from the flank, and somebody shouted that the other platoon commander had been hit. I ran forward with my platoon over a small ridge, when a Spandau opened fire on us. We all dropped to the ground, but I was a yard or two in front, and I was forward of the ridge and my platoon was just behind it. I thought to myself, "I've had it," but then I heard a corporal shout, "Come on, lads, after Mr Wallace," and they all charged up after me. They cheered as they came – it was one of the few times I've ever heard them cheer. A German in a position higher up stood up with a grenade, but somebody shot him, and the others ran away down the other side of the slope. We'd captured the peak, and so we dug in.'[12]

By the evening of the 27th, all three peaks were in British hands, and Hawkesworth bustled his division on towards the Foglia. For the weary infantry, the marching seemed worse than the fighting; from the Metauro to the Gothic Line was only twelve miles as the crow flies, but nearer twenty on foot. There were one or two sharp little actions, but casualties were light, and the advancing troops picked up many prisoners from the bewildered 71st Division. By midday on 29 August, the leading battalions, 2nd Hampshires and 5th Sherwood Foresters, with the supporting tanks of the North Irish Horse, were lined up at Colbordolo and Monte Fabbri on the south bank of the Foglia, looking across the river at the Gothic Line.

The other leading division of V Corps, the 4th Indian, had started early on 25 August, since it was somewhat behind the main start line of the advance and needed extra time to catch up. This division had been allotted the most mountainous sector of all, and with it on the march was one of the most

unusual units of the British Army. This was the 85th Field/
Mountain Regiment, a Kiplingesque column partly mounted
on horses, and hauling its mountain guns on mules led by
Basuto drivers. Two batteries were equipped with the famous
3·7 howitzer screw guns – 'the guns that are built in two bits',
of Kipling's poem – and one with the American 75-mm. pack
howitzer.

The division pushed forward swiftly, though its advance was
marred by a tragic misunderstanding with a unit of the Italian
Corps of Liberation, which was spread as a light screen in front
of the advance. As the 2nd/11th Royal Sikhs of the leading
brigade advanced to the small town of Acqualagna, the Italians,
after a telephone conversation with an officer inside the town
itself, reported that it was clear of Germans. When the unsus-
pecting Sikhs approached the town walls, they were hit by a
storm of fire from the surrounding heights. The company commander and three platoon commanders of the leading company
died instantly, and others were wounded. Another company,
advancing to clear the town, was fired on in error at point-
blank range by the confused Italians, and it was not until the
evening of 25 August that the position was clarified. By that
time, the Germans had indeed withdrawn, but the misunderstanding had cost the Sikhs more than seventy officers and
men.[13]

On the same night, the leading battalion of the division,
1st/9th Gurkhas, crossed the Metauro, and on the next day a
British battalion, 1st Royal Sussex, entered the medieval town of
Urbino, the birthplace of Raphael, and was cheered through
the streets by its 20,000 excited inhabitants. Six miles beyond
the town lay the Foglia. As they closed up to the Gothic Line,
the Royal Sussex received a foretaste of the days ahead. Heavy
and accurate artillery fire poured from the German positions
across the river, and there were short fierce fire fights, in which
the supporting armour lost seven tanks before the bank was
cleared.

Nearer to the Adriatic, the Canadians, on their narrow front,
had also crossed the Metauro unopposed, and pushed on into
country strewn with blown buildings, destroyed roads, and
wrecked buildings. They had a stiff fight at Monteciccardo, but

by the morning of the 29th they, too, were in the Foglia Valley, facing the Gothic Line.

Among those who watched them as they drove north from the Metauro was the rubicund, sun-helmeted figure of Mr Winston Churchill, who was visiting the front with Alexander. He observed the fighting from the cover of a stone farmhouse only recently evacuated by the enemy, and he wrote later:

'The Germans were firing with rifles and machine-guns from thick scrub on the farther side of the valley about five hundred yards away. Our front line was beneath us. The firing was desultory and intermittent. But this was the nearest I got to the enemy and the time I heard most bullets in the Second World War.'[14]

Farthest east of all, the Poles, moving with their customary dash, caught a German parachute regiment in the open and in the act of retiring, and inflicted heavy losses as they cleared the right flank of Eighth Army's advance. Thus by 29 August the preliminary phase was over, and the three attacking Corps faced the Gothic Line. It was a discouraging prospect. Along the north bank of the Foglia, the Germans had constructed an elaborate killing ground, designed to herd the advancing troops on to the Spandaus, rifles and mortars which waited for them in unseen positions. From Colbordolo, where 46th Division waited for the next and grimmer phase of the assault, an officer of the North Irish Horse reported:

'When we looked down on, and across, the River Foglia to Monte Gridolfo, it must be confessed the situation looked anything but pleasant.

'All houses had been razed to the ground, trees and vines felled, and avenues prepared between extensive minefields for a hail of machine-gun fire. . . . The assault across the River Foglia and up the bare slopes beyond appeared suicidal.'[15]

★ ★ ★

The Germans who waited on the other side of the Foglia, however, were worried and confused. The fact that the Eighth Army attack had hit them while they were in the act of retiring made

it difficult for them to judge whether the attack was a genuine
offensive, or merely a follow-up to occupy the ground that they
had left.

The Allied artillery support impressed them by its weight, if
not by its effect – 25,000 shells, they estimated had fallen on
positions which Herr's 76th Panzer Corps had safely vacated –
but they decided at first that this indicated no more than a local
tactical move to try to drive a wedge between the 71st Division
and Heidrich's parachutists. After another day, there was more
anxiety, and the Tenth Army Chief of Staff, Wentzell, reported
to Kesselring: 'I think it is going to be quite an affair on the
Adriatic coast.'[16]

Meanwhile, however, Fifth Army, making its elaborate
threatening motions with heavy troop concentrations and
increased air activity on the central front, was sowing doubts in
German minds. Kesselring, in particular, thought that the
Adriatic attack was some kind of Allied diversion connected
with the invasion of the south of France and would not be
strongly pressed. He worried more about another Anzio, and –
ironically in the circumstances – feared a landing up the coast
at his rear.

Into this sea of uncertainty now dropped one piece of real
evidence of Allied intentions. It was Leese's order of the day,
with its revealing phrase that 'secretly . . . we have moved right
across Italy an army of immense strength and striking power –
to break the Gothic Line.' A copy of this had come into Kesselring's possession. For a day, the German command looked
at this sheet of paper, and wondered if, perhaps, it was no
more than another British deception. But by the evening of
the 28th they decided it was genuine – and the orders went out
immediately to concentrate the attention of Tenth Army on the
Adriatic. Late that night, von Vietinghoff, hurrying back to
his command from his ill-timed leave, was told by Herr on the
telephone:

'On the basis of the captured document, it is now certain that
the enemy intends to carry out a big push to the plains of the
Po.'[17]

Von Vietinghoff cannot have been happy about the situation
of Tenth Army. The speed of Keightley and Burns with their

two corps – and especially of Hawkesworth with 46th Division – had pushed the Germans back to the Foglia three days ahead of their programmed withdrawal. Von Klinckowstroem's curtly-received warnings to Wentzell about the Gothic Line seemed now to have more point. The German reserves – 26th Panzer Division and 29th Panzer Grenadier Division from Fourteenth Army – were still at least a day from the main defence works. General Wilhelm Raapke's 71st Division, which had withdrawn across the Foglia, was tired, mauled, and below strength. The possibility of a great Allied triumph suddenly loomed above the Tenth Army staff as they struggled to man the Line which Hitler expected never to be broken.

5
The Dream of Vienna

The possibility that after all their hopes, fears, suspicions, and disappointments, the Allies might yet triumph in Italy had once more seized Churchill's mind. But it had occurred also to the Americans, and each side immediately manœuvred to fit Alexander's hypothetical victory into its own set of strategic calculations.

The United States moved first. As early as 7 August, the American Joint Chiefs of Staff predicted that 'the campaign . . . will probably result in a weight of effort and force on the east flank, this pointing towards continued operations to the eastward. It is considered more possible that an advance to the westward would provide greater support for the two major operations. . . .' These, as the Americans made clear, were Eisenhower's Overlord operations in north-west Europe, and Dragoon, the forthcoming invasion of the south of France.[1]

A fortnight later Churchill was in Rome, where, after a conference with Brooke, Wilson, and Air-Chief-Marshal Sir Charles Portal, he announced that he was 'utterly opposed to the proposal that General Alexander's army should move westward.' He was also determined that its operations should not be hampered by the withdrawal of further forces.

On 26 August, the Americans issued a polite but firm reminder that it had been decided at the Sextant conference in Cairo in December 1943 that Overlord and Dragoon would be the supreme operations for 1944, and that 'nothing would be undertaken in any other part of the world to hazard the success of these operations'. Suspicions of Britain's Balkan policy were still darkening Marshall's mind.

The definition of what would or would not 'hazard the success' of the operations in France, however, gave Churchill room to argue, and on the 28th he again returned to his attempts to convince Roosevelt. He told the President:

'I am sure that the arrival of a large army in Trieste and Istria in four or five weeks would have an effect far outside purely military values. Tito's people will be waiting for us in Istria. What the condition of Hungary will be then, I cannot imagine, but we shall at any rate be in a position to take full advantage of any great new situation.'[2]

To the South African Premier, Field-Marshal Smuts, who shared his views, Churchill was more explicit:

'. . . I hope to turn and break the Gothic Line, break into the Po Valley, and ultimately advance by Trieste and the Ljubljana Gap to Vienna. Even if the war came to an end at an early date I have told Alexander to be ready for a dash with armoured cars.'[3]

Back in London after his Italian visit, Churchill received Roosevelt's reply. It was judiciously non-committal:

'It is my thought that we should press the German Army in Italy vigorously with every facility we have available, and suspend decision on the future use of General Wilson's armies until the results of his campaign are better known, and we have better information as to what the Germans may do. . . .'

The Prime Minister, however, was now in no mood to suspend decision. He replied unequivocally on 31 August that if Alexander achieved victory, the only possible employment for the Fifth and Eighth Armies would be a movement 'first to Istria and Trieste, and ultimately upon Vienna'.[4]

There was another soothing telegram from Roosevelt, but the President must have been well aware that Churchill would yield no further. The Prime Minister had stood by, unwilling but loyally, while Alexander's armies were stripped of seven vital divisions. But if, in spite of this, Alexander now defeated Kesselring, Churchill would insist on exploiting that success in the way he wished.

Others might see the offensive against the Gothic Line as a great holding operation, or simply as the chance to kill more Germans, but to Churchill the object was still Vienna. His motives have been much discussed. He himself said after the war that he had hoped to use British military powers 'to influence the liberation of south-eastern Europe'. His critics see this as merely a post-war rationalization of his favourite strategic theory, born at Gallipoli, of hitting at Germany through the underside of Europe. They assert that his proposal to invade Austria was made without political considerations, and simply because it was his personal obsession that this was the best military way to defeat Germany.*

Even in the summer of 1944, as the Allied armies waited to make their assault on the Gothic Line, Vienna was a word which divided British commanders from each other, as well as from their American colleagues. The British C.I.G.S., Brooke, did not think that the capture of Vienna was possible. To him the value of the new Italian offensive was that it would force Hitler to reinforce Kesselring at the expense of German armies on other fronts. Brooke had seen Alexander in London in July, and had criticized his failure to smash up Kesselring's retreat north of Rome, recording later in his diary:

'I am afraid Alex did not like this much, but it is desirable to make him face the facts instead of his dreams of an advance on Vienna.'[5]

And he wrote to Wilson in August:

'I do not see Alex advancing on Vienna this year unless he does it in the face of a crumbling Germany.'[6]

Thus as the Allied divisions prepared to attack the bare slopes across the Foglia, they were in an extraordinary position. There was no agreement, either between the United States and Britain, or even between the British Prime Minister and his own C.I.G.S., as to how it would be desirable or practicable to exploit their victory, if they won it. Their objective was an imaginary line drawn across the north of Italy from Venice to Brescia, where, under Wilson's directive of 5 July, they would await 'further instructions'.

But Churchill, not Brooke, was directing British war policy, and if Alexander now inflicted a decisive defeat on Kesselring in the Apennines, Churchill's letter to Roosevelt on 31 August made it clear what those 'further instructions' would

* This argument is briefly discussed in Appendix D.

be. His desire to forestall the Russians may have been, as his critics assert, a myth. But the attack on the Gothic Line was not a myth. Thousands of men were to die in it during the next eight weeks. If Alexander succeeded, both he and Churchill would expect his armies to drive on to the east, and whether Churchill had originally intended it as a political move or not, a British military presence in Austria would be a political factor of incalculable importance which Stalin would have to take into account. Much would depend on how decisively Alexander could defeat Kesselring, and, quite as important, how quickly. If the German armies in Italy were swiftly routed at the Gothic Line, Alexander in Vienna might change the history of Europe.

The tremendous 'ifs' of the operation still abounded; there were 400 road miles between Venice and Vienna, through steep mountains, over difficult roads, and with the bad time of the year drawing nearer. Those on the spot in Italy, however, were more optimistic than Brooke about the chances of success. Harding, Alexander's Chief of Staff, had his eyes fixed on the Upper Danube basin as a goal from the time he arrived in Italy in January 1944. The withdrawal of the divisions for the invasion of the south of France had been a sad blow, but it was his opinion that if the Germans could be broken between the Gothic Line and the Po, Austria might still be reached, 'provided,' he said later, 'that all our resources had been concentrated in driving along the axis Florence–Bologna–Trieste–Klagenfurt–Vienna'.[7]

The troops themselves shared this feeling of confidence to a surprising extent. 'Drive slowly if you want to see Vienna', said the big white-lettered notices warning drivers not to make dust visible to enemy artillery south of the Foglia, and there were many soldiers, especially in Eighth Army, who were confident that the coming attack would take them there.

However, for the high command, Alexander's success was still only a hypothesis. For the moment, the question of a long-range strategy to develop it had to rest. The possibility of a British-led victory, with Alexander and Mark Clark driving side by side in triumph down the Ringstrasse – with all that this would mean in political, diplomatic, and human terms – was yet open. But first there was a battle to be fought.

The men who held the issue in their hands were lined up, facing each other across the narrow stream of the Foglia. They were given little more than perfunctory attention by the world's Press, whose fascinated gaze was absorbed by the larger-scale struggle in north-west Europe. Even among those who waited to make the assault, and among those who waited to receive it, few had any inkling of what might be at stake.

On the Allied side, there were Poles, already angry and bitter at the threatened obliteration of their way of life by Soviet Communism; Canadians and British eager to finish the job and get home; Greeks, proudly conscious that they were the living proof that their country was still fighting; Gurkhas and Sikhs from the hills of India and Nepal, to whom the problems of European politics were so remote as to seem non-existent. Farther west waited the Americans, whose own government mistrusted the role which they would be called on to play in the event of victory; and the Brazilians, whose gesture of solidarity with their great northern neighbour had brought thousands of their men to fight in Italy. Yet all of them, no matter how far away their homes from the northern Apennines, would be touched in the years to come by the shadow of the battle that was now to be fought.

For the German armies in Italy, history had reserved a last sardonic joke. They were to put up a superb resistance. 'A famous page in German military history,' Kesselring called it later. But every German bullet that killed an Allied soldier, every German mine that blew up an Allied vehicle moving north, every German anti-tank crew that cheered as it watched another Sherman or Churchill explode in flames, was making a tiny but significant contribution towards the establishment of Stalin's European satellite empire. Every day that Alexander was held back from Vienna made it more and more easy for the Russians to rule eastern Europe. This was the German nightmare, yet the harder the Germans fought in Italy, the nearer and nearer they came to making it come true.

These ironies, however, were hidden from the soldiers on each side of the river in the last days of August 1944. The battle was now to be joined. Its outcome would depend on many things . . . the skill of Kesselring and Alexander, von Vietinghoff and

Leese, Herr and Hawkesworth; the morale of the troops; and, most of all, perhaps, the nature of the battleground and the weather.

★ ★ ★

To Leese in the dying hours of August, the outcome seemed to depend on speed. The sharp and hurried retirement of Raapke's 71st Infantry Division indicated that the Allies had achieved surprise. It might be that the Germans were not yet ready to man their defences. Leese now ordered both the Canadians and V Corps to patrol actively at daylight on the 30th, and to try to gatecrash the Gothic Line in accordance with Eighth Army's original plan.[8] *(Map 2.)*

Ahead of the two corps, across the Foglia, lay the steep, green, bulky masses of Monte Calvo, Monte Gridolfo, and, farther east, Tomba di Pesaro and Monte Luro. Behind these features, the streams of the Ventena, Conca, Marano and Marecchia, ran successively across the coastal corridor into the Adriatic. Between the Conca and the Marano swelled the formidable-looking ridges of Gemmano and Coriano. Beyond that the fixed defences were sparser, and the flat country of Romagna and Emilia, and more distant still, the plains of Lombardy, beckoned to the impatient armoured cavalrymen of the British 1st and the Canadian 5th Armoured Divisions.

The country north of Pesaro narrowed into a bottleneck little more than three miles wide as the Apennine foothills reached down more closely to the sea. The approaches to this corridor were guarded, first of all by the Gothic Line proper, with its range of defended heights rising just beyond the north bank of the Foglia; later by the Gemmano and Coriano ridges. This bottleneck, if the Allied plan was to succeed, must be forced and held open by the infantry, while the Shermans of the armoured divisions poured through it to what seemed the better country beyond. Here, and here only, was the ground for the armoured breakthrough of which Eighth Army dreamed.

In 4th Indian Division, on the left of the Allied line, there was no need to urge the need for speed. The Indian battalions wait-

ing for the assault looked out across the bare slopes of the
north bank of the Foglia towards Monte Calvo and the white
ribbon of road which climbed up towards the village of Tavoleto
and the higher ridge beyond. There was no movement north of
the river, and no fire was directed on Indian patrols.

The commander of the assaulting 5th Indian Brigade was a
bold man. At dawn on the 30th, without artillery support, the
3rd/10th Queen Mary's Own Baluch Regiment – men from the
barren, stony province in the north-west of the Indian sub-
continent – splashed across the gravelly bed of the Foglia and
took the first fortified outpost of the Gothic Line, Monte della
Croce, after little more than a scuffle with its scanty German
garrison.[9] It was an astonishing success. The battle for the
Gothic Line had begun, and the disorganization of the Germans
was such that the Allies had already won a foothold across the
Foglia without cost.

The Germans, however, were collecting themselves, and as
soon as the Baluch tried to push beyond Monte della Croce they
came under heavy fire. Two German counter-attacks were
made during the morning, and one Baluch platoon was forced
off the captured position. Then the tanks which had crossed the
Foglia with the infantry came up in support, and by late afternoon the Baluch advanced through a spouting curtain of
mortar fire and re-took Monte della Croce.

During the same afternoon, the rest of the two corps moved to
the assault. All morning the Kittyhawks, Spitfires, Bostons and
Baltimores of the Allied Air Forces had bombed and strafed
German gun positions north of the river. Stick after stick of
bombs smashed into the geometrically-planned killing grounds,
tossing dozens of mines high into the air, and exploding many
others in columns of mud and dust.

Hawkesworth ordered the two leading brigades of 46th
Division to cross the Foglia immediately. These were Kendrew's 128th Brigade, and the 139th, commanded by Brigadier
Allen Block. By early afternoon one of Block's battalions, the
2nd/5th Leicestershire Regiment, was across the river but
pinned down by heavy fire and restricted in movement by an
extensive minefield. The Leicesters' company, however, kept a
tight grip on its small bridgehead, although tanks which were

brought up to support it were held up by the minefield and were unable to get forward. The company had forty casualties during the next few hours, and when another company was brought up to help, it, too, was severely shelled and its commander was killed. Further movement in daylight was now deemed impossible.

General Hawkesworth himself, coming up to look at the situation, was almost killed when a shell landed a few yards in front of his jeep, causing several casualties. Imperturbable as ever, he manœuvred the jeep past the shellhole and finished his reconnaissance. He then agreed with the Leicesters' plan to continue the advance at night. It proved successful.[10]

In the darkness a Leicesters' company, aided by assault pioneers, opened a path through the minefield under heavy machine-gun fire, while the rest of the battalion moved down the shell-torn slopes of Monte Fabbri and across the Foglia.

Meanwhile, on the right of Block's brigade – and in the centre of the 46th Division line – the 5th Sherwood Foresters had as their objective the fortified village of Monte Vecchio, which was on a hill about 600 feet high rising steeply half-a-mile north of the Foglia. This was a considerable obstacle – a gradient of about two-in-three, its sides barren both of trees and of folds in the ground which might give cover from German defensive fire.

A battle patrol of the Foresters, quickly followed by a full company, pushed across the river, sustaining a few casualties from mortar fire. The Germans had machine-gun posts in five houses on the slopes, but all were silenced by a smart and gallant attack by a single Forester platoon. The lower slopes were soon virtually cleared of the enemy, but the main mass of the hill and its village still loomed above. The Foresters, too, amid the crump of mortars and the rip of Spandaus, waited for the fall of night.[11]

On the right of the divisional line, 128th Brigade was having a similar experience. The way was led by 2nd Hampshires, who, like the leading battalions of Block's brigade, had pushed across the Foglia in the afternoon against surprisingly light opposition. The battalion advanced until it straddled the road at Belvedere Fogliense, not far from the north bank. Then, as the German defenders collected themselves, the Hampshires were hit by very intense mortar and machine-gun fire, and waited for darkness. The night of 30 August would obviously be crucial for the German defence of the main works of the Gothic Line.

As night fell, the three battalions across the river moved once more to the assault. The Leicesters made their way through the minefield and seized the high ground in front of them, pushing on in the dawn light to take the hamlet of La Cantina, and probing towards the village of Mondaino, high on the spur which dominated the surrounding country.

The Foresters, after losing men in an attempted flank attack through a minefield, advanced under cover of a heavy barrage and entered the village of Monte Vecchio. For the Hampshire Brigade, however, was reserved the most spectacular and significant deed of these hours. The 2nd Battalion, returning to the attack at night, had successfully cleared the machine-gun posts on the ridge ahead of them, and at dawn the 1st/4th Battalion passed through blazing haystacks and burning houses, surrounded by sprawled dead, to attack Monte Gridolfo, the sector's biggest defence bastion.

A Hampshire company was soon pinned down by fire from concrete emplacements and swept by bullets from enfilading Spandaus in a valley on its right flank. This was just such a situation as the German defence planners had foreseen – one which presented a problem almost insuperable in the ordinary terms of a staff-college exercise. It was solved by the kind of bravery which no exercise can reasonably envisage.

A platoon commander, Lieutenant G. R. Norton – an officer seconded from the South African Union Defence Force – ran forward alone, killing the three Germans in the first machine-gun position with a grenade and then, with what seemed a charmed life, working his way forward to another emplacement containing two Spandaus and fifteen riflemen. He cut down the two machine-gunners with his Thompson gun, and killed or took prisoners the amazed infantrymen. His own men were now at his side as he cleared another strong point, taking more prisoners. Though he was now wounded and weak from loss of blood, he went on up the valley where his platoon stormed the remaining enemy positions.[12] Norton's luck and courage had defeated the intentions of the Gothic Line planners. Rarely can one junior officer have done so much to sway the fortunes of a campaign. The citation for Norton's Victoria Cross made the point clearly:

'Lieutenant Norton displayed matchless courage, outstanding initiative, and inspiring leadership. By his supreme gallantry, fearless example, and determined aggression, he assured the successful breach of the Gothic Line at this point.'

By evening, the Hampshires of Kendrew's brigade were in Monte Gridolfo, and the Leicesters of Block's brigade were tackling the stubborn problem of Mondaino, a small town less than a mile to the south. A company advancing on Mondaino up the valley on its north side found itself caught in crossfire from Spandaus on both sides and in front. Both its company commander and second-in-command were killed as they scrambled forward to make a reconnaissance.

In the darkness, the Leicesters slowly fought their way out of the trap, storming a group of burning houses to make the battalion master of the valley. By daylight another Leicester company was inside the town, and only snipers and small parties of stragglers remained to be dealt with. In the eight days since they crossed the Metauro, the Leicesters had lost eleven officers and 200 men in dead and wounded; the Foresters had lost fifty. The German resistance, though fierce, had been surprisingly short. The Gothic Line was well and truly pierced, and the British infantry had rarely done a better job.

6
The Cracking of the Line

The fighting on the flanks had been equally severe. Far down on the left of V Corps, on the eastern edge of Eighth Army's line, 4th Indian Division engaged in a bitter struggle for Monte Calvo and the German defence bastion of Tavoleto. This was the most mountainous part of the sector chosen by Eighth Army for the assault, and the division, which included three Gurkha battalions, was probably the nearest approximation to specialized mountain troops that Leese had under his command.

The divisional commander, Major-General Arthur Holworthy, a regular Indian Army officer, was himself a mountain specialist. He had commanded an Indian infantry brigade on the Ruweisat Ridge in the Western Desert in 1942, and the following year formed the Mountain Warfare Training School in the Lebanon. His promotion had been rapid; he became a major-general only a year after being made brigadier.

General Keightley, having given Holworthy the steepest mountains as his axis of advance, gave him also a wide measure of decision as to how he should deal with them. Holworthy wrote later:

'The Army Commander did not wish the left-hand division of the army to move any distance into the hilly country, but V Corps commander felt that a wide movement was more likely to find weakness and so enable the Line to be pierced. He therefore gave me full discretion as to how far into the difficult country I should go. There was no restriction, provided the left flank of Eighth Army was protected.'[1]

Holworthy had made use of this discretion in his approach to the Foglia, but by the time the river was crossed and the hamlet

of Monte della Croce seized in that first surprising morning of
30 August, the inescapable facts of the geography of the Gothic
Line made the field for tactical decision of this nature a narrow
one indeed. *(Map 2.)*

One mile north of Monte della Croce, on still higher ground,
stood the village of Monte Calvo; beyond that a road wound its
way north-west along a ridge which finally merged into another
transverse ridge running east and west, with the small town of
Tavoleto at its centre. Thus on the map, the Monte della Croce–
Monte Calvo–Tavoleto complex is roughly like a T, slightly
angled to the north-west, with Monte della Croce at the base of
the upright stroke, Monte Calvo half-way up it, and Tavoleto in
the centre of the horizontal stroke. The position was difficult to
outflank; from positions on both strokes of the T, the German
artillery could instantly be brought to bear on movement in
front of it, or on either flank.

Tavoleto itself was the key to this position, as the Todt
engineers had clearly recognized. Holworthy faced a difficult
problem.

'On both sides of Tavoleto,' says the divisional account, 'the
advantage of ground had been studiously exploited by the
enemy with a variety of fortification devices – anti-tank ditches,
wire obstacles, machine-gun pits, forward sniping guns, and
trench systems. The glacis had been cleared to provide an open
field of fire. Thickly sown minefields covered all approaches.
On the left of Monte Calvo, the enemy defences were organized
on a mountain basis; instead of fixed and continuous lines the
forward positions were held by outpost groups protected by
intricate defensive fire lines. German counter-attack forces
waited in sheltered reserve areas in the rear.'[2]

The easy capture of Monte della Croce had shown that the
Germans were far from organized, and Holworthy realized the
need for speed. He pushed forward the Baluch battalion, with a
Sikh battalion on their right, towards Monte Calvo, and tried to
threaten the German flank by sending 1st/9th Gurkhas up the
valley to the right of the Monte Calvo ridge. In the constricted
country of the Gothic Line, however, the Gurkhas' movement
quickly became entangled with that of a British brigade on their
right, and they were seriously delayed.

On the 31st, the assault on Monte Calvo began in earnest with a crash shoot by the reinforced divisional artillery, supported by squadrons of fighter bombers which pounded the German positions with high explosive and then searched the ruins with cannon fire. The advancing Baluch however met fierce resistance from the German infantry as they toiled up the ridge during the long, hot summer morning.

Holworthy, eager to get on to Tavoleto, fretted at the delay. He noted in his diary:

'Another hot and sticky day – disappointing as regards Monte Calvo – 4th/11th Sikhs did not push on as they might have done to take town by night or at first light – stayed put all morning 1,000 yards east of town – 1st/9th Gurkha Rifles wide turning movement blocked by Div on our right and did not come off – 3rd/10th Baluch still short of Monte Calvo as attack put in at 1200 hours after air and artillery bombardment held up by Spandau and mortar fire 400 yards from town.'[3]

As darkness came, however, the Baluch and Sikh battalions were pushing into and around the village, while the Gurkhas were moving fast up the valley to the east. Monte Calvo was held by troops of the battered German 71st Infantry Division which had been bustled back from the Metauro during the previous week; they were tired and disillusioned and in no mood to be caught again by the speed of another unexpected Allied advance. They pulled back quickly at nightfall, and the German guns put the seal on their withdrawal by opening fire on the village.

An eye-witness wrote: 'The village was a shambles. Wire obstacles had been crushed by the tanks. Broken shutters, window-frames and drainpipes swung in the breeze. Tileless roofs allowed clouds of dust and smoke to rise above the village. A bell from the church tower lay in the rubble, but the altar was still intact. Piles of barbed wire and rail dumps revealed that the Germans had not finished work on their defences.'[4]

Tavoleto, however – the toughest proposition of all – still lay ahead. By nightfall on 1 September, 1st/9th Gurkhas reached the crest of the ridge 1,000 yards south-east of the little town, and 2nd/7th Gurkhas of 11th Brigade were brought up on their left. The next day, while another Gurkha battalion of 7th Brigade captured the village of Auditore four miles west of Monte Calvo, the Gurkhas outside Tavoleto crouched in whatever holes they had been able to scratch in the ground and waited for night.

Holworthy had decided on a midnight attack, using 2nd/7th Gurkha Rifles and 2nd Queen's Own Cameron Highlanders of 11th Brigade. The divisional artillery, assisted by an additional two field regiments, laid down a heavy deception shoot well away from the projected line of attack. But now occurred one of the spontaneous reactions from troops which sometimes make havoc of military plans.

Parties of Germans supported by tanks attacked downhill towards the Gurkhas, but were beaten off by heavy fire before they reached the Gurkha positions. A company of Gurkhas, commanded by a British subaltern, followed them out into the open and scrambled over the village wall. With grenades and kukris, the Gurkha company, moving like shadows in the darkness, began to clear the houses one by one. At brigade headquarters just outside the town, the death-screams of Germans, and the thud of grenades from Tavoleto were listened to by mystified officers who had no idea what was happening. The battle went on for four hours; at the end of it the streets of the town were strewn with German and Gurkha dead. The only Germans alive were prisoners – fewer than thirty Gurkhas were still able to stand, but they had taken Tavoleto.[5]

★ ★ ★

On the right flank of V Corps, the Canadians had also had a bloody but successful struggle. Burns, the Canadian Corps commander, had received the reports of Canadian patrols which penetrated the minefields already blown up and scattered by three days of bombing, and he, too, was eager to rush his Corps through the Line before it could be properly manned. He advanced with the 1st Canadian Infantry Division on the right and the 5th Canadian Armoured Division on the left. Troops of both divisions crossed the Foglia in the late afternoon of the 30th.

Ahead of them lay the looming heights of Tomba di Pesaro and Monte Luro – the ragged but formidable eastern edge of the hill mass which extended down through Monte Gridolfo, where 46th Division was now struggling, down to Monte Calvo, which 4th Indian Division was then about to attack.

After a couple of hours, things looked so good for the three leading Canadian regiments – the West Nova Scotia, the Perth, and the Cape Breton Highlanders – that a conference at Corps headquarters was seriously examining the possibility of capturing the Monte Luro heights that night and pushing straight on to the Conca, nearly seven miles ahead.

Then, however, the Germans seemed to grasp for the first time that this was a full-scale attack, and not merely a feint or a reconnaissance in force. There were three small towns on the Canadian front just north of the river – Montecchio, Osteria Nuova, and Borgo Santa Maria – and from the hills behind these the enemy guns swept the advancing Canadians as they stumbled through the minefields in the flats which bordered on the river. The Canadian official account gives a vivid picture of the unpleasantness of the next few hours:

'The attempt made by the West Nova Scotia Regiment to reach Point 133, north-east of Osteria Nuova, turned into a sad débâcle. With all its companies caught in a large minefield midway between the river and the lateral road, the battalion staggered helplessly under a storm of fire from the enemy's automatic weapons, mortars and artillery, ensnared in precisely the sort of killing-ground which the designers of the Line had intended to create. Unable to move, the West Novas had to be withdrawn, suffering almost as many casualties getting out of the minefield as they had while becoming involved in it.'[6] The regiment had lost seventy-six men – twenty of them killed.

On the left, too, in the fight for Montecchio, the Cape Bretons had heavy casualties, three times being driven back to the Foglia by withering German fire. The Perths, however, were more successful. They fought their way on to a small height behind Montecchio, and pushed on to higher ground to the north-east.

The alarms of the night were many. Supporting tanks floundered in a minefield until dawn, but by noon on the 31st the Irish Regiment, coming in on the right through the ground held by the Perths, drove the enemy from his remaining positions on the heights above the shattered, smoking rubble of Montecchio, capturing more than 120 officers and men.

In the centre, Princess Patricia's Canadian Light Infantry, supported by British tanks of the 48th Royal Tank Regiment, enveloped Osteria Nuova after a bitter struggle with the German veterans of the 1st Parachute Division – of whom nearly 250 were taken prisoners.

The success of the day was marred, however, by a portent of what was to come in the days and weeks ahead. North of Osteria Nuova, almost half-way to Tomba di Pesaro, was the height of Point 204. It was intended to seize this position by a joint attack of the British Columbia Dragoons and the Perths. But the Perths, losing men in scores to an inferno of shell and mortar fire, were not able to move without being annihilated. The big grey Shermans of the Dragoons pushed on alone across the open countryside in front of their objective – and received a swift and bloody lesson on the rashness of armour operating against prepared positions without infantry. The regiment's half-hundred tanks advanced bravely up the slope of Point 204, swept and enfiladed by anti-tank fire from the heights on their left. One by one, the Shermans were hit; troop after troop, squadron after squadron came under the lash of the German 89-mm. guns, firing projectiles with a tungsten-carbide core – twice as hard as steel – which smashed at 3,400 feet a second into the tanks, turrets, petrol tanks and ammunition bins. Soon twelve tanks were burning on the slopes; two dozen more were disabled; at the end of the day only eighteen were still able to fight. Regimental headquarters was wiped out, and among those who died was Lieutenant-Colonel F. A. Vokes, brother of Major-General Christopher Vokes, commander of the Canadian 1st Division.

At night, the Perths fought their way forward, and with them came the tanks of Lord Strathcona's Horse to relieve the battered Dragoons. The situation was now contained; but looking back, twenty years later, it seems clear that the pattern of the campaign of the Gothic Line had already been set.

On the first day of September, however, only the mass of Monte Luro stood between the Canadians and the Adriatic, where, under Leese's plan, they were to take over from the Poles.

First the Strathcona tanks, supported by the 4th Princess Louise Dragoon Guards – these were fighting now as an ordinary infantry battalion – were paying the debt of the British Columbia Dragoons on Point 204. A joint tank–infantry attack caught the confident Germans on the point of a counter-attack and in the open; the machine-guns of the Shermans played along their ranks as they crouched in folds of ground or along the thin hedgerows; more than 120 were killed[7] and bull-dozers had to be used to dig their graves.

The capture of Point 204 cleared the left flank for the advance of Vokes' 1st Division on Monte Luro. A joint force of Canadian infantry, the Loyal Edmontons, and British armour, the 12th Royal Tanks, attacked the well-constructed trench system on the heights and found it virtually deserted. Kesselring had seen the danger to the German 1st Parachute Division as the Canadians thrust out their spearheads towards the coast. He was pulling them back quickly, and in the next few hours von Vietinghoff was ordered to withdraw 76th Panzer Corps – the left wing of the German Tenth Army – to the line of the River Conca. During the morning of the 2nd the Poles had occupied Pesaro, and moved on towards Cattolica; then they were pulled back into army reserve as the Canadians reached the Adriatic. Before dawn on 3 September, the Royal Canadian Regiment of the Canadian 1st Brigade had actually crossed the Conca, making a small bridgehead north of San Giovanni, three miles inland from Cattolica.[8] *(Map 2.)*

Along the whole of the front, the situation looked very promising indeed. The main works of the Gothic Line were now behind the advancing infantry, and while the Germans had certainly not been routed, they had lost heavily in both dead and prisoners.

'It had been a great success for Eighth Army,' Alexander wrote later. 'By a combination of surprise in preparation and dash in the attack, they had swept through a fortified line which had been twelve months in preparation almost as though it were not there.'[9]

For the tired and depleted Allied infantry, however, there

was little respite. Ahead of them lay the most vital task of the campaign. They had now to hold open the gate for the 1st British Armoured Division in its anticipated dash to the plains of Lombardy. In the exhilaration of these days of early September, the task did not seem too difficult. Kesselring was in trouble – possibly the biggest trouble he had been in during the whole of the war in Italy. But Kesselring in trouble was a dangerous opponent. Several times in the Italian campaign – at Cassino, Anzio, Lake Trasimene – he had revealed his toughness and adaptability under pressure. He moved swiftly now.

He had already brought 26th Panzer Division to stem the advancing Allied tide, and the infantry components of the division, thrown in hurriedly, had suffered severely. He now moved in 98th Infantry Division from its reserve position near Bologna, and the famous 29th Panzer Grenadier Division was transferred from Fourteenth Army at the centre. Perhaps the most significant move of all, however, passed almost unnoticed by both sides. The German 5th Mountain Division, in accordance with OKW orders, was being transferred to the French frontier, where the high command still feared an attack linked with the invasion of the south of France. Ironically enough, its move had been hampered and delayed by incessant Allied air interdiction on the roads north. Now part of the division was brusquely halted, and its 100th Mountain Regiment – an élite Austrian unit – was brought back to the Adriatic.[10] There it was disposed upon a ridge called Gemmano.

7
A Foot in the Gate

Eighth Army as a whole was now beginning to wheel ominously left, against the ridge system which thrust out ragged spurs just north-east of the northern bank of the Conca. This was precisely what the planners did not want to happen, and the urgent need of opening the way for 1st Armoured Division through the gap to the east of Coriano was very clear.

On 3 September, after a stiff fight in the dry shingle bed of the Conca, the 6th York and Lancasters of 139th Brigade crossed the river and fought their way up the slopes beyond to capture the little village of San Andrea.

Hawkesworth now demanded one last great effort from the weary and depleted infantry of 46th Division after their ten days of continuous fighting. Five miles north of San Andrea ran the stream of the Marano; here, if it could be reached quickly, was the gate for the armoured division. Hawkesworth ordered the Hampshire battalions of 128th Brigade to seize crossings over the river at Ospedaletto,[1] and form a flank west to contain the enemy, so that the armour could go through next day. Under very heavy fire, 2nd Hampshires climbed on to the slopes just below San Clemente, little more than a mile north of the Conca. Now, however, the German reinforcements, and the dominating positions of their artillery on the heights to the left, began to exert inexorable pressure. Two companies of 5th Hampshires, attacking Castelleale a couple of miles ahead, came under fire from several kinds of artillery, with a hail of bullets from small-arms positions. They held on along the road as long as they could, but casualties were too heavy, and there were no fresh infantry to push through. They were pulled back to San Clemente, a mile east of the Coriano ridge. The crossing at Ospedaletto was still in enemy hands. That was the end of the 46th Division advance. Hawkesworth had got a foot in the gate, but he had not been able to open it. The next day would tell whether a foot in the gate would be enough. *(Map 2.)*

The heights of Coriano and Gemmano loomed on the left, and from them the Germans still dominated the so-called corridor between the hills and the sea. With the left flank in enemy hands, and the river crossing ahead fiercely resisted, the omens looked bad for 1st Armoured Division. To see how this situation had developed in this way, it is necessary to go back four days and look at the progress of another British division which was now also in the fight.

★ ★ ★

The fierce German resistance in front of Tavoleto at the end of August meant that the general advance of V Corps was being to some extent inhibited by the delay on its left flank. To maintain the momentum of the attack, Keightley brought in the 56th (London) Division from its reserve positions just south of the Foglia, about 8,000 yards from the Gothic Line.

The division was commanded by Major-General John Yelde Whitfield. It had seen very heavy fighting at Anzio earlier in the year, and had been sent to the Middle East to rest and refit. This was its first action since its return to Italy. The division included a brigade – the 169th – of three battalions of the Queen's Royal Regiment, and Whitfield himself was a former Queen's officer.

On 31 August, the division was ordered to take over from 138th Brigade on the left sector of 46th Division and to advance through them to the Monte Cappella ridge just west of Mondaino, and thence forward to Montefiore, a small hill-town which overlooked the River Conca and its tributary the Ventena.

The emphasis in Eighth Army, and particularly in V Corps,

which had the Canadians to keep up with on the right, was still on speed. Belief in the breakthrough of the armour, which had been strengthened even among the pessimists by the German discomfiture of the past few days, was now stronger than ever. Nothing was to be allowed to slow Eighth Army as it gathered itself for its leap to the River Po. Whitfield remembered this emphasis later:

'There's a certain amount of more or less flat country between the hills and the sea, and they hoped to get through that without having to be involved in the hills. I can still see the way the corps commander kept putting his hand on the map and saying: "We mustn't get involved in the hills. We can get along on this flat bit and the army commander reckons that we may get a race up that right-hand side."'[2]

This was a misunderstanding between Keightley and Whitfield, natural enough in the hurry and confusion of battle, but ominous in its effects. Whitfield thought that he was being warned off the hills. Keightley did not intend this.[3] He was emphasizing speed, but he did not wish to gamble with security. The results of this failure to appreciate each other's intentions became apparent in the next few days.

Meanwhile, however, Whitfield was moving swiftly. He gave the task of taking Monte Cappella to the Queen's Brigade. One battalion, 2nd/6th Queen's, attacked on 1 September. The summit was reached by the leading company without loss, but the next company up met heavy machine-gun fire from positions hidden in trees and houses, and its company commander was killed.[4]

These positions were cleared later, and a dozen prisoners were taken. This handful of men was not without significance. They were from the 98th Division, which had been hurried down from Bologna, and they had taken over their positions only the previous day. Their presence was a clear warning that the advance of 56th Division might not be as trouble-free as the optimists hoped.

For optimism there still was, and it was growing. Eighth Army seemed resolutely to turn its eyes away from the long brooding flank of ridges and hills on its left. It was recognized that the nature of the country might slow V Corps a little, but it was now believed that the anticipated breakthrough would be made by the Canadians on the right. Whitfield was now ordered to have ready a mobile force to exploit this success, if and when it came. This force was to be commanded by Brigadier Otho Prior-Palmer, and consisted of brigade headquarters of his 7th Armoured Brigade, 2nd Royal Tank Regiment, a squadron of 44th Reconnaissance Regiment, a battalion of lorried infantry, and a field regiment of artillery. Prior-Palmer was universally known in the army by his Sandhurst nickname of 'Minnow', and Whitfield christened his new command with the codename Minforce.[5]

Minforce came into being in the early hours of 2 September, but the long day which followed dampened the hopes which had been held for it. German resistance stiffened in front of 56th Division; enemy guns and mortars pounded the Monte Cappella ridge, and the Queen's Brigade made no significant advance. On 3 September, after so brief an existence, Minforce was disbanded, its units returning to their parent formations.

Nevertheless, the intelligence reports still proclaimed that the situation was favourable, that the enemy was weak, and that one last heave would put Eighth Army into the plains of Lombardy and the valley of the Po. Whitfield's divisional order on the 3rd – the one which dissolved Minforce – defined its intention as 'to pursue the enemy to Bologna and destroy him'. And it began with the unequivocal words: 'A breakthrough is occurring on Eighth Army front both on the Canadian Corps front and on the right of V Corps. . . .'[6]

Whitfield proposed now to advance to the line of the Marano – where, as we have seen, Hawkesworth was at this moment making his own vain bid to seize the crossing at Ospedaletto. After the Marano was reached, the advance – it was really envisaged as more of a pursuit – would be headed by the tanks of the 7th Armoured Brigade.

The advance was to be made on a two-brigade front, with 167th Brigade on the right and 168th Brigade on the left. Now, however, the interlocking nature of this jagged front of ridges, hill towns, and valleys became apparent; 168th

Brigade was unable to move until 4th Indian Division, far out on the left, had cleared the ground north of Tavoleto. Even by the evening of 4 September, the situation there was confused, and 168th Brigade was still out of the battle at midnight.

Meanwhile, Whitfield's hopes rested with 167th Brigade. This was to advance in three bounds – first, the complex of roads just south of Montefiore; second, the Gemmano ridge south of the bend of the Conca; third, the Mulazzano ridge north of the Marano. (*Map 2.*)

The brigade attack began in the early hours of 4 September, and by half-past nine in the morning the 8th Royal Fusiliers had safely achieved the first bound. The 7th Oxford and Buckinghamshires went on the north, and by late afternoon Montefiore was captured, with more than 100 prisoners from the German garrison.

Whitfield decided to wait no longer for 4th Indian Division to clear the way, but switched 168th Brigade over to the right of 167th. Both brigades, however, were ordered to try to by-pass the long, imposing Gemmano ridge which loomed on their left; only if there was enemy interference was it judged that it might be necessary for 167th Brigade to capture it.[7] Whitfield was keeping uppermost in his mind the emphasis of his superiors that he 'must not get involved in the hills'.

Nevertheless, he did send the 7th Oxford and Bucks up to Gemmano 'purely,' he said, 'on the principle that every commander is responsible for his own security.'[8] On the morning of 5 September, the battalion had two companies on the slopes of the ridge, but they were under heavy pressure and could get no farther. A battalion was not enough. It was becoming clearer and clearer that the Gemmano ridge could neither be by-passed nor easily captured.

This was not surprising. In the optimism which had run through Eighth Army in the past three days, the tremendous importance of Gemmano for the German defence of the Conca valley had been more or less discounted. The ground along the top of the ridge, and the high ground around Croce, a mile to the north, gave the enemy magnificent fire positions dominating the roads in the valley below, and reaching out to interdict movement in the narrow corridor between the ridge and the sea. Here, and along the Coriano feature which ran to the north of Croce, must Kesselring fight if he was to hold off disaster. Already he had massed beside the Adriatic the elements of seven divisions – 26th Panzer, 1st Parachute, 71st, 98th, 162nd, and 278th Infantry Divisions, and the excellent 5th Mountain Division.

The two brigades of the British 56th Division, and 46th Division struggling on the slopes of San Clemente, had already in the past few hours felt the chill shadow of Gemmano behind their left shoulders. The momentary pause, the delay in going straight for the ridge, had helped the Germans to arrange their units upon and behind it as they were hurried piecemeal into battle. Whitfield felt strongly afterwards that he had acted in the spirit of his instructions, and that he had tried to carry out his part of the Eighth Army plan, with its emphasis on speed.

If this plan was to work, the armour must now break through. The date selected was 4 September. The position could hardly be described as one of exploiting success. Hawkesworth and 46th Division had not reached the Marano; Whitfield and 56th Division were only on the lower slopes of Gemmano, and did not yet hold the high ground around Croce. The gate through which 1st Armoured Division must pass was barely ajar, much less open. The German troops, tough, brave, resilient, waited in their excellent positions dominating the two roads which ran west from Morciano along the Conca valley. Every crossroad, every stretch was registered; the exact ranges were filed comfortably away in the minds of the commanders of the German batteries of 88-mm. guns.

Yet in Eighth Army, there was a thrill of anticipation. Hundreds of men in the tired infantry battalions had died in the past nine days to get this far, but it was passionately believed that this would not be in vain. The long, exhausting, bloody struggle in Italy seemed almost over; now it was the turn of the armour to peel back the German front like a ragged strip of tin from a sardine can, and finish the job. Waiting and watching in the corners of ruined farmhouses and in slit trenches, the anxious German and British infantry heard in the night of 3 September, distantly at first, but growing louder and louder, the roar of the engines of hundreds of tanks.

8

The Armour

'Dash and doggedness alone no longer make a soldier, Bayerlein; he must have sufficient intelligence to enable him to get the most out of his fighting machine.'

> Field-Marshal Erwin Rommel, in conversation with General Fritz Bayerlein, 17 May 1944.

The 1st Armoured Division, which was the tool with which Leese now meant to split open the German front and drive to the River Po, had not been in battle since the end of the Tunisian campaign in May 1943. After a year in Algeria, the division had moved to Italy in June 1944, staying at a training area about fifty miles from Bari on the southern Adriatic coast.

The units which composed it bore some of the most famous names in the British Army. The three armoured regiments were the Queen's Bays, the 9th Lancers, and the 10th Hussars. The divisional reconnaissance troops were Churchill's former regiment, the 4th Hussars, whose cavalry record stretched back through the Charge of the Light Brigade at Balaclava to Wellington's campaign in the Peninsula.

The names of the infantry battalions were also distinguished. The battalion attached to the armoured brigade was the 1st King's Royal Rifle Corps. There were two infantry brigades in the division – the 18th, with the 1st Buffs, the 9th King's Own Yorkshire Light Infantry, and the 14th Sherwood Foresters; and the 43rd Lorried Brigade, made up of three battalions of the almost legendary Gurkhas.

The division was commanded by Major-General Richard Amyatt Hull, a young man of thirty-seven who had won a fine reputation, first while commanding the 17th/21st Lancers early in the war, and then successively the 12th Infantry Brigade and the 26th Armoured Brigade in North Africa.

This was his first action as a general officer, and he was well aware that in spite of his glittering order of battle, his division had to face the problem of lack of battle experience in Italian conditions. First, as we have seen, the four cavalry regiments had not fought at all for fifteen months – and never in Italy. The battalions of the 18th Infantry Brigade had seen action at Anzio and later south of Florence; but the Gurkha brigade was fresh from Palestine, and had not seen a shot fired in anger during the whole war. Hull's own comment sums up his feelings:

'If a Staff College student had suggested that as a solution for re-forming an armoured division, he'd have got nought out of ten.'[1]

Hull had as his armoured brigade commander Brigadier Richard Goodbody, a gunner officer of the Honourable Artillery Company, who had an excellent fighting record from North Africa, and who had spent two months on the Italian front, studying the particular conditions of armoured warfare.

In June, Goodbody launched 2nd Armoured Brigade on an intensive programme of training in the art of co-operation between armour and infantry. His method, as described in a regimental account, was a model for the Italian campaign:

'The infantry were the senior partners. They first decided how a position should be attacked, and were then given an appropriate number of tanks to support them. The rest of the tanks were responsible for helping and supporting the leading tanks from behind. The infantry scoured all bushes, hedges, and ditches to clear out any bazooka-men or snipers who might be in a position to pick off tanks or their commanders at ranges of a hundred yards and less. The bazooka was a highly-effective anti-tank weapon used by infantry. It consisted of a long tube out of which was fired a hollow-charge projectile that was capable of penetrating the armour of any British or American tank. One man could carry it and it was effective up to ranges of seventy-five yards. The Germans were very artful in its use and the bazooka-men and snipers sometimes held their fire until the leading troops were a mile or more beyond them. To overcome this it was necessary for the attacking troops to advance in great depth, so that when the leading infantry reached the objective their rear had only recently crossed the start-line. In this way the infantry and the tanks were well spread out over the ground just won and in a position to help each other to deal with the snipers. All-round observation in each tank was vital, because the enemy were just as likely to fire from either flank, or from behind, as they were from in front.

'There was no hard-and-fast rule as to who should lead. It might change as much as three or four times in a mile, depending on the terrain and on whether opposition was more likely to be anti-tank or anti-infantry. In this way the best anti-tank tactics possible in the circumstances were superimposed, as it were, on the infantry tactics. Each partner was aware of the difficulties and the limitations of the other. If in the event tanks suffered heavy casualties, they saved the lives of many infantrymen and their sacrifice was worth while. All this sounds easy, as generalizations usually do. It was the mass of small details that had to be solved correctly which made the complications.'[2]

These tactics were admirably suited to Italian conditions. When, eventually, they were finally used in battle in the spring of 1945, the result was the encirclement and annihilation of the German armies south of the Po. That moment, however, was still eight months away. The Eighth Army plan for the Gothic Line envisaged something much faster than these tactics were likely, initially, to produce. Hull's division was intended to make a classic armoured breakthrough, pouring through a gap in the enemy front in the way in which Guderian in 1940 and Patton in 1945 showed it could be done in France and Germany.

The division was going to have to be both brilliant and lucky if it was to make this dream come true, for the Eighth Army planners seemed to take little account of previous experience. Italy, in general, had proved highly unsuitable country for armoured operations of this kind, and the country north of the Gothic Line, alluring though its green patches might appear on the map beside the brown contours of the mountains, was probably the most unsuitable of all.

This was a flaw in thinking which was to have the most savage consequences, and yet it suited the psychology not only of Eighth Army but also of the armoured regiments themselves. Its roots stretched into the past – the recent past in the case of Eighth Army, but more distant years for the cavalry regiments.

First, the cavalry. It has been fashionable to depict the British cavalry officer in the years before 1939 as looking wistfully back to the days of the horse, ill at ease with, and contemptuous of the clumsy armoured fighting vehicles with which he was now equipped. However true this may or may not have been of the pre-war years, by 1944 it was no longer the case in a fighting sense.

The officers and men of the 2nd Armoured Brigade – indeed, of every other armoured brigade also – had served in tanks for up to five years of war. Most of them had never as much as seen an army horse; almost all of the men, all the junior officers – but fewer of the senior officers – had been trained at the great tank training centres at Barnard Castle and Catterick on the northern moors, or in the Royal Armoured Corps Officer Cadet Training Unit at Sandhurst, where armoured professionalism was brought to a very high peak.

The cavalry tradition, however, lingered on in other ways – seemingly innocuous echoes of the past, but not without significance. There was still, even now, something left of the ingrained sense of cavalry superiority – not in fighting quality, for in view of infantry casualties this would have been grotesque – but of a sort of social superiority within the army.

The old tradition of cavalry exclusiveness had arisen in part from the social importance in British life of the horse; the cavalryman rode while the infantryman walked. This still applied. The armoured trooper did not have to plod along roads and ditches, draped with the laborious paraphernalia of war – a rifle, a spade, boxes of ammunition, a blanket, a water-bottle. These things he was able to carry on his vehicle, with many other minor but significant comforts which would have hopelessly over-burdened the foot soldier.

His armour, of course, did not protect him from death. It

merely made some kinds of death less likely, and others more likely. He could ignore the machine-gun bullets he heard pattering on the outside of his tank, but a single anti-tank gun which meant nothing to an infantry platoon could destroy a troop of tanks in less than a minute, leaving the crews helplessly trapped in their burning steel boxes. In battle, both infantryman and trooper took the same chance, but the trooper had a more comfortable journey to the battleground.

The trooper was also a specialist. Every member of a five-man tank crew could drive the tank, operate its wireless, load and fire its gun. Each man was an integral part of an efficient fighting machine; indeed, unless he was reasonably good at a job which demanded a fair degree of intelligence, he would rapidly be displaced from a tank crew and found other military employment.

The sense of being a military *élite*, too, was fostered by the idea of the employment of armoured divisions in what might be called the post-Guderian days, after the massive German scything movement across France in 1940 which had almost destroyed the British Expeditionary Force. In the British Army conception of the armoured division, the slogging battles of attrition were not the role of an armoured regiment. This was the traditional cavalry one of pursuit, exploitation, and destruction – words much more glamorous and evocative than could be found for the role of the infantry.

In 1944, British armour was in some ways half-way between its cavalry past and the sheer professionalism which the present and the future demanded. The three fighting squadrons in many armoured regiments were still referred to as 'the sabre squadrons'; in some regiments tanks were always known as 'chargers'; the order given for a tank crew to get into its vehicle was 'mount'; and, occasionally, the commander of a knocked-out tank would report that he had been 'unhorsed'. These things were not harmful in themselves, and in many ways might even be considered useful in making some kind of bridge with a regiment's past. Words, however, and especially military words, are not unimportant; and although the officers and men of British armoured regiments were by now thoroughly at ease with the tanks in which they had to fight, there were times when it seemed that they still heard the bugles calling from the cavalry lines of not so very long ago.

This applied most of all to the officers. Although by 1944 the cavalry regiments were recruiting subalterns from a wider and wider social field, the ideal officer was not expected to be an earnest or scientific professional, but something rather lighter and gayer. *Insouciance* was perhaps the quality still most admired and sought in a cavalry subaltern.

The principal test of a regiment or brigade was: 'will they "go"?' And by 'go' was meant the combination of dash and *élan* which was judged the most vital quality of an armoured cavalry force.

This belief had been strengthened by the warfare in the desert which was still fresh in Eighth Army minds. There in the clean open spaces, the regiments had manœuvred and fought in the classic tradition, relatively unhampered by the claustrophobic nature of the ground which they were to find in Italy. British armour, under the carefully-controlling hand of Montgomery, had learned the lesson of Guderian. It might be said that in some ways it had learned it too well. Army commanders with armoured divisions waiting in their reserves were eager to out-Guderian the Germans; the breakthrough was the be-all and end-all of armoured cavalry operations.

British armour in Italy, however, was not fighting, like Guderian, an old-fashioned, out-thought enemy with little knowledge of tank warfare. Nor was it advancing along the great empty roads of northern France, or the long bare ridges of the Western Desert. The conditions of tank warfare were changing, and the technique of anti-tank warfare was developing day by day. The infantry bazooka alone, properly and bravely handled, spelt the end of the tank's brief reign over the battlefield. The anti-tank gun, firing its high velocity projectile from prepared positions, always had the advantage of the tanks it aimed at.

As far as the British and American armoured divisions were concerned, these disadvantages were accentuated by the inadequate nature of the vehicles in which they had to fight. Two main types of Allied tank were in service in Italy – the British Churchill and the American Sherman. The 38-ton Churchill was used in tank brigades whose role was mainly infantry support, while the 30-ton Sherman equipped the armoured divisions. By 1944, the Sherman was obsolescent in relation to the German tanks which mainly opposed it in Italy.

It was usually still equipped with a 75-mm. gun, for although supplies of Shermans with the improved 76-mm. cannon were now arriving in Italy, they were being doled out to regiments on the basis of only two or three to a squadron. Official United States figures[3] for the performance of the standard 75-mm. gun against German tanks make lamentable reading.

The comparative tables allow the 75-mm. Sherman *no* penetration at any range against the frontal armour of a German Panther or Mark I Tiger tank, though the Panther's own improved 75-mm. could blast a shot through the front of the Sherman at 3,000 yards.

The best chance for a 75-mm. Sherman was to hit a Panther or Tiger in the side, where it was able to penetrate at ranges of 4,000 yards and 1,900 yards respectively. The Panther and Tiger, however, could effectively engage the Sherman in the flank at ranges of about 5,000 yards.

With the 76-mm. Sherman, the picture became brighter, though the German still had some advantage. A 76-mm. Sherman could penetrate the front turret of a Panther at 600 yards and of a Tiger at 1,200; the Panther could do the same to the 76-mm. Sherman from 3,000 and the Tiger from 1,800. In fact, in the type of closed country where tanks fought in Italy, these long ranges rarely obtained, so the 76-mm. Sherman with its effective penetration at 600 yards was nearly the equal in hitting power of its bigger adversaries.

The Sherman was mechanically reliable and light enough for tank recovery crews to tow away and quickly repair. The 55-ton Tiger had great engine problems, and many had to be abandoned to the advancing Allies when they broke down, since their great weight made them difficult to recover quickly.[4] This meant that the Germans lost the tank but not the crew, whereas British or American tank squadrons often had to give two or three Shermans, and a consequent proportion of dead and wounded among their crews, in order to knock out one giant Tiger.

The Sherman had one more disadvantage. It burned easily. With its petrol protected only by the thinner armour on its sides, the flash from even a glancing blow could turn it in a moment into a blazing torch. The German tank and anti-tank crews had a sardonic name for the Sherman tanks which rolled into their sights. They called them 'Ronsons' – automatic lighters.

The ingenuity of British and American tank gunners, however, went some way to redress the balance which the under-gunning of their tanks had tipped against them. The official tables might show no penetration against a Panther or Tiger, but the man in the gunner's seat of a Sherman soon learned that these monsters had weak spots, especially on the turret ring where the enemy gun revolved on its traverse above the hull, and where a direct hit, even if it did not penetrate, would fuse the metal and jam the gun. This needed a cool head and a sharp eye, however, whereas almost any enemy hit on a Sherman was fatal.

Thus by autumn 1944 in Italy, the Allied armour, numerically superior to the enemy's though it was, could no longer be a decisive weapon in any battle where the Germans were able to put up a long resistance from prepared positions. Only in the most favourable conditions, when the enemy front had crumbled to a disastrous extent, could the tank again become an invincible armoured horse, rather than a vulnerable mobile gun. What had now to be discovered was whether these conditions yet operated in the Gothic Line. The question which faced 2nd Armoured Brigade, as it moved north in August towards the sound of the guns, was not '*Will* they go?', but '*Can* they go?'.

9
Frustration

On 31 August, the 300-odd tanks – Shermans and the lighter
Stuarts – of the 1st Armoured Division moved forward to a
staging area near Senigallia, north of Ancona. The plan was
that they would halt there for a twelve-hour rest, and then continue to a concentration area near the River Foglia, where they
were due to be assembled by the morning of 3 September.

The narrow dusty tank track from Ancona to Senigallia,
however, became blocked by a ditched tank, and the last of the
tired and sweating tank men did not reach the staging area until
day broke on the 2nd. The Foglia was still forty miles away, and
there was hardly any time for sleep.

'It was obvious,' says the 9th Lancers' account, 'that all was
not well. Presumably we were to start exploiting very soon, and
we were not there.'[1]

The planned twelve-hour rest for the weary crews was cut in
half. By afternoon the columns of tanks and lorries were again
on the move north, winding slowly on, nose to tail, through
dust-clouds so thick that visibility was down to five yards. There
was a staging point on the River Metauro, and the dust-masked
men rushed down to the river to bathe as they arrived in the
late evening. They had had virtually no sleep for thirty-eight
hours, but at ten minutes after midnight they were ordered to
move again at once.

Two routes were planned for them. The first, codenamed
'One-Bar', was for the lorries and soft transport. It had been
constructed by the engineers along razor-edged mountain
ridges, along a track so difficult that the heavier vehicles had to
reverse to get round each corner, leaving the rear of the column

sitting in fretting inactivity amid the settling clouds of white, choking dust. In addition, a strange hot wind blew so hard that the drivers of vehicles on the more precipitate part of the track felt uneasy for their vehicles. By the time the last vehicle reached the Foglia, the drivers had been at their posts for fifty hours. Only a handful of vehicles had been lost, overturned and rolled ruthlessly, sometimes burning, off the track and down into the rocky valleys.

For the tanks, the journey had been even worse. Naturally, the lorries had been allotted the better road, and 'Boat' was a good deal more difficult than 'One-Bar'.

The tank crews had a scant two hours' rest beside the Metauro before they tackled this route. The dust flung up by the sliding, churning tank tracks of the Shermans was so thick that drivers in the rear of the column could not see at all, but drove by listening above the roar of their own engines to the bellowings of the tank in front. Sometimes a tank would slew to the side of the road, one of its tracks ripped from the bogies by some too-exacting turning strain. Here and there a tank attempted an impossible gradient to try to get round some obstacle on the track, and rolled over and over into the side of the valley while its bruised and shaken crew clung hard to the ammunition racks inside the turret.

The noise as the column of tanks crept slowly through the hills towards the Foglia was frightening – the ear-splitting thunder of hundreds of engines of 450 horse-power, all in low gear. The tanks were burning between four and five gallons of petrol to a mile, and many ran out of fuel.

By daybreak, the head of the column had wound its way to the heights which looked down on the narrow stream of the Foglia. A Bays' officer described the moment:

'The bottom of the valley was still enveloped in a violet gloom, illuminated fitfully by the gun flashes of our artillery in contrast with the daylight which was striking the hill-tops beyond. It could be observed that our guns were across the river and were firing in support of what had apparently become a steady and methodical advance by the infantry.'[2]

By 8 a.m. on 3 September tanks were rumbling into leaguer positions south of the river. The exhausted crews snatched some sleep, while the fitters worked ceaselessly to bring in those which had been stranded during the night, or had developed mechanical defects during the journey. By evening the last of the movable tanks had straggled in, and the position was better than might have seemed possible during the nightmare approach march. Nevertheless, it was far from reassuring. The brigade tank state showed that the three armoured regiments, which normally totalled 52 Shermans each, were now down to: Bays 45, 9th Lancers 47, 10th Hussars 44.[3] Twenty tanks – roughly 13 per cent of the armoured strength – were out of action, knocked out not by the enemy but by the ground on which they had to fight. Some of these made their way into regimental areas in the next few days. Meanwhile, however, while the exhausted tank crews slept and the fitters toiled, the divisional reconnaissance regiment, the 4th Hussars, were already beginning the opening phase of the division's operations in the Gothic Line.

★   ★   ★

The Hussars had arrived in leaguer about eight miles south of the Conca at 4.30 a.m., after their own appalling marathon approach march. These tank crews, too, were eager for sleep, but before they could settle down the regiment was told to move at once. It was ordered to reconnoitre the Conca, find crossing places for the division, and then continue to Coriano to open up the way for the armoured brigade.[4]

The commanding officer, Lieutenant-Colonel R. C. Kidd, issued his own orders, maps were hurriedly marked, and at first light the forty-six Shermans and forty-two turretless Honey tanks moved off. The leading squadron, deploying across country towards the Conca, found marshy ground immediately, and within a couple of hours the whole squadron was stuck fast. The next squadron, following up, also became helplessly bogged down. The regiment, the 'eyes and ears' of Hull's division, had two squadrons effectively out of action before it had even seen the enemy.

At ten o'clock in the morning, Kidd sent off his remaining

squadron – 'C', commanded by Major H. L. White – ordering
it to keep to the road at all costs. These tanks advanced successfully until they reached a small bridge across a narrow
valley. The bridge was partly destroyed, but the road behind
the tanks was so narrow that it was impossible to turn round.
Gingerly, the tanks crossed the bridge one by one, and half the
squadron got across before the ramshackle structure collapsed,
hurling one tank into the river below.

The half-squadron already across pushed on towards the
Conca, while the tanks left on the other side reversed out as best
they could, and set off across country, fortunately contacting
the rest of the squadron later. The tanks now climbed up to the
ridge above the Conca, and came under heavy enemy artillery
fire. Little was known in the squadron about the situation on
the ground, and two troops were sent up to spurs overlooking
the valley. Two tanks stripped off their tracks on the way, and
when the remainder reached the spurs, they found them
occupied by a Hampshire battalion of 46th Division. It was the
front line.

However, the squadron was at least at the Conca, and an
N.C.O. in a Honey was sent back to where Kidd in his own
tank, 'Dauntless', was waiting with the two squadrons which
had now laboriously extricated themselves from the marsh. He
arrived late in the afternoon, and the regiment, with him in the
lead, set off across a difficult route. In the darkness he lost his
way. The regiment's own account tells of the frustration of the
situation:

'It was a black moment for everyone. Kidd realized that to go
on wandering about the hills in the darkness would be folly, so
he ordered the column to halt and a message was passed to the
division that they were waiting for visibility to improve.
Everyone was depressed. In their first day, begun with such
high hopes, the reconnaissance regiment, presumed experts in
path-finding, had managed to move only a few miles towards
the enemy and had got itself hopelessly lost. It was difficult to
know what to do until an obvious course presented itself. Quite
in the tradition of the 4th Hussars, Kidd summoned some of his
officers to 'Dauntless', opened some wine, and held a party – in
the circumstances rather a melancholy one. It did, however,

have the effect of cheering spirits to a small degree, and then, as if to prove that the party was the correct action, White's voice came over the wireless to say he was sure his rear troop could hear the noise of tanks, and that he was sure the regiment must be close. Division was at once informed that the 4th Hussars were advancing again. Guided only by relayed reports on the sound of the tanks, the column crawled slowly on through the inky darkness. It climbed a long slope, found a road, turned down it, and soon afterwards found the tail of C Squadron.'5

The reunited regiment moved on down a patchwork of narrow tracks and drove on across the wide, shallow, stony bed of the Conca. At 5 a.m. on 4 September, the tanks were nearing Coriano. But further frustrations were now in store. The rest of the armoured division was now coming forward behind the 4th Hussars, and the regiment was ordered to halt and pull off the road. A position was found in a field about a mile from Coriano, and there the 4th Hussars sat all day. The Hampshire Brigade of Hawkesworth's 46th Division was just in front of them, struggling on the shell-torn slopes round Castelleale, and the Hussars supported them with fire and smoke where possible.

The enemy artillery soon found the range of the lines of tanks, and they were heavily shelled, losing one or two men killed through the long day. Late in the afternoon the motor battalion, the 1st K.R.R.C., arrived and took over the ground. The 4th Hussars withdrew. Few of its officers and men had slept for sixty hours; all were disappointed and frustrated. It had been a bitter demonstration of the difficulties of armoured cavalry in the Gothic Line. And yet in some ways it had not been such a hopeless failure as the tired Hussars thought. *If* 46th Division, after all, had reached the Marano, and *if* the weary and diminished Hampshires had managed to press on past Castelleale, the leading regiment of Hull's division was there in its proper position and at the right time, ready to exploit. There could have been worse results to the uncertainty and confusion of the previous night.

10

The First Check

A little to the south of the field where the 4th Hussars waited in frustration during 4 September, the tanks of 2nd Armoured Brigade were now launched on their own vital part of this momentous day. The three armoured regiments had crossed the Foglia during the 3rd, and the crowded and inadequate roads, packed with the trucks, water-carts, armoured cars, ambulances and motor-cycle dispatch riders of two army corps, were already casting their malign spell over the movement of the tanks.

When the commanding officer of the Bays, Lieutenant-Colonel D. V. H. Asquith, took the regiment's reconnaissance troop north of the river to look at the ground, he found that the road he had used was now the main axis of the Canadian Corps, and the traffic on it was so dense that he was unable to bring the tanks back. He was separated from the regiment for most of the day, but finally found positions for all the tanks just to the north of the Foglia.[1] Forty-four of the fifty-two tanks were now with the regiment, and the Bays crossed the Foglia in the late afternoon. The weary tank crews settled down once more to try to snatch some sleep. The 10th Hussars had crossed during the morning, and the 9th Lancers in the evening.

At eight o'clock Goodbody went to divisional headquarters to get the orders for his brigade. His first task was to lead the division over the River Conca, a few miles to the north, crossing it about four miles from its mouth. He would then cover the concentration and deployment of the division immediately north of the river, before it passed through 46th Division in the first phase of the anticipated breakthrough.[2]

Astonishingly little, however, was known about the progress

and positions of the British infantry. In particular, it was uncertain whether 46th Division had, in fact, reached the Marano. But the information available, vague and scanty as it was, agreed on one thing. The Germans were tired and badly mauled. Pursuit was the key-word for the operation.

Hopefully, Goodbody decided to move up during darkness and to secure by first light a firm base in the area of San Savino. From here he would be well-placed to pass through the 46th Division crossings over the Marano, if the infantry had succeeded in seizing them.

The brigade advance was to be led by the tanks of the 10th Hussars and the infantry of the 1st King's Royal Rifle Corps, with some guns of the 11th Royal Horse Artillery (Honourable Artillery Company). Then would come the Bays, with the 9th Lancers in the rear. The roads were so thick with traffic that only one route could be used, following by-roads twisting along the flanks of Monte Gridolfo. Guides and lamps were positioned along the route, but the approach march was, if anything, even worse than the previous day's marathon to the Foglia.[3]

Gathering in the darkness about the tanks of the squadron leaders, the tank commanders marked the talc covers of their maps with coloured chinagraph pencils. Wireless silence was broken half an hour after midnight. The advance started an hour later. The small bridges and culverts along the narrow roads collapsed one by one beneath the crushing weight of the lines of Shermans. The next five miles took six hours to cover. Communication along the column was hampered by an unlucky choice of wireless frequency for the Bays. This was also being used by the B.B.C., and the unfortunate wireless operators and tank commanders, huddled in their turrets with their map cases shaking under the shielded turret lights, had to strain their ears to hear their orders above the voices of announcers reading the news, and the regular blare of martial music.[4]

At eight o'clock in the morning, the 10th Hussars reached the south bank of the Conca, to find a bizarre situation in the middle of the ford which was to be their crossing place. This was being blocked by vehicles of 1st Armoured Division headquarters, whose crews were making tea and unconcernedly playing a gramophone.[5]

The Hussars' colonel, Lieutenant-Colonel D. R. B. Kaye, went forward on foot and cleared a way through for the regiment, and the tanks rolled on for another mile. Then Canadian tanks were seen ahead, supporting infantry in contact with the enemy. Far from being near the Marano, the infantry were still only 4,000 yards north of the Conca, and south of the Coriano ridge. Five miles away to the south-west, the high ridge of Gemmano erupted into towering brown pillars of earth and stone as the fighter-bombers of the Desert Air Force peeled off to drop their bombs upon it. It was clear that this, too, was still in enemy hands.

The Hussars and the 1st K.R.R.C. were now halted on high ground beside the Canadians, and any movement to the west was greeted by immediate enemy fire. Behind them, the rest of the brigade was slowly crossing the Conca, but the optimism of the previous night was melting swiftly. The brigade was clearly not going to pour through any 46th Division gap over the Marano. It would have to make its own gap.

Goodbody was still hampered by inadequate information, but there was no time to be lost, and at midday he issued new orders. The two lorried infantry brigades of the division were still south of the Conca, but he decided to attack at once with two armoured regiments – the Bays and the 10th Hussars – keeping the 9th Lancers and most of the infantry of the 1st K.R.R.C. in reserve to exploit success. Both the Bays and the 10th Hussars would each have one company of the K.R.R.C. under command, and they would be supported by four field regiments of artillery, the self-propelled guns of the 11th R.H.A. (H.A.C.), and four medium batteries.[6]

The attack was so hurried that reconnaissance was impossible, and the regimental commanders and squadron leaders had to do the best they could with a quick look at the map. Goodbody's plan was that the brigade should pass through the 46th Division positions on the San Clemente ridge and advance to the high ground near Vecciano, just east of Marano. It would then seize its own crossings over the river and exploit beyond.

The obvious weakness of this plan was the lack of sufficient infantry, but its virtue was speed. Its validity rested entirely on the correctness of the information that the Germans were indeed in confusion and on the run. This would now have to be proved.

Even as the brigade prepared to advance, however, it became obvious that its start line, running along the road from Cevolabbate to San Clemente, was still either in enemy hands or considerably interdicted by his guns. It was changed to a new one, running from a point a mile east of Coriano south-west to San Savino.

The Bays, who were waiting in a vineyard, had a great deal of ground to make to their left to reach the new line. One squadron moved off in line ahead down a narrow lane, the grey hulls of the Shermans smothered with branches loaded with black grapes, which the crews had draped over them as camouflage. As soon as they started, they were confronted by a long column of supply lorries coming down the lane in the other direction, but they managed to drive across country and regain the road and the start-line farther up.[7]

The other Bays' squadron, moving along the valley just north of the Conca, was instantly in trouble. As the tanks moved into sight, the German anti-tank gunners on Gemmano to their left and at Croce in front of them began to make good practice. The tanks came under steady fire from armour-piercing shot. For the first time since Tunisia in 1943, the crews heard the express-train roar of the near-miss in front of them or behind, and saw the long furrows ploughed up around them as the gunners found the range. To be hit by one of these hurtling solid projectiles meant a terrifying, bone-shattering crash, and the probability that the flash from the disintegrating molten metal would ignite the ninety-gallons of petrol or diesel carried in the side tanks, or the charge in one of the high-explosive shells which were clipped round the turret walls. Even a glancing blow from an armour-piercing shot would gouge metal from the turret side like a finger rubbing along a pat of butter, producing a brief rosy glow on the inside of the turret wall as the steel became white-hot at the point of impact, and then cooled.

The road on which the tanks were moving had deep ditches on either side, and the big Shermans could only press on, returning the fire as best they could. The squadron rear-link radio tank, which was its contact with regimental headquarters, was hit at once, so that the tanks were immediately cut off from the regiment. One by one, three more tanks were lost, but the others succeeded in climbing the winding road to Coriano and the start-line. Here they were attacked by German infantry with bazookas, and another tank was knocked out and its commander killed. The tanks now came under heavy shell-fire, and as they crossed the start-line two tanks of squadron headquarters mistakenly turned away from the leading troop and took the road for Coriano by themselves. These tanks were commanded respectively by the squadron leader, Major H. W. Hibbert, and Captain J. C. McVail. McVail's own account[8] of what followed reveals the confusion of the fighting:

'We moved forward cautiously on the corners and quickly on the straight expecting any moment to meet the troops who were coming up on our right. Our plan then was to left wheel and close the squadron on to us after we had made contact with the squadron on the right. Unfortunately, as we were then out of communication with our C.O. . . . ., we did not know that this squadron and the 10th Hussars to the right of them had been held back by heavy enemy fire.

'As we moved forward we machine-gunned everything – hedges, ditches, houses, haystacks, in fact every possible place which might conceal the enemy, and when we came to a village we put H.E. into the corner houses while our scatter gunners machine-gunned the doors and lower windows of the houses, the commander at the same time tommy-gunning the top windows. These tactics at first proved successful and the noise and confusion must have frightened the enemy as several of them ran out of their ditches and foxholes and tried to run for it, but many of them were caught in our fire.

'Just south of San Savino we had our first piece of real excitement when a bazooka man leapt out of a ditch behind Major Hibbert's tank and tried to knock him out. Major Hibbert shot him with his pistol. We continued on, and north of San Savino we passed by a few feet a Mark IV tank with its 75-mm. gun trained on to the road. We then realized that we were cut off and in a desperate position, and every time we halted and tried to make a plan we were fired on from every conceivable angle and we had to move on. Also in the back of our minds we could visualize the Mark IV creeping out from its position and startling us from the rear. Eventually we reached K 13 at S. Maria and when Captain McVail's tank went round the corner and the dust cleared he was confronted by a Mark IV tank reversing as fast as it could go down the road. The two tanks halted with guns pointed at each other at a range of fifteen yards. Captain McVail's tank opened fire with an H.E. which he already had in his gun. Troopers Corbett and Jumps, the loader and gunner, then got off four more shots (two A.P. and two H.E.) before the German could reply. The Mark IV brewed up and one man baled out. He tried to make a bolt but was machine-gunned by Corporal Hutchin and Captain McVail and was killed before he got back to his friends. At this moment Major Hibbert's tank was hit and immobilized and the crew baled out. The road was now blocked in two directions. Captain McVail's tank pulled over to the left of the road to a house behind which Major Hibbert and his crew were hiding and a conference was held. Fire was still coming from all directions and it was only a question of seconds before the other tank was hit. Lance-Corporal Grist was sent to Corporal Hutchin to tell him to dismount with the tommy-guns and as much ammunition as possible. We then ran for cover just as our own divisional artillery barrage opened fire. During this barrage we think our tank received a direct hit and was 'brewed'. We lay in the barrage together unable to move until someone spotted a dug-out near by, and gradually, one by one, we ran for it and took cover.'*

Back at regimental headquarters, the Bays' commander, Asquith, had now been told of the plight of Hibbert's squadron. He ordered the other squadron, which was waiting at the start-line, to give it assistance. This move, too, led to trouble. As they manœuvred on the side of the hill to find fire positions for support, many of the tanks lost their tracks in the loose, sliding earth. The remainder were then ordered to advance in accordance with the original plan. They had covered only three-

---

* Hibbert and McVail, after an adventurous time behind the enemy lines, rejoined the regiment on 7 September. McVail was killed a fortnight later.

quarters of a mile when they were again halted by heavy and accurate fire.

On the right, the 10th Hussars were also in considerable difficulty. As they began their own advance they were caught in a heavy concentration of mortar fire. The commanding officer's tank was hit, and six tank commanders – among them the second-in-command, Major M. F. Morley, and the adjutant, Captain The Viscount Ednam – were wounded. The ground also claimed its victims among the tanks. Eight Shermans and the observation post tank of the 11th R.H.A. (H.A.C.) were lost. The intense enemy shelling made it impossible to recover these tanks during the day.[9]

The 9th Lancers, moving up at the rear of the brigade, were surprised to see so many tanks of the leading regiments still struggling on the start-line at 6 p.m. Goodbody ordered them to come up between the Bays and the 10th Hussars and to try to capture San Savino. As the drivers, tired and red-eyed from lack of sleep, rolled the Shermans forward, the same story was repeated. Two tanks overturned in a gully; several others bogged down on the hillsides. The Lancers advanced for half a mile, but by then it was getting dark.[10]

The brigade now asked for infantry to hold the ground which had been gained, but neither of the divisional infantry brigades was far forward on the crowded roads. The Buffs were the nearest, and they were hurrying up, but they could not be there until half-past ten. The tanks fell back slightly in the darkness to the ridge between San Clemente and Cevolabbate. It was virtually the start-line from which they had planned to launch their drive to the River Po. The brigade was much depleted. The Bays had only twenty-one Shermans in leaguer; the 10th Hussars thirty; the 9th Lancers twenty. Duly at 10.30 p.m., the Buffs arrived and took over the ground.[11]

It had been a bitter day. If things had gone as planned, Hull's division would now have been moving north towards Bologna and Ferrara. Hull himself had been presented during the day with strongly-conflicting information about the possibilities of breakthrough. Hull knew the 46th Division commander, Hawkesworth, very well, having previously served as a brigade commander in a division commanded by him. He had great confidence in Hawkesworth's judgement, and Hawkesworth had told him: 'I can promise you that when I say "Go" there will be a clear gap for you to go through.'

When, therefore, the news came through from both 46th Division and V Corps that the gap was there, and that the moment was ripe for exploitation, he was puzzled by the reports from the reconnaissance regiment, the 4th Hussars – who were, of course, up with the forward positions of the infantry – that the situation was *not* favourable. He thought at first that the Hussars were perhaps being unduly pessimistic, but events rapidly disillusioned him of this theory.[12]

There was no gap. This was no blame to Hawkesworth and his exhausted infantry, who had borne the brunt so far of the Gothic Line campaign, and who were now near the end of their strength. They were eager, the whole of Eighth Army was eager, to let the armour through, and finish an arduous and bloody campaign. In these circumstances, men's judgement becomes affected, and there seems no doubt that the infantry report that the moment was favourable for breakthrough was premature, at the very least. Hull himself said that Hawkesworth told him afterwards that he had felt like a man out hunting who had held the gate open for his friend and then let it slam in his face.

Under these circumstances, the armoured attack had been a failure. It had been made by regiments having their first taste of Italian battle conditions, over highly difficult ground, without adequate infantry support, and on inaccurate information. The Germans were not on the run from the Coriano and Gemmano ridges. Kesselring had brought his last reserve over from the central front. This was Major-General Fritz Polack's excellent 29th Panzer Grenadier Division. Its 71st Panzer Grenadier Regiment had reached the Coriano ridge early on 4 September, to greet the British armour.

Nevertheless, on the other side of the hill, things always look different in war, and the Germans were more disturbed by the abortive British attack in the vital Coriano area than the facts would seem to have warranted. Kesselring, who had surprisingly been away visiting the Fourteenth Army front during the day, returned to his headquarters in the evening and found there was talk of further withdrawal. He flew into a somewhat theatrical rage, threatening to replace senior officers who were 'retreat-minded'.[13] The Tenth Army commander, von Vietinghoff, eventually calmed him, but his public anger had no doubt had its effect. There was no further talk of German withdrawal from the Coriano ridge.

11

San Savino: 5 – 6 September

On 5 September, however, it was still believed that in spite of
the resistance of the previous day, the San Savino ridge was only
lightly held, and a new plan was made to capture it. In making
his dispositions for this operation, Goodbody was once more
restricted in his tactical approach by a serious lack of infantry.
It was ironical that he, whose training had been formulated
upon the closest armour-infantry co-operation, should now be
forced by circumstances to deliver an armoured attack, supported by only the slenderest infantry forces, upon a prepared
enemy position. For neither of the divisional infantry brigades
was yet forward, and on the morning of the 5th it even seemed
likely that the 1st Buffs, who had come up to relieve the Bays on
the San Clemente ridge the previous night, would revert to the
command of the 18th Infantry Brigade.[1]

A mile to the west of the San Clemente ridge, the San Savino
ridge thrust out a tongue of high ground from San Savino itself
in the south, through the little village of Passano, to Coriano at
its tip. Goodbody now planned to advance with the remaining
tanks of one of his armoured regiments towards Passano. If the
German resistance was broken here, he would once more be
able to take the brigade to the River Marano, cross it, and
exploit. (Map 2.)

He chose the 9th Lancers to lead this advance, supported by
the 1st King's Royal Rifle Corps – the only infantry under his
command.

At eight o'clock in the morning the regiment was formed up.
Two squadrons were in position 500 yards in front of the cross-
roads at Cevolabbate. Their role was to give support to B

Squadron of the Lancers, which was to make the assault on San Savino. They waited an hour for infantry, but none had yet reached the position, and it was decided, in view of the need for speed, to attack without them.[2]

Three troops of B Squadron – nine tanks in all – moved into the assault just after nine o'clock. Only two tanks were bogged on the way down into the treacherous defile which lay between them and San Savino, but when the others got through it, they were immediately attacked by bazookas from patches of vines and haystacks.

Gradually, leapfrogging their way forward by fire and movement, the tanks moved up to the edge of the cemetery which was on the left of the village and at the southern end of the ridge. They reported a great many bazooka-men and snipers, particularly in a sunken road beside the cemetery. They were now also under heavy fire from armour-piercing shells, and a troop-leader's tank was destroyed by a shot from a German Mark IV tank. A corporal commanding a turretless Honey tank managed to get into position to sweep the sunken road with his Browning machine-guns, but after a few moments the Honey was hit and the crew were killed.

A platoon of the 1st K.R.R.C. had now arrived. This handful of infantry, magnificently led by a young subaltern, gave such effective support during the hours that followed that the Lancers were able to hold on to their positions. The Germans themselves were now under great pressure, and some of the bazooka-men and snipers began to surrender, causing the tanks great difficulty as there were no infantry to take charge of the prisoners.

Goodbody's brigade headquarters were well up with the fighting at Cevolabbate, and Goodbody himself went forward to watch the 9th Lancers' attack. Brigade headquarters was under steady mortar and shell fire all morning. At ten minutes past eleven, a particularly heavy concentration fell around the command tank. This was a Sherman equipped as a head-quarters, with tables inside the turret instead of the bulky 75-mm. gun, but with a wooden dummy gun outside the turret so that it was not easily identifiable as an important target to enemy anti-tank gunners. By ill-luck, a shell hit the wooden gun, smashing it back into the turret where the brigade second-in-command, Colonel J. R. Macdonell, was working. He was killed instantly. Macdonell, a former commander of the 9th Lancers, who had already won two D.S.O.s, was one of the most popular officers in the brigade. The news was not given to the regiment during the San Savino attack, because it was judged to be too great a shock.[3]

Goodbody was now receiving repeated requests for infantry from the Lancers' commanding officer, Lieutenant-Colonel R. S. G. Perry. These demands were being passed on to 1st Armoured Division. At least a battalion was necessary to capture San Savino, let alone advance farther down the ridge, but nothing was yet available.

The Buffs were again the nearest. They still were dug in at their overnight positions near San Clemente, and orders did not come for them to move forward until the evening. Meanwhile the tanks, very vulnerable to German infantry stalking them with bazookas, had to be protected against counter-attack in their precariously-held positions. What could not be done by infantry had to be done by gunfire. An officer of E Battery, 11th R.H.A. (H.A.C.), working from an exposed jeep, held the Germans at bay for hour after hour. Switching fire from point to point with formidable accuracy, he brought down the shells of six artillery regiments – a total, with those of his own battery, of more than fifty guns – wherever the Germans tried to gather for counter-attack. The armour held on until darkness.[4]

The Buffs were now brought forward, but their leading company was caught in a British barrage and suffered some casualties. Then they were fired on in error by a battalion of 56th Division, operating on their left, before they were able finally to take over the Lancers' position.

The Lancers had once more been frustrated in their bid to advance, and yet within the vital limitations imposed by lack of infantry, they had done well. Eight tanks had been lost, either destroyed or ditched; one officer was taken prisoner and another – Second-Lieutenant The Viscount Stuart – died of his wounds; one N.C.O. – Corporal Moffatt, who had tackled the Germans in the sunken road with his Honey – was killed, with two or three other ranks. But they had destroyed two German

tanks, killed thirty Germans, and taken sixty prisoners.[5] It was a
clear indication that the Germans on the ridge could be disturbed and could be worried. Had infantry been available, the
day might have had a very different end. Probably the brigade
would not have reached the Marano. But a further advance
along the San Savino ridge would have made the Germans
think hard next day about the possibilities of holding south of
the river.

During the night of the 5th, the two remaining infantry
battalions of the 18th Brigade put in an attack on San Savino,
but with only moderate success. They dug in on the reverse
slopes while their commanders decided what to do. And then,
blowing in the faces of the tired infantry crouched in their slit
trenches all along the Eighth Army line, the rain began to fall.

★ ★ ★

The San Savino-Coriano ridge, on the morning of 6 September,
still lay across the path of Eighth Army, blocking its advance to
the Marano and beyond. In particular the Canadians, who had
struggled up the slopes of the Misano ridge which ran a couple
of miles east of Coriano, could get no farther, since the enemy
retention of the Coriano ridge exposed their left flank and their
rear to his fire as soon as they moved beyond it.

Leese was now presented with a formidable problem. He
could either pause to gather his army for a massive stroke at the
German positions in front of the Marano – a pause which was
the antithesis of his previous emphasis on the need for speed –
or he could continue to thrust the Canadian Corps against the
Rimini positions to the east, taking the risks entailed in attacking with an open flank on the left of their line.

He decided to pause, although this was clearly at variance
with the way in which the progress of the campaign had been
anticipated. Nevertheless, it was the right choice. Leese had
few reserves for the Canadians, and they had been fighting
valiantly for ten days. Their casualties had been heavy; in the
past four days alone, for instance, the 1st Infantry Brigade had
lost 300 men. To continue the Canadian offensive in these

circumstances would have been hazardous. The Germans had won a respite.

Leese met the Canadian Corps commander, Burns, on the morning of 6 September, and told him what he had decided. Burns was to plan now for a major assault over the Marano, and for this he would be given the assistance of a good portion of Leese's scanty reserves – the 4th British Infantry Division, the 25th Army Tank Brigade, and the 3rd Greek Mountain Brigade, which had just arrived from the Middle East. Keightley's V Corps was to clear the left flank, and to drive the Germans from the Gemmano and Coriano Ridges.[6]

Meanwhile, however, Hull's 1st Armoured Division, with its infantry thrust up against the cemetery at San Savino, and nothing much in depth behind it, was in an awkward position. It was essential for the corps and army plan that the gains at San Savino should be held. Another battalion of the 18th Infantry Brigade, the 9th K.O.Y.L.I. (Yorkshire Dragoons), commanded by Lieutenant-Colonel S. J. Linden Kelly, took over the line which ran through the shattered Italian graveyard. There was little room for deployment, and for the next two days and nights, in a little infantry epic, the division was fought on a front of only two companies, while the Germans attacked again and again in an effort to dislodge the K.O.Y.L.I. from their toe-hold.

Tremendous artillery support was brought in to help the British infantry – all the divisional guns, reinforced by extra ones from Eighth Army, and the 75-mm. cannons of the armoured regiments as required. While the companies fought grimly on amongst the smoke and flame and pulverized graves, they could see equally fierce fighting raging on the heights to their left, as the struggle for Gemmano mounted in intensity.

The K.O.Y.L.I. suffered very heavy casualties, more than 170 being killed or wounded in the forty-eight hours, but they held on until, from sheer exhaustion, the German attacks slackened. By then the street which ran through San Savino was piled with dead. At the end of the struggle, British infantry who walked amongst the ruins found that wherever a whitewashed wall was standing, it was smothered in scarlet from British or German blood.[7]

Even while this struggle was taking place, another factor now imposed itself upon the situation. On the morning of 6 September, the meteorological officers of Eighth Army frowned over their charts. It looked, they said, as though it would rain for some days.[8] As the skies opened, the fine powdered dust of the country roads turned into quagmires of slime. Behind Eighth Army, one by one, the weakened bridges over the Foglia toppled into the surging brown flood which the little river had now become. All along the front, as infantry, supply trucks, and tanks floundered in the mud, and the army engineers toiled desperately to make bridges and roads, the movements of Eighth Army began to slow.

12

Croce and Gemmano:
6 – 10 September

Keightley, whose V Corps had been given the task of clearing
Eighth Army's flank, had already begun to tackle the problem
of the Coriano ridge. During 5 September, while the 9th
Lancers were making their attack on San Savino, he decided to
outflank the enemy positions on the ridge by reaching out to
capture Montescudo, a small town on the heights which lay
about three miles to the south-west.

This task fell to Whitfield's 56th Division, which, it will be
remembered, already had 167th and 168th Brigades across the
River Conca. At one o'clock on the afternoon of 5 September,
Whitfield issued verbal orders. The two brigades were to attack
with two battalions each; they were to secure a start line from
San Savino to Croce by 5 a.m. on 6 September; then the tanks
of 7th Armoured Brigade, reinforced by the remaining two
infantry battalions of the two brigades, would pass through
and continue the advance to Montescudo.

The way to Montescudo, however, passed between the high
ridges of Gemmano and Croce, and earlier failure to capture
the former now began to exert a baleful influence upon Whitfield's operations. From this ridge the Germans dominated the
Conca valley and the roads running west from Morciano towards Montescudo. The Royal Engineers had done something
to nullify this enemy advantage by building a long diversion
south of San Clemente, which was shielded by intervening
ground from the binoculars of the sharp-eyed watchers
on Gemmano. As much transport as possible passed along

this temporary track. The Germans shelled it steadily, but they could not see what they were aiming at, and the guns did not have the devastating effect of short-range observed fire.[1] (Map 2.)

On the German side, von Vietinghoff was well aware that Whitfield's attack posed a danger to his flank, and as 56th Division moved towards Croce, German units from four divisions – 26th Panzer, 29th Panzer Grenadier, 98th Infantry, and 5th Mountain – were brought hurriedly into the line to block the path of the British infantry. From Gemmano and Croce, the German artillery observers watched the roads, for even if some of the supply transport could be diverted up temporary tracks, the troops had to advance in view of the guns. (Map 2.)

The 1st London Scottish of 168th Brigade, after passing through Morciano on 5 September on their way towards Croce, swiftly came under fire from the heights on their flanks. The leading companies had to scramble from their vehicles and disperse, while the battalion transport – as much of it as was not already in flames – got off the road as well as it could. There were many casualties, and there would have been more if the battalion had not been keeping strictly to the proper interval between vehicles, so that the German guns did not find a bunched target.[2]

During the night, confused and chaotic fighting raged around the little hamlet of Croce. An hour after midnight, the 1st London Irish seized the locality of Palazzo, a mile to the north, but a savage German counterattack drove them out again. The London Scottish had advanced beyond Cevolabbate and were across the road from San Savino to Croce at two points.

Meanwhile the 9th Royal Fusiliers of 167th Brigade had managed to enter Croce during the night, but they, too, were at once expelled by a strong German attack. They attacked again at 3.30 a.m. but gained only a little ground before intense Spandau fire halted them. Dawn found the Royal Fusiliers in possession only of the outlying part of Croce, while to the north the London Irish held positions just outside Palazzo. During the morning of the 6th the tanks of 7th Armoured Brigade supported the 9th Royal Fusiliers forward against Croce, and shortly before midday the village was again in the hands of a Fusilier company. Two enemy counter-attacks were beaten off, and during the afternoon the British garrison of Croce grew to two infantry companies and a troop of tanks.

The 8th Royal Fusiliers, slightly in rear of the Croce positions, was now asked to help the 9th. The battalion, like the companies of the 9th in Croce itself, had been subjected all day to violent mortaring and shelling – 'some of the heaviest and most concentrated,' an officer wrote later, 'that it had ever experienced.' Two companies of the 8th moved up to the area of Croce church, and were instantly struck by a torrent of enemy fire. One company was quickly reduced to a strength of sixty men. It began to dig in as a German counter-attack, led by 129th Tank Battalion of 29th Panzer Grenadier Division began. An eye-witness described what happened:

'Soon after dark the enemy counter-attacked in strength, sending one tank straight down the main road. At this time it had not been possible to get any anti-tank guns forward and the PIAT was the only weapon available. Two platoons were overrun and the company headquarters surrounded. The company commander and a platoon commander who had just been briefed for a patrol escaped from the church and joined up with the remaining platoon, which, although it had not been involved, numbered only eighteen men. The situation was very confused after this fighting, so the company commander sent a recce patrol, under an officer, to the church to discover the enemy's strength with a view to counter-attacking. They were met with a hail of machine-gun fire and grenades at several points, and reported the area strongly held – obviously a stronger force was needed to retake the position. . . .'[3]

Another enemy attack, however, was developing on the two companies of the 9th Battalion inside Croce. After a night of confused struggling, the remains of these two companies were withdrawn on the morning of the 7th. The Germans were once more in firm control of Croce.

Early in the afternoon, 167th Brigade was ordered to recapture Croce. The task was given to the 8th Royal Fusiliers, supported by the 9th. The Fusiliers were pulled back from their outlying positions, so that the divisional artillery could bring down massed fire on the enemy positions for ten minutes before the counter-attack went in. The whole of the 8th Battalion was withdrawn while the British guns did their job. German artillery observers, however, were equally active. As the battalion formed up for its attack, a storm of shells fell on the area. There were very heavy casualties, and when the British barrage stopped at zero hour, the companies were too badly hit to advance. They asked for a postponement, but were ordered to continue with the attack. A quarter of an hour later, they moved forward, and a fighting patrol reported that Croce was empty. The two companies entered the village, but their elation was premature. The Germans had pulled back their infantry to escape the British bombardment, but they had left a Tiger tank and a self-propelled gun behind. These swept the advancing companies with fire. Men were falling everywhere, and one of the two companies was now reduced to a strength of three men. There were still twenty of the other company on their feet, and these twenty-three men prepared to hold Croce. The village was being systematically devastated by the German guns, but troops of the 44th Reconnaissance Regiment were brought in, followed by the 1st Battalion of the Welch Regiment from 168th Brigade. The depleted Fusilier battalions were now pulled out, leaving Croce once more in British hands, after one of the fiercest struggles in the regiment's history.

'That battlefield,' wrote an officer of the 8th Battalion, 'presented a terrible sight. Dead, enemy and Fusiliers, lay across each other where they had fallen fighting at close quarters: blackened hulls of burned-out Sherman tanks, Bren carriers lying on their sides, not to mention the usual flotsam of battle. . . .'[4]

During the day, another success had been gained a little way to the north-west of Croce. The London Scottish of 168th Brigade had seized the Palazzo-Croce ridge in the early hours of the morning, and shortly after 5 a.m. they took Palazzo itself. They beat off a heavy counter-attack and took many prisoners, but they were being steadily fired on from both flanks and during the day their casualties began to mount. In spite of this, in the early evening they pushed another company forward and took the small group of buildings known as Casa Menghino, a key position between Croce and Palazzo.[5]

Thus on the night of 7 September, the prospects looked good, and the men who had died in the last two days around Croce did not seem to have died in vain. Whitfield, with the London Scottish, had driven a salient into the German line, and now his Queen's Brigade was moving up towards Montescudo. This move, if it succeeded, would turn the German line, and force the enemy to pull out of his Gemmano positions. The German defences were showing signs of strain. At this vital point, however, nature offered Kesselring invaluable aid. The rain continued. The roads crumbled and vanished, and the movement of 169th Brigade towards Montescudo was ordered to be postponed for twenty-four hours. It would, in fact, never be resumed – and it would be a long and bloody week before British troops entered Montescudo. To see why this was so, we must look at what was happening on the other side of the river from Croce, on the Gemmano Ridge.

The Gemmano Ridge was the anchor point of a German line of defences which ran north through San Savino and down the Coriano Ridge to the Adriatic. In the early days of September, Kesselring brought back one of his best units – 100th Mountain Regiment, which was recalled, as we have seen, while on its way to the Franco-Italian frontier – to garrison it. This was an excellent Austrian formation, well-trained and of fine morale. The regiment consisted of a reconnaissance battalion and four ordinary infantry battalions, each contaning about 600 men, and well-supported by artillery and armoured units.

The ridge itself, about a mile long and 1,500 feet high, consisted of four main heights. At the eastern end, the village of Gemmano stood on Point 404; 500 yards to the west, with a single house on top, was Point 414; 300 yards farther west, surmounted by a wooden cross, Point 449; and 1,000 yards farther on, above the tiny hamlet of Zollara, Point 402. Slightly to the east of Gemmano village rose the smaller height known as Villa.

Below the ridge flowed the little stream of the Ventena, an innocent-seeming line on the map, which did not reveal its steep and awkward banks, or the fact that it became a formidable torrent after heavy rain. Three subsidiary ridges ran up from the valley of the Ventona towards the Gemmano Ridge; one emerged between Gemmano and Villa, one near the west end of Gemmano, and one, the Farneto Spur, up to the wooden cross on Point 449.

The village of Gemmano offered relatively easy entry only on its western side – the side where the main body of the enemy garrison was stationed. On the eastern side, the slopes up to the village were steep, smothered in thorny scrub, and ended at a thick, ancient, twenty-foot-high wall. There were caves in the slopes, and the village contained cellars prepared as defensive positions.

The Germans had disposed their four battalions upon the principal heights; the reconnaissance battalion held the left-hand, or Farneto Spur; one infantry battalion occupied Point 402; another Point 449; and the third, Gemmano village and Villa. From these heights, looking down at almost every move of their advancing enemies, nearly 3,000 German troops waited for the British infantry to attack.[6]

Eighth Army intelligence, however, had failed to grasp the importance which the Germans put on the Gemmano position, the number of enemy troops which held it, or the determination with which they would fight. Whitfield's orders of 4 September had still spoken of by-passing Gemmano if at all possible, but two days later it was clear that this could not be done.

The two brigades of 56th Division which were now fighting around Croce, on the other side of the Conca, were constantly harassed from the German positions overlooking them from Gemmano. Still not aware of how strongly Gemmano was held, Whitfield sent his 44th Reconnaissance Regiment up to Villa to act as a flank guard for his operations at Croce. The 44th came under very heavy fire, but they did reach Villa, and their patrols towards Gemmano convinced Whitfield that more was needed. It still seemed to him, however, that it might be possible to capture Gemmano without too much difficulty, for he had no accurate information on the size of the German garrison.[7]

The task of taking the village was now entrusted to a single battalion, the 7th Oxfordshire and Buckinghamshire Light Infantry. This battalion had already been on the slopes of

Gemmano on 5 September, but had been pulled back and put under command of 7th Armoured Brigade for the anticipated advance to Montescudo. Now, soon after midday on 6 September, the battalion was brought back under command of 167th Brigade and ordered to take Gemmano.

Their attack went in during the late afternoon, and by darkness they had succeeded in pushing their way up the steep eastern slopes, with severe casualties from the German defensive fire, and establishing themselves in Gemmano itself. This surprising success, however, was soon checked. The Germans had drawn back to give their counter-attack more momentum, and during the night, in confused and bitter fighting, they drove the British infantry out of Gemmano, down to the ridge of Villa.[8]

Gradually the Gemmano situation was escalating. It had begun with a reconnaissance in force by the 44th; then a battalion attack by the Oxford and Bucks; and now it was clear that at least a full brigade would be needed. Whitfield ordered the Queen's Brigade, whose attack on Montescudo had been delayed by the rain, to assault the Gemmano position on 8 September.

There was now a much keener appreciation of what 56th Division was facing in this jumble of formidable ridges, and the attack was planned with great care. It was to be led by 2nd/6th and 2nd/7th Queen's – 2nd/6th on the left to clear Points 414 and 449, and 2nd/7th on the right to capture Gemmano village and Borgo. They would be supported by 4·2-inch mortars, the medium machine-guns of the 6th Cheshire Regiment, two squadrons of the 8th Royal Tank Regiment, and the whole of the divisional artillery. The other infantry battalion of the brigade, 2nd/5th Queen's, was held in reserve, to be ready next day to attack Zollara, along the line of the Farneto spur.

It rained heavily all morning on the 8th, but the rain had slackened when the two assaulting battalions moved off towards Gemmano at two o'clock in the afternoon. No transport could move along the quagmires that the roads had now become, but the brigade received 130 mules to carry stores and ammunition for the attack.

The bloody efforts of the 44th Reconnaissance Regiment and the 7th Oxford and Bucks had given the brigade commander,

Smith-Dorrien, invaluable knowledge of where the German defensive fire was likely to fall, and the two attacking battalions were carefully directed up the slopes to Gemmano so as to avoid it as much as possible. Meanwhile, as the divisional artillery and heavy mortars pulverized it, the top of the ridge erupted into towering brown columns of flying earth and stone.

Whitfield himself watched the attack with Smith-Dorrien, standing in a slit trench at Montefiore, across the valley. To the two commanders, sweeping the ridge with their binoculars, the scene was strangely like that of an artificial battle at the Aldershot Tattoo – the spectacular explosions along the skyline, the tanks labouring up amongst the shell-bursts of defensive fire, the tiny figures of the infantry moving antlike up the side of the ridge.[9]

On those slopes, the two battalions were losing men fast. Murderous machine-gun fire from the trees and shrubs below Gemmano was cutting down the 2nd/6th as they clambered towards Point 414. Smoke from blazing haystacks drifted across the line of advance, and Spandaus and German snipers were firing from front, sides, and rear. As the leading company reached the small group of houses which was its first objective, the company commander, Major G. E. Smith, and two other officers were killed. The battalion struggled on to within 200 yards of the top of Point 414, and waited for darkness.[10]

Watching from Montefiore, Whitfield was worrying about the German positions in the long façade of buildings which crowned the ridge up which 2nd/7th Queen's were climbing towards Gemmano village. He ordered a heavy artillery battery to concentrate on them, and within a few minutes the entire façade was battered into ruin, the whole front of each house crumbling into heaps of rubble at the impact of the 155-mm. shells.

Late in the afternoon, under very heavy fire, 2nd/7th Queen's got a company into Gemmano, where it was subjected amongst the ruins to desperate and repeated counter-attacks by the German garrison. Casualties were mounting steeply on both sides, and another company went forward to help. The company commander, Captain David Rossiter, collected together the survivors, about forty men, and established this little force in two houses at the rear edge of the village, while a few more men occupied a ridge outside the village to cover the entrance. It had been a bloody day for the Germans as well as the British infantry in Gemmano, and by midnight their last exhausted counter-attack against Rossiter and his men had ceased.[11]

Meanwhile, on the left, 2nd/6th Queen's had renewed the attack on Point 414 at eleven o'clock. German snipers were busy picking off men by the red light of burning haystacks. The 200 yards between the British infantry and the top of Point 414 took almost four hours to cover, and the commander of the attacking company, Major R. K. Purdon, was killed. His body was found on the objective next day, his hands still grasping the Bren gun which he had carried into the attack.[12]

All through 9 September, 2nd/6th Queen's held on to Point 414, capturing almost forty prisoners, but finally the company was almost surrounded. It was ordered to fight its way out, and the night of 9 September found the battalion, reduced now to two composite companies, on the slopes south and east of their objective.

September 9 was also a bitter day for the remaining battalion of the brigade, 2nd/5th Queen's. The battalion began its attack up the Farneto spur during the morning, moving in single file up the stony course of the Ventena stream at the foot of the Gemmano Ridge. All went well for nearly two miles, until they were opposite the hamlet of Farneto, where two companies branched off up separate defiles and immediately ran into serious trouble. Both were swept with fire from the front and flanks, and it was clear that they had run into a well-sited German ambush.[13]

Every effort by the battalion to get up to Farneto during the day was stopped by intense German fire, and the infantry were showered with mortar bombs as they crouched and died in the stony gullies waiting to advance. After a long night on the slopes, while the wounded were carried back and ammunition brought forward, the thirty remaining men of one company made another desperate effort to get forward. Organized in two small platoons commanded by a major and a sergeant respectively, they advanced some way against heavy opposition, but were finally withdrawn during the afternoon of 10 September.

The brightest feature of these three days of blood and toil came from 2nd/7th Queen's. During the morning of the 9th, the battalion managed to reinforce Rossiter's little garrison at the end of Gemmano village with another company. Between them they cleared both Gemmano and Borgo, so that the eastern end of the ridge was in British hands.[14]

Now, however, the struggle of the Queen's Brigade for the Gemmano Ridge was over. The strength and fierceness of the German resistance in the past few days had forced great changes in the Eighth Army plan. The divisions were to be regrouped for new roles, and other battalions would now have to continue the struggle for the western end of the ridge, and for Point 449 and Zollara.

13
American Sympathy

For Leese, the outlook at the end of this first week of September was discouraging. The desperate German defence around Croce and Gemmano and along the Coriano Ridge was yielding them good dividends. The little spotter aircraft used by the Royal Artillery to direct the fire of the guns reported considerable numbers of enemy troops moving south across the Conca on the afternoon of the 8th, and it was clear that Kesselring meant to fight on for Gemmano as well as for the positions north of the river.

Thus the toughest defences still had to be broken by Eighth Army, which had already been much weakened by the past fortnight's fighting. Since 25 August, when the three corps had surged over the Metauro, Eighth Army had lost 8,000 men in killed, wounded, and missing.[1] It had also lost a hundred tanks, though in view of the great numbers available, this was less important. The Germans, of course, had also suffered heavy casualties, losing 3,700 men in prisoners alone. But Leese was attacking over terrain where it was estimated that the attackers needed a superiority of at least three to one, so that the ratio of casualties could hardly help but be in Kesselring's favour.

Even more important than Eighth Army's losses, however, was the fact that Leese's original army plan was now distorted out of all recognition by the fierce German resistance. Leese had intended that the Canadians should seize Rimini and the coastal sector, freeing that flank so that Keightley's V Corps could crash on to Bologna and Ferrara. Now V Corps was entangled in a bloody stalemate on its own flank, while the Canadians for their part were held back from Rimini by the unresolved struggle on their left. Thus the roles of the two corps had been more or less reversed by the circumstances of the battle, and it seemed clear that Eighth Army's offensive would need to be reconstructed.

Alexander himself visited the front on 8 September. He was trying to choose the exact moment at which to launch General Mark Clark's Fifth Army offensive in the central Apennines. His original assumption had been that Clark would not be ordered to attack until Eighth Army had broken through into the plains beyond Rimini, but the stalemate in front of Coriano changed his mind.

'It was clear to me,' he reported, '. . . that we could not continue our advance on to Rimini until we had driven the enemy off the Coriano Ridge. This would need full preparation and would probably take two or three days more. I explained the situation in a signal next day, 9 September, and concluded by saying that for these reasons I had decided to unleash Fifth Army who would now go ahead with their offensive in the centre. The enemy's forces there were as weak as we could ever expect them to be, and he was obligingly withdrawing from the high ground north of Florence without serious resistance, which saved us time and trouble. As soon as Fifth Army had forced the enemy back to the Gothic Line they would launch a full-scale attempt to break through, and by that time I hoped Eighth Army would be just about ready for their attack on the Rimini positions and that we should be able to prevent Kesselring from shifting reserves from one army front to another by keeping up a series of heavy blows by our two armies in turn. The weather had improved and I hoped for a fine spell. . . .'[2]

The entrance of Fifth Army into the battle would signal a new phase in the Allied effort in Italy. The issue was not yet decided, but it was being keenly watched in London and, with surprising sympathy, in Washington.

★ ★ ★

One of the many ironies of the autumn campaign in Italy was that at this moment, when the campaign itself had faltered, and the early optimism about it was dying, the American

Joint Chiefs of Staff were coming round to Churchill's point of view about how Alexander's hypothetical victory should be exploited.

Churchill, Roosevelt, and the Allied military leaders, met for the Second Quebec Conference on 12 September. The British leaders had sailed from the Clyde in the *Queen Mary* a week before, and had used the voyage to reach agreement on the proposed strategy to lay before Roosevelt. Once more Churchill was eager that Alexander should be given every chance of developing his operations into central Europe. He was worried about plans to withdraw Alexander's three Indian divisions from Italy to reinforce a proposed amphibious operation aimed at capturing Rangoon in Burma. Vienna still beckoned to him as the ultimate British goal in the one major theatre which still had a British commander, and where the majority of the troops on the ground were from Britain and her Empire.

'I was very anxious,' he said, 'to forestall the Russians in central Europe. The Hungarians, for instance, had expressed their intention of resisting the Soviet advance, but would surrender to a British force if it could arrive in time. If the Germans either evacuated Italy or retired to the Alps, I much desired that Alexander should be enabled to make his amphibious thrust across the Adriatic, seize and occupy the Istrian peninsula, and try to reach Vienna before the Russians. It seemed much too early to start sending his troops to south-east Asia. The C.I.G.S. agreed that there should be no question of withdrawing any of Alexander's troops until Kesselring had been driven across the Piave. Our front would then be considerably less than half its present width. For the time being only the first of the Indian divisions needed for the assault on Rangoon would be taken from Alexander. I was discontented even at this prospect. . . .'[3]

The conference began at midday on the 12th with an opening statement by Admiral Leahy, Roosevelt's personal Chief of Staff. He began, rather ominously, by saying that part or all of Mark Clark's Fifth Army should be transferred to France, if it could be used there effectively in the attack on Germany, though the timing of the transfer would clearly have to depend on the outcome of Alexander's Italian offensive. This remark-

1. Field-Marshal Kesselring (left) with his Chief of Staff General Westphal

2. General Alexander

3. General Mark Clark

4. Lieut.-General Sir Oliver Leese

5. British infantry patrol in San Clemente

6. Tanks of 2nd Armoured Brigade moving up into the Gothic Line

7. Vickers machine gunner firing on Gemmano

8. Self-propelled gun on a mountain road near Mondaino

9. Shermans of 7th Armoured Brigade out of action in the ruins of Croce

10. German dead in Zollara, on the Gemmano Ridge

11. American infantrymen move up to the Gothic Line

12. British infantry of 78th Division in the mud: October 1944

13. Tiger turret commanding part of the Futa Pass

14. American dead in the castle ruins on Monte Battaglia

able statement, however, was followed by another which made the British breathe more easily.

'If General Eisenhower indicates that he does not require a part or all the United States forces now in Italy, they should then be utilized to clear the Germans from Italy and to assist British forces in operations to the north-eastward towards Vienna.'

This was certainly a tremendous advance on the previous American position, and the British seized on it eagerly. Brooke, the C.I.G.S., told the conference that he believed that the Germans might fail to disengage successfully into the Alps, and might take a heavy beating in the northern Italian plains, leaving the Ljubljana Gap and the road to Vienna open in the coming months. He pleaded that all of Fifth Army should remain in Italy, and he also raised the question of the availability of landing craft in the Mediterranean for any attack on the Istrian peninsula.

There was now another, welcome, surprise. Admiral King, the commander-in-chief of the United States Fleet, replied that although the American assault shipping was in fact provisionally allotted to projects in the Far East, it was not yet under orders. And, astonishingly, he added that he, too, 'had in mind the possibility of amphibious operations in Istria'.[4]

The Americans, in fact, were being generous in victory. The war was going well, and seemed to be moving at mounting speed to a triumphant climax. The setback at Arnhem was still a week ahead and it was not yet clear that a long hard winter lay before the Allies. The American-backed invasion of the south of France, which had caused such dissension in August, had been, in terms of ground gained and prisoners taken, a formidable success. The American Joint Chiefs of Staff had won point after point in the recent military dialogue with their Allies, and it would hurt them little to be co-operative now.

The conference went on in an atmosphere of mounting cordiality. General Marshall assured Churchill that there was, in fact, no intention at all of withdrawing Fifth Army from Italy at this time, and King confirmed that an option on the important landing-craft in the Mediterranean could be retained, so long as a final decision on their use could be reached by 15 October.

'It went off most satisfactorily,' Brooke noted in his diary that night;[5] and next day Churchill cabled jubilantly to the War Cabinet:

'The conference has opened in a blaze of friendship. The Staffs are in almost complete agreement already. There is to be no weakening of Alexander's army until Kesselring has bolted beyond the Alps or been destroyed. . . . The idea of our going to Vienna, if the war lasts long enough and if other people do not get there first, is fully accepted here.'[6]

All depended now upon Alexander and his Fifth and Eighth Armies. General Wilson, the Supreme Commander, had already sent the Combined Chiefs of Staff a report which offered two possible outcomes to the battle; either Kesselring would be routed, in which case Alexander would push on to the Ljubljana Gap, or the Germans would make an orderly withdrawal, in which case Alexander would be restricted during the winter to clearing the Lombardy plains.

The fighting ahead of Fifth and Eighth Armies was to be amongst the fiercest that either army had ever known. If Alexander was to succeed, he must succeed quickly. But, on the other hand, he could not afford another check due to over-optimism about the strength and quality of the German resistance.

The strength of the German defence was now making Alexander's shortage of men appear even more chronic. There was little to replace the weary and depleted divisions which had hurled themselves against the German line. However co-operative the Americans might be now, the original decision to withdraw seven divisions a few weeks earlier had stretched Alexander's capabilities to their limit. To overcome this situation, he had needed a quick breakthrough, good weather, and good luck. He had had none of these. Now he needed men, and, almost desperately, he cast about to find them.

On Alexander's behalf, Wilson had asked during August for permission to equip three Italian divisions for use on defensive fronts. This permission was granted by the Combined Chiefs of Staff, but with reservations which made the concession virtually meaningless. The Italian divisions could be equipped – but only from Italian equipment, supplies captured from the Germans, or what was already available in the area. On no account must the supplies given to the Italians affect in any way the operational and reserve requirements of the invasion of the south of France.

'With the reservations thus imposed on equipment,' Wilson reported, 'the immediate utilization of additional Italian divisions was made virtually impossible.'[7]

The best news available for Alexander was that the British 78th Infantry Division was being brought back to Italy from the Middle East, and would be available for him by the end of the month. Wilson's hopeful requests for more United States divisions were fobbed off with the instruction that he must wait and see what happened in France before any decision could be taken on reinforcements for Fifth Army. Clark did, however, get two more divisions – one of Brazilian troops, whose state of training and combat readiness was an unknown quantity, and with them the 92nd U.S. Infantry Division, which was composed entirely of Negro troops, and whose unsuitability for campaign conditions was later demonstrated in a near-disaster on the Serchio River early in 1945.

The strangest reinforcements of all, however, were for the Poles. Alexander asked for more men for Anders's Polish Corps on 8 September, and informed Wilson that he understood that 11,000 Poles captured while fighting with the German Army in Normandy had been screened as suitable to fight now for the Allies. It was planned immediately to receive a first contingent of 4,000 for retraining and distribution to units. In one of the most bizzare moves of the campaign, these men, who only a few weeks before had carried German weapons and drawn German pay, soon began to arrive to join their compatriots in Alexander's new assault on Kesselring's Gothic Line.

14
Coriano and Gemmano: 10 – 14 September

Under Eighth Army's new plan, its main effort was to be redirected into the coastal strip round Rimini, which was protected by a line of German defences running through the fortified village of San Fortunato, about four miles north of the River Marano. Before any assault could be carried across the Marano, however, it was necessary to secure the long line of the Coriano Ridge on the army's left flank.

Leese planned a three-phase battle. In the first phase, Keightley's V Corps would continue its attacks at Gemmano and Croce with 46th Division and later with 4th Indian Division, in order to hold von Vietinghoff's attention on the southern end of the German Line. Meanwhile the armour of both V Corps and the Canadian Corps would assault the Coriano Ridge, while 56th Division attacked at Croce to protect the left flank.[1] (*Map 2.*)

In the second phase, the 4th British Infantry Division would pass through the Canadian armour and advance over the River Marano, accompanied by Hull's 1st British Armoured Division.

The third phase envisaged that the Canadian Corps would capture San Fortunato, and with V Corps on its left, advance to the River Marecchia, which flowed into the sea at Rimini. The army reserve, the New Zealand Division, accompanied if possible by the Canadian Armoured Division, would then move swiftly on Bologna and Ferrara.

Meanwhile the shell-torn, smoking ridge of Gemmano,

scarred by its shattered hamlets and strewn with the swollen corpses of men and animals, still stuck like a sword in Eighth Army's side. One of the reasons that the Eighth Army attack on Coriano had been delayed until the evening of the 12th was in the hope of a favourable outcome at Gemmano, and the battle for the ridge was in no way diminished when 46th Division replaced 56th Division on its slopes.

Hawkesworth's division assumed responsibility for the area on 10 September. The 2nd/4th King's Own Yorkshire Light Infantry of 138th Brigade began by an attempt to clear the western side of the Borgo on the same day, but received heavy casualties in violent house-to-house fighting. The 6th Lincolns, given the formidable task of capturing Point 449 and Zollara, were badly cut about by a storm of German shells as they moved up to attack, but managed to get one company up to the wooden cross on top of the hill, advancing through a screen of smoke while the Germans on their flanks swept them with machine-gun fire.[2]

During the night, the Germans swarmed back on to the hill, and there followed a day of confused and bloody fighting, in which the K.O.Y.L.I., taking over from the hard-pressed Lincoln company, lost and regained the hill several times. Three battalions were now crowded into the buildings and cellars of Gemmano village, as the Durhams of 139th Brigade were brought in, followed on the night of 12/13 September by the York and Lancasters of 138th Brigade. Ground was taken and retaken and taken again in a score of savage little actions, and the pattern of the fighting was so chaotic that brigade and even battalion headquarters often had no idea whether points on the map were held by British or German troops. The defenders of the ridge, the Austrians of 100th Mountain Regiment, fought brilliantly and bravely, scrambling down to the protection of the reverse slopes as the British guns pounded the top of the ridge, and then running back to their trenches in time to play their Spandaus along the first lines of British infantry when the shelling stopped and the assault began.[3]

On the early morning of 13 September, when Eighth Army, waiting no longer for victory at Gemmano, began its attack all

along the line to the north, the main heights along the Gemmano Ridge were still in enemy hands. All around the bullet-
chipped cross on Point 449, the dead, khaki and field-grey,
lay heaped, unburied, in score upon score; at their centre a
soldier of the Lincolns whose hands were still frozen in death
round the cross itself, which he had reached in his battalion's
first attack.[4] Few regiments of Eighth Army had ever known
fiercer fighting than that on Gemmano, and on 13 September
it seemed as if it might go on for ever. On that same morning,
however, across the River Conca at Croce, the Queen's
Brigade of Whitfield's 56th Division scored a success which
transformed the whole situation on the southern flank of the
German line.

★ ★ ★

The role of 56th Division in Leese's attack, as we have seen, was
to secure the flank round Croce while the Canadian and British
armour assaulted the line of the Coriano Ridge which stretched
to the north. Croce itself had already changed hands five times,
but was now held by British troops. The whole area was being
continually pounded by the artillery of both sides, and the dead
who lay round the area in hundreds were being blown to pieces
by the ceaseless rain of shells. An officer of 2nd/6th Queen's
described the barrage as 'so intensive that it was impossible
to distinguish any single explosion'.[5] The gruesome landscape of
Croce was one of the few in the war which recalled the scenes of
Flanders to senior officers who had served there between 1914
and 1918. It was, said Whitfield, 'the dirtiest battleground I saw
during the war'.

Whitfield decided to begin his attack by seizing the ridge
on which stood the villages of Casiccio and San Marco,
a little more than a mile north-west of Croce, and also the
high ground round Casa Fabbri, farther to the north. The
task was given to the Queen's Brigade, which had had a bare
two days' rest since its fierce struggle across the valley at Gemmano. The brigade was to be supported by the Royal Tank
Regiment battalions of the 7th Armoured Brigade, which

was itself reinforced by an armoured regiment, the 7th Hussars.

In the first phase of the attack, 2nd/7th Queen's were to advance on the right towards Casa Fabbri, while 2nd/6th Queen's cleared the Il Palazzo and Casa Menghino areas which had remained disputed ever since they had been seized by the London Scottish of 168th Brigade a few days earlier. Then 2nd/5th Queen's would advance through Il Palazzo to San Marco and Casiccio. In the second phase, the brigade would seize the whole of the Fabbri ridge. A stunning barrage of three thousand 25-pounder shells would be fired in support of each of these phases.[6]

The troops opposing the renewed British assault were mainly those of the German 98th Infantry Division, which had been seriously weakened by the loss of nearly 900 prisoners in the last twelve days.

The attack by 2nd/6th Queen's began in the early hours of 13 September. It started well, and just after 4 a.m. the battalion seized the areas round Casa Menghino and Il Palazzo. By 6 a.m. the German infantry recovered themselves, and a strong counter-attack drove 2nd/6th Queen's out of Il Palazoz, though they hung on to Casa Menghino. Three hours later, supported by the tanks of the 7th Hussars, the British infantry surged forward again, and Il Palazzo was once more in their hands.

Moving on through heavy fire, the Shermans of the Hussars reached San Marco and thrust out to within a quarter of a mile of Casiccio, but German anti-tank guns began to pick them off and three tanks were soon burning just short of the objective.

Meanwhile, on the right, the greatest achievement of the day went to 2nd/7th Queen's, and their supporting Shermans of the 2nd Royal Tank Regiment. The battalion was directed towards the Casa Fabbri, and they were badly hit by enemy fire as they moved forward at 6 a.m. All the officers of the leading company were wounded in the first ten minutes, and two officers in the next company were killed, while casualties among N.C.O.s and men were very heavy. The reserve company, commanded by Captain David Rossiter – the

officer who had held the houses of Gemmano against the
German counter-attacks five days before – now came forward.
They, too, came under intense mortar and small-arms fire.
Rossiter was killed as he crossed the start-line, but his men went
on.[7]

They were supported by a squadron of tanks of 2nd R.T.R.,
which in the smoke and confusion of the early morning fighting
became somewhat detached from them, but made a brilliant
contribution to the day. An officer with the squadron described
what happened:

'. . . We moved off just after first light. There was a very
heavy concentration of artillery fire in the valley, together with
a smoke-screen to shield us from San Savino. This, together
with the half-light, made it very difficult to see more than a few
yards and we were worried by the fact that we had no infantry
with us and would have to manœuvre amongst enemy positions
without being able to see them until we were well within
bazooka range. But we had no casualties from this cause, and
found out later that we had very good cause to be thankful for
the poor light. Three tanks stuck in the ploughed land within a
few yards of the startline, but these were the only casualties we
had in getting up on to the objective. The right leading troop
was hung up by bad country in the valley, and the two remaining tanks of the other leading troop got up on the ridge completely by themselves. They had come right through the main
infantry positions and then had to turn and fire backwards
among the tanks of the rest of the squadron in order to help
them get forward, which they soon did. We found out afterwards that the route which we had travelled was occupied by
more than 300 enemy infantry, who were taken completely by
surprise.

'In about ten minutes from the start of the attack, the nine
remaining tanks of the squadron were all concentrated at the
northern end of the Fabbri Ridge. As the light grew and the
smoke cleared, we saw that we were splendidly placed; looking
back at the whole of the enemy's reserve positions along the
Coriano Ridge, and overlooking any movement that he
made. . . .

'We were actually on Fabbri Ridge for about two hours

before any infantry joined us; they had run into enemy infantry as soon as they moved off from the start-line. . . .

'We had a number of excellent shots at enemy moving about in and behind San Savino, and during the morning an enemy Mark IV tank appeared moving down the hill. We must have fired about 80 or 100 rounds from all the tanks in the squadron at it and hit it repeatedly. The crew abandoned it. We also brewed up a half-track near some haystacks, which caught fire, revealing two enemy 88-mm. anti-tank guns concealed in them. . . .

'We remained to help the infantry consolidate and were relieved about 3 a.m., by which time, nearly twenty-four hours since we started, every man in the squadron had fallen asleep.'[8]

The combined efforts of infantry and armour in their rear had considerably disconcerted the German infantry of 98th Division, and 2nd/7th Queen's alone took more than 300 prisoners during the day, mainly from 117th and 289th Grenadier Regiments. The battalion's commanding officer, Lieutenant-Colonel M. E. M. MacWilliam, saw clearly that a gap had been torn in the German line, and that the position was ripe for exploitation. He tried to make contact with his brigade commander, Smith-Dorrien. At this vital moment, however, Smith-Dorrien, who had just been in conference with Whitfield at the brigade tactical headquarters, was killed by a shell while giving orders over the wireless.

The 9th Royal Fusiliers of 167th Brigade relieved 2nd/7th Queen's during the evening of the 13th, and the battalion marched the weary way back to a reserve area at San Andrea, shelled all the way by German guns. 'Everyone,' wrote a member of the battalion, 'was completely exhausted but would have marched twice the distance to get out for a few hours.'[9] The day's fighting had cost the battalion six officers and 100 men in dead and wounded.

★ ★ ★

Along the line of the Coriano ridge to the north, the attack had also made good progress. The shattering salvoes from seven hundred guns had done much to daze the German defenders. Hull's 1st Armoured Division, attacking the section of the ridge from San Savino to Passano, registered quick gains. The 18th Lorried Brigade, supported by the 9th Lancers in an attack on Savino, were firmly in the village by midnight, though confused fighting went on until dawn. Farther north, the 43rd Gurkha Brigade, riding into action on the backs of the tanks of the Queen's Bays, took Passano, and at the end of the line the 11th Canadian Infantry Brigade was locked in hand-to-hand fighting with 29th Panzer Grenadier Division inside the village of Coriano. The day cost the 11th Brigade 210 men – the Cape Breton Highlanders alone losing eighty-five. But at the end of it Coriano was in Canadian hands, and the stage appeared to be set for the next phase of Leese's plan – the advance of the 4th British Infantry Division and the 1st British Armoured Division over the Ripabianca Ridge just behind Coriano to secure crossings over the Marano.

It had been a bad day for Kesselring, and his divisions, pounded by the British artillery, harassed by infantry and tanks, and systematically battered from the air – 500 tons of bombs were dropped on them by the Desert Air Force during the day's 900 sorties – had sustained heavy losses.[10] Kesselring himself was in no doubt about the seriousness of the position. He was in process of moving the 20th Luftwaffe Field Division from Viareggio and the famous 90th (Light) Panzer Grenadier Division from the Franco-Italian frontier to the Adriatic front, but this move was still not completed and the reinforcements would not be available next day. In addition, 356th Infantry Division, also, as we have seen, being transferred from the central front to help von Vietinghoff, was having to march at night down Route 9 from Imola, because the railway line was being destroyed with precision by the Desert Air Force, who also made the road unusable by day.

In his telephone conversation with von Vietinghoff at the end of 13 September, Kesselring's usual optimism seemed to have deserted him. The exchange is reported in the Tenth Army war diary:

Kesselring: 'I have just returned and heard the terrible news. Will you please inform me of the situation.'

Von Vietinghoff: 'The depth of the penetrations cannot be ascertained with accuracy as yet. . . . The front has been greatly weakened.'

Kesselring: 'We must realize that tomorrow will be a day of great crisis.'

Von Vietinghoff: 'We are certain of this; all day we have been racking our brains about how to help, but we have nothing left. . . .'[11]

The night brought new fears for the German command. After a tremendous barrage by the guns of both 46th and 56th Divisions, reinforced by those of the Army Group Royal Artillery, the battalions of 168th Brigade advanced more than 6,000 yards against spasmodic German resistance, and in a few hours were firmly established on the high ground above the River Marano. The Germans of 98th Division, now so shattered and pulverized as to be scarcely a cohesive force, abandoned Casiccio. There began, at last, to be evidence of the disintegration of some German units; the commander of 114 Reconnaissance Unit, left to cover the last ridge before the Marano, was captured with most of his headquarters.[12]

September 13 saw the gates of opportunity swing creakily open once more for Eighth Army. With the Canadians firm in Coriano and 56th Division looking down on the Marano, the way seemed clear for the next move. The 4th British Infantry Division and Hull's 1st Armoured Division should now cross the Marano, bursting further open what seemed to be a cracking front. Yet by the end of the day, the chance was gone. Once more, the inability to develop success cost Eighth Army dearly.

The first blow came when the tanks of 1st Armoured Division discovered that the little stream of the Rio delle Fornaci, which seemed no more than a hairline on the map, had been fed by the rain and was now a thick brown torrent racing between steep banks, impassable to armour. A group of Royal Engineers, working in front of the infantry in the steep ravine leading down o the stream, managed to get an Ark* bridge across during the

---

* A turretless Churchill tank, fitted with ramps, which could be driven into place to bridge a narrow gap.

night, but the advance of the armour was held up until then.[13]

Even more important, however, were the delays suffered by the 4th British Infantry Division as it came forward to its assembly area behind the Coriano ridge, ready to pass through the Canadian positions and push on over the Marano. The division was led by its 12th Brigade, which consisted of the 2nd Royal Fusiliers, the 6th Black Watch, and the 1st Royal West Kents. Several factors now contributed to the delay in getting this brigade into a position to attack. The Black Watch and the Fusiliers were delayed on their way to the assembly area by intense shelling and mortaring of the approach roads and tracks. Moreover, according to the account of the 2nd Royal Fusiliers, the time required for the infantry to march to and assemble behind the Coriano Ridge had been underestimated.[14] When the battalions eventually reached the assembly area, which was in a dried-up river bed, they were again heavily and accurately shelled and mortared, and there were many casualties. It was now late on a hot evening, and the tired infantry would have had to attack due west, with the evening sunlight dazzling them. The attack was postponed until early next morning.[15]

Meanwhile, however, the Germans were desperately strengthening their position. North of the Marano lay yet another of the seemingly endless ranks of ridges which confronted Eighth Army. This was the Mulazzano Ridge, and here von Vietinghoff was hastily feeding in 356th Division at the end of its frantic march to the rescue. This was considered by Allied intelligence to be a good German division, though by no means at full strength. Companies were down to forty or fifty men, with only one mortar for each. During 13 September, 356th Division was being shuffled, piecemeal, into place; when Eighth Army attacked next morning, it would not find the broken front which the events of the previous twenty-four hours might have led it to expect.

At the southern end of Kesselring's defence line, however, the Allied advance on 13 September had a decisive effect. As 56th Division increased its pressure beyond Croce, the German position at Gemmano, south of the River Conca, became increasingly untenable. During the 14th, the German infantry of 100th Mountain Regiment began quietly to evacuate the positions which they had defended so stubbornly, unaware that a third Eighth Army division had now been given the task of clearing them from the ridge.

This was Holworthy's 4th Indian Division, which since the capture of Tavoleto on 4 September had been engaged in a grim battle across the Pian di Castello ridge three miles due south of Gemmano, moving through bitterly-contested mountainous country in driving wind and rain. By 13 September, the division was about a mile south of the Gemmano Ridge, and the V Corps commander, Keightley, sent for Holworthy. He had now decided to pull 46th Division off Gemmano and to push them along the north bank of the Conca to help 56th Division exploit the success at Croce. The task of taking Gemmano was to be given to 4th Indian Division, and it was vital that it should be done quickly.

'Corps commander wanted tonight,' Holworthy wrote in his diary after the meeting, 'but told him I could not get reconnaissances, preparations, artillery support, etc., laid on in time, so he said: "All right, tomorrow night."'

Holworthy was well aware of the formidable reputation of the ridge and its German defenders, and he prepared his attack with meticulous care. He chose the 2nd Queen's Own Cameron Highlanders of the 11th Infantry Brigade as his assaulting battalion, and he proposed to support them with a heavy and intricate artillery programme designed to mislead as well as daze the Germans. Five field regiments of artillery, two medium regiments, one heavy battery, sixteen 4·2-inch mortars and a platoon of medium machine-guns pulverised the ridge before the Camerons went in. The battalion objective was Point 449, and the little hamlet of Zollara just below it received 2,000 shells as the preliminary to the assault. Meanwhile, a series of crash shoots was organized on suspected enemy positions, while other guns laid down deception barrages to deceive the German defenders into thinking the attack was coming in other places.[16]

The Camerons went forward just before midnight on 14 September. Their commanding officer, Lieutenant-Colonel Alistair Noble, wrote later:

'The concentrations started at 22.25 hours with a great crash, and B and C Companies got away. Opposition was light, as most of the Boche had cleared out earlier. B and C cleared the village and some caves where it was known the Boche were, and A Company, with a platoon of D, which was brought up to make certain, were dug in on Point 449. It was said that the Boche had to all intents and purposes gone, so we felt that we had been deprived of our pound of flesh and not fully avenged the losses of 46th Division. However, we killed some Boche and took twenty-one prisoners of war, all at no cost whatever to ourselves, which was most gratifying. . . .'[17]

Noble and his Camerons were well aware of what other battalions had sacrificed on Gemmano. When day came they removed ninety-one British dead from Point 449 alone, and when Leese sent his congratulations on their success, Noble replied that 'the success of the operation was very largely due to the hard fighting of our predecessors and to the excellent support which we were given'.

So, almost as an anti-climax, the Gemmano Ridge passed into British hands. 'A good show,' Holworthy noted laconically in his diary and added: 'Gemmano full of dead and smells like another Cassino.'

The battle roared on to the north, and within twenty-four hours the only men left in the villages of Gemmano and Zollara and Borgo along the ridge were the men who would never leave.

They sat, wedged side by side, in the ruined cellars of the old stone houses; sprawled in piles in the doorways of barns; lay in untidy heaps in the little peasants' houses where they had crawled to die. After the fighting had moved on, a medical officer of 46th Division, Captain James Speer, went up with his orderly to these eerie villages of the dead. Most corpses, now, were German, for more than 900 of the enemy were thought to have died on the ridge, and burial parties had already cleared most of the British dead.

Speer and his orderly, quite alone, walked through the silent square and cobbled paths of Gemmano.

'There was,' he recalls, 'a big corner house, probably a shop or a café, which looked out on the river valley on two sides. The walls had been smashed front and back, and it was packed with corpses. The wind on top of the ridge was blowing straight through the house from front to back, and all the broken shutters were banging, but there was no other sound. We went outside, and there was a little outhouse there with another dozen dead men inside. I kept feeling that I would hear someone shout, or talk, but there was nothing. When the wind dropped, it was absolutely quiet. That's what I remember most, the quiet, and the smell.'[18]

15
Breaking Strain

Fierce and grim though the fighting for the Gemmano and Coriano Ridges and their approaches had been, the week which lay ahead of Eighth Army when Leese's new offensive began on 13 September had worse to offer. Kesselring was now being forced back to the vital anchor points of his main line of defence in front of the Marano, and he must fight furiously for these if he was to avoid disaster. From 13 September onwards the German command had also to reckon with the growing threat on the central front of Mark Clark's Fifth Army as it began to advance north of Florence. The Fifth Army operations, for the sake of the unity of the narrative, will be described in later chapters; but it is important to remember when studying the Eighth Army campaign that Clark's offensive many miles away to the west was from now on a vital factor in Kesselring's ever-fiercer resistance on the Adriatic front.

The week between 13 September and 20 September was one of confused fighting, swaying over a complex map, criss-crossed with jumbled ridges and winding streams. For those who fought on the ground itself, it was only a little less confusing. There was no clear line, no consistent grain to the country across which Eighth Army advanced. There were no great roads whose significance was clear to all; no big communications centres; no railheads. Only the names of tiny and seemingly insignificant hamlets leap into the unit war diaries and regimental accounts – Trarivi, Mulazzano, Cerasolo, Ospedaletto. Sometimes they were not even hamlets, but the names of single houses which happened to crown some hill or knoll, commanded the head of some miniature valley. But all of them had one thing in common. Somewhere, dug in within their boundaries, would be a Spandau post, or a mortar section; an 88-mm. gun or a Tiger tank.

From south to north, the Allied divisions now moved forward across this patchwork map of rural Italy ... 46th Division, 56th Division, 1st British Armoured Division, 4th Division, the Canadian Corps, the Greek Mountain Brigade, and the New Zealanders.

At the ragged edge of this slowly-moving front, each house, each hamlet, each little height required a separate attack – by platoon, or company, or squadron, or battalion, or brigade. Each of these attacks cost men. On every day of this week, Eighth Army lost an average of 750 men in killed and wounded – roughly the equivalent in fighting men of an entire infantry battalion daily. These losses would not have seemed decisive in the First World War, to soldiers soaked in the terrible statistics of the Somme. But to Eighth Army, they were crippling.

The Bedfords, and the Queen's, and the Somersets, and the Black Watch, and the Queen's Bays, and the Canadians, and the Gurkhas, and the Greeks who fell, not in one great battle, but in slowly mounting dozens and scores, could not be replaced. Alexander had virtually no reinforcements for his British, Canadian, Indian, and New Zealand divisions. If Vienna was to be reached, as Churchill still dreamed, these were the men who must get there, and they were growing fewer and fewer every day.

There was also another factor. It is a truism in war that 'it is always the best who are killed first'. This may or may not be true in a moral sense, but it is certainly true in a professional military one. The infantry subaltern who first gets up from a safe position to run towards an enemy post; the first soldier to follow him out into the open; the tank commander who leaves safe ground to work round on a flank and surprise the enemy – these are the men who die first in battle. Eighth Army had been fighting for over a year in Italy, and many of these men were dead already. Many more would die in the next week. Yet such men were especially needed now, in the coming offensive. No army can attack without them, and for Eighth Army the offensive spirit was even more vital. Victory over the Germans was coming; the whole army knew it. On the radio, exultant voices proclaimed it; in the army newspapers which were delivered up to the front, the war maps of Europe showed the driving arrows of the Anglo-American offensive in the west, and of the Russians in the east. Whatever happened in Italy, the war would soon be over.

It is one thing for a soldier to die bravely with his back to the wall, or to fall in a storming offensive which turns the tide of war. But it is another thing altogether to get killed by being a little over-zealous in the last few weeks or months. The larger strategic plans of men like Churchill or Smuts meant little to the men on the ground. They would, of course, fight on, doggedly and courageously, conducting themselves with a high professionalism. But sometimes, at vital moments in the coming days, the willingness to take a shrewdly-calculated gamble was no longer there.

The Germans, too, were suffering terrible losses. But, as we have seen, the actual numbers on each side were not very different, and attack demanded a ratio of roughly three to one. The German psychological situation might seem, however, to be even more precarious. It must have been clear to many of Kesselring's troops that Germany could no longer win the war. Strangely enough, however, this very belief helped to strengthen their will to fight. The Führer's strategy was not difficult for them to understand. He was fighting now for peace on reasonable terms, buying time with his soldiers' lives, so that the V-weapons, of which the German troops were constantly told, could force the Allies to stop the war. The young Germans who manned the slit trenches against Eighth Army, many of them now very young and indoctrinated since childhood with Hitler's insane sense of national glory, knew clearly what they were fighting for. They were battling for the best possible future that their Führer could snatch from his encircling enemies.

Nevertheless, however surprisingly good their morale, the position on the ground of the German troops was dauntingly difficult. They were being flayed and pounded from the air and the Allied artillery, and levered one by one out of their positions on the ground. Only the autumn rain could save Kesselring now, and like his master at Berchtesgaden, he was playing desperately for time.

Every Spandau post which held on for an extra hour against a British or Canadian infantry company was bringing nearer the time when the rain, blessed on one side, cursed on the other, would make movement impossible in the North Italian plain. Juggling his shrinking resources, keeping a cool and calculating head, and buttressed by the brave sagacity of von Vietinghoff, Kesselring now committed his tired but hard-fighting units to the task of slowing Eighth Army down.

★ ★ ★

The stream of the Marano straggled between the two armies, from about two miles north-west of Montescudo at the left end of the line, through Ospedaletto in the centre, until it entered the Adriatic between Riccione and Rimini. After it was crossed, only the Ausa and the Marecchia would lie between Eighth Army and the Lombardy Plain of which it had dreamed for so long. The crossing of the Marano had originally been planned for 4 September. Ten days later, the moment seemed near.

Part of Keightley's V Corps was already thrusting towards it. Keightley had taken 46th Division off Gemmano in order to attack Montescudo, and on 14 September the Leicesters of Block's 139th Brigade, supported by a squadron of tanks, advanced through the 56th Division positions west of Croce, along the line of high ground which stretched from Croce through the hamlet of Poggia to the hill villages of Monte Colombo and Montescudo itself. Gemmano at this stage had not yet been taken by 4th Indian Division, and the long menacing feature on the left flank of Block's brigade was smothered in smoke from the Allied artillery in order to confuse the German gunners.

The Leicesters took Poggia before noon, and five hours later, amid violent enemy shelling, captured Monte Colombo as well. However, Keightley's move in switching 46th Division from Gemmano had been countered by a similar move by the German command. They had moved the Gemmano garrison, 100th

Mountain Regiment, to Montescudo, and when the 5th Hampshires of 128th Brigade passed through the Leicesters at Monte Colombo just before midnight on 14 September, they found these formidable opponents waiting for them.[1]

The Hampshires began well by catching a German platoon talking on the crossroads at Trarivi, just outside Montescudo, killing many of the enemy before the Germans realized what had happened. But the main German positions in the houses outside the town held firm, and a long and bitter day loomed for the Hampshire brigade. Soon after dawn, a Hampshire company commander got his men into the outskirts of Montescudo, but another company of 2nd Hampshires was brought to a standstill by fierce German resistance round Trarivi, while the enemy guns controlled from Point 475, a smooth round hill just beyond Montescudo, put down a carpet of shells. Trarivi had to be cleared of 100th Mountain Regiment house-by-house, and not until the evening of 16 September was it fully in British hands. At dawn on the following day, 2nd Hampshires took Point 475. It was now 17 September, and at the left end of the army line, all German resistance south of the Marano was finished.

★ ★ ★

On the right of 46th Division, however, 56th Division, which had done so well on the last ridge before the Marano on the night of 13/14 September, now paused before exploiting. During 15 September, activity along the divisional front was limited to reconnaissance and active patrolling, while the infantry dealt with any small pockets of Germans south of the Marano. Useful work was, of course, done – the river was found passable by armour, being only knee-deep and no obstacle at all to infantry. But during all this day the Germans of 356th Division were establishing themselves more firmly on the Mulazzano ridge on the other side of the Marano, and every hour spent by 56th Division on its deliberate preparations for the attack was gold in Kesselring's pocket as he arranged his reserves. British soldiers are traditionally slow to exploit, and these particular infantrymen were tired, depleted, and too thin on the ground. Nevertheless, on the mysterious other side of the hill, Kesselring's infantry were just as weary, and much more worried. A quick push across the Marano on the 15th, instead of meticulous reconnaissance, might have yielded surprising dividends.

The attack across the Marano upon the Mulazzano Ridge began at midnight on the 16th. The leading troops crossed the river without difficulty, reaching Mulazzano itself, but then pocket after pocket of firm enemy resistance held up the advance for the rest of the day. Next day the German resistance in front of the division stiffened still more, and violent enemy counter attacks on the slopes west of Mulazzano swept the front line to and fro until evening. Kesselring was winning valuable time as he raced to reconstruct his line in front of the Lombardy Plain. Once more, the pattern of the past two weeks seemed to be about to be repeated; that of a fierce German resistance in the difficult, hilly country on Eighth Army's left flank, holding up and in-hibiting operations farther north. If this was to happen, the advance of the 4th British Infantry Division and the Canadian Corps towards the northern end of the German line would be put in serious difficulty.

The 4th Division, as we have seen, had itself made an un-fortunate pause on 13 September, but on the 14th it was ready to advance again. Early that morning, with the Black Watch on the right and the Royal Fusiliers on the left, the division attacked across the Fornaci ravine which lay between it and the Marano. By evening, the two battalions were established on a ridge look-ing down on the Marano. It had been a stiff day's fighting, especially for the Churchill tanks supporting the infantry, which were roughly handled by the 88-mm. guns of the defending German Tigers. One well-sited Tiger destroyed seven Churchills during the afternoon, until its jubilant commander stood up in his turret and was at once killed by a sharp-eyed Fusilier captain with a rifle shot at a range of 250 yards.[2]

Before midnight, the Royal West Kents passed through, and seized a bridgehead over the Marano at Ospedaletto, although the bridge itself was blown as they moved up.

On the morning of 15 September, the divisional commander,

Ward, put his 28th Infantry Brigade through the Ospedaletto bridgehead to attack the straggling ends of the Mulazzano feature in front of them. The 2nd/4th Hampshires of the brigade captured San Patrignano on the left, while the 2nd King's (Liverpool) Regiment attacked the hil on the right. In three hours, both battalions were on their objectives, but were still overlooked by enemy positions on the Mulazzano Ridge to their left, and beyond that, from the looming heights of the tiny independent Republic of San Marino. They were moving across open rolling ground and had to endure heavy enemy shelling as they advanced.[3]

By the end of the day, however, 4th Division had a grip on the north-eastern end of the jumble of foothills between the Marano and the Ausa; its next task was to cross the latter stream. Early on 16 September, the reserve battalion of 28th Brigade – the 2nd Somerset Light Infantry – prepared to pass through the King's and the Hampshires to attack yet another feature, the Frisoni Ridge, which looked down on the Ausa.

The night was one of confused fighting along the ridge and its approaches, lit by the red light of burning haystacks and blazing vehicles. A violent German counter-attack by infantry in armoured lorries drove the Somersets back from their advanced positions, and shelling and mortaring were so heavy that no further advance was possible after dawn.

During the afternoon of the 16th, Ward decided that the enemy gun and observation positions at Cerasolo, a little to the south-west, must be cleared before he could advance across the Ausa. The small village of Cerasolo had originally been one of the objectives of 1st Armoured Division, but Hull's men had not yet reached so far. *(Map 3.)*

At dawn on the 17th, Ward attacked it with the 2nd/4th Hampshires, and during the morning Cerasolo was captured, with about fifty prisoners. On the same night, the Black Watch stormed and took the Frisoni Ridge, and the leading elements of Ward's division closed up to the Ausa. During the day the Royal West Kents of 12th Brigade moved up once more from their positions at Ospedaletto. They started their crossing of the Ausa at midnight, and by dawn, after a brisk night's fighting in which they took fifty prisoners and had twenty-six casualties, they had three companies over the river, supported by two troops of tanks of the North Irish Horse. Farther up on the right, the 2nd Bedfords of the division's 10th Infantry Brigade also crossed the river and advanced a further 500 yards before beginning a bloody struggle with German infantry and machine-gunners on the next ridge.

The night was remarkable for a new element injected into the fighting by the Allied command. The Germans were no longer given the cloak of darkness to disguise their troop movements from the searching fire of Allied guns. On a moonless night, the Allies created artificial moonlight. Batteries of searchlights, positioned on the newly-captured Coriano Ridge, illuminated the battlefield in front of the British infantry, so that enemy movements could be clearly seen.

The innovation both surprised and perturbed the German defenders.

'Since 2200 hours an enormous number of searchlights has been lighting up our forward areas . . . making it most difficult to carry out moves,' said the next day's morning report of 29th Panzier Grenadier Division. On the same morning, the 76th Panzer Corps commander, General Herr, reported to von Vietinghoff that 'this new enemy trick of lighting up the battle-field has harassed our moves and blinded our people'. The subsequent telephone conversation between the respective chiefs of staff of Tenth Army and Army Group C reveals the extent of the German discomfiture.[4]

Tenth Army: 'Last night he did the weirdest thing I ever saw. He lit up the battlefield with searchlights.'

Army Group: 'From the sea?'

Tenth Army: 'No, on land. He turned on a display like Party Day in Nuremberg.'

Army Group: 'Really from the land, not the sea?'

Tenth Army: 'From the Ospedaletto area.'

Army Group: 'Couldn't you get them any way?'

Tenth Army: 'No.'

Army Group: 'They can't have been as far away as all that.'

Tenth Army: 'Anyway, we couldn't get them. I must discuss the matter with the army artillery commander.'

Army Group: 'They will do that again tonight.'

Tenth Army: 'I don't know what we're going to do about it. We may detail a few 88-mm. guns to deal with them. . . . Couldn't we send a few aircraft over?'

Army Group: 'I'll see what I can do.'

Tenth Army: 'It's a great worry to the boys to be lighted up and blinded and not be able to do anything about it.'

★ ★ ★

Meanwhile, on the left of the army line, a new problem loomed for Eighth Army. It was clear to the troops who were now struggling forward in its shadow that the little neutral mountain republic of San Marino – one of the most ancient states in Europe, with a record of independence going back for seven hundred years – was being used by the Germans to provide observation posts for artillery. This was, in fact, the case; Kesselring had demanded the use of State territory at the beginning of September. The little town, perched on the 2,500-foot height of Monte Titano, was crammed with people. In addition to the Republic's usual population of 14,000, more than 120,000 Italian refugees from the surrounding countryside crowded its steep slopes.[5]

As Eighth Army moved across the Marano, it was clear that this dominating position must be taken. The task was given to Holworthy's 4th Indian Division on 17 September.

'Corps Commander early this morning gave us new role to get San Marino road centre starting tonight,' he wrote in his diary that evening. '5th Brigade will have to do it. It is a chancy business – if we surprise the Boche we will get there, otherwise we may be stuck under direct observation from hill town of San Marino and its towers. Corps and everyone seem very optimistic about whole front – absurdly so, I think. They confidently expect a breakthrough tomorrow morning all along the front and the Boche, they say, has no reinforcements. In my opinion, he has more than they think.' He added, ominously: 'Looks like rain this evening.'

The 3rd/10th Baluch battalion of 5th Brigade crossed the Marano unopposed near Faetano, on the border of San

Marino, early on the 18th, and 1st/9th Gurkhas moved through to seize Points 345 and 366, two commanding heights just ahead. These heights, however, were strongly held by two battalions of 993rd Grenadier Regiment, in the German 278th Infantry Division.

Just after 5 a.m. the Gurkhas fought their way on to Point 345, and two companies went on to Point 366 under heavy Spandau fire. The track up which they advanced was so bad that the only ammunition available was what could be carried in eighty porter loads. After a long fire fight with the Germans on the steep, cliff-like sides of Point 366, the Gurkhas began to run out of ammunition. The two companies were now in a precarious position. Attempts were made to pull them back, but they came under heavy Spandau fire. At this point a Gurkha rifleman, Sherbahadur Thapa, with his section commander, seized a Bren gun and charged one of the Spandau posts, killing the German machine-gunner. A German infantry section counter-attacked at once, wounding the Gurkha section commander. Rifleman Sherbahadur Thapa drove back the attack with his Bren gun, and then ran to the crest of a ridge, from where, lying in the open, he poured fire against a German company preparing to counter-attack the Gurkhas. For two hours he held up the German attack. Then, as the companies below him safely withdrew, he saw two wounded Gurkhas lying between him and the Germans. Under heavy fire he dragged one back to safety. As he returned for the second man he was killed by a Spandau burst. He had won the second Victoria Cross of the Gothic Line campaign.

The 1st Field Regiment of the divisional artillery now came to the rescue of the Gurkha battalion, firing smoke and high explosive to cover the withdrawal and break up the German counter-attack. The Gurkhas had had a bad morning, losing sixty-three men, but they had kept their grip on most of the high ground. German shelling increased steadily all day, and Holworthy himself, visiting the battalion tactical headquarters to watch the battle, was shelled heavily all the way there and back.[6]

The next day, 19 September, the Camerons of 5th Brigade put patrols up the hillside above Faetano, and on the 20th they worked their way into the winding streets of the city, killing twenty Germans and capturing more than fifty by the evening. They lost thirty-six men in killed and wounded, but San Marino had been taken at a much smaller cost than many of those who looked at its looming heights from the valley had imagined.[7]

16
The Last Ridge

There had been a grim little joke running through Eighth Army for the last week that 'Jerry's retreating all right, but he's taking the last ridge back with him'. But now, after all the disappointment, the army was at last in front of the final ridge before the Lombardy Plain. After this obstacle was passed, the military geography of the area would, it was believed, change to Kesselring's disadvantage, with the country flattening out, and the gap between the foothills and the coast growing wider and wider.

Nevertheless, the last ridge was a considerable obstacle. It thrust across the Eighth Army front, running north-east towards the coast from the northern borders of San Marino. On the left, just north of the tiny republic, it began as the confusingly-named Ceriano (not to be mistaken for Coriano) Ridge, and then ran above the line of the River Ausa through the bulky mass of the San Fortunato feature, crowned by the village of the same name, which reared almost 500 feet above the surrounding country. *(Map 3.)*

This line of high ground had been prepared by the Germans as the last fixed defence before the plain. It was known to Allied Intelligence as 'the Rimini Line', and it was controlled by the fortress village of San Fortunato. Along this line, von Vietinghoff's Tenth Army turned once more to fight, looking anxiously at the sky, while the rain made itself felt in occasional small drenching showers, filling the stony beds of the mountain streams and rivers, and making the narrow roads daily more treacherous and greasy. As we have seen, von Vietinghoff had already committed 356th Infantry Division and the 20th

Luftwaffe Field Division from the centre; now he began to pack the centre of the Rimini Line, just west of San Fortunato, with the leading elements of the 90th (Light) Panzer Grenadier Division, which had won a celebrated name in the fighting in North Africa, and had been reconstituted after the defeat of the Afrika Korps. The division had been moved down from the north-west of Italy, where it had been sent during the summer in response to Kesselring's obsession with the fancied danger to the Alpine crest positions.

It was commanded by Lieutenant-General Ernst Gunter Baade,* one of the best fighting generals, and also one of the most unconventional, in the German Army. This officer, who seems to have had a Montgomery-like aptitude for catching the imagination of his troops, usually wore a khaki kilt over his uniform riding breeches, with a pistol hanging in place of the sporran. He had a habit of leaving behind him at any forward command post which he occupied a bottle containing his own name, that of his adjutant, and also of his dog.[1] Like Montgomery, however, he was more than a showman. He had won golden opinions from fellow-generals during the fighting at Cassino, and his well-trained division was probably the best in von Vietinghoff's army. From the German point of view, no better choice could have been made to strengthen the vital centre of the Rimini Line.

The British V Corps could now feel the breeze from the plain blowing in their faces as they moved forward from the Marano up to and across the Ausa. Although 46th Division, still embroiled around Montescudo, was lagging a little on the left flank, farther north the leading battalion of Whitfield's 56th Division crossed the Ausa on the afternoon of 18 September and next day began their attack on the Ceriano Ridge. To the right of Whitfield, Hull's 1st Armoured Division also crossed the Ausa at Monte dell'Arboreta, near the north-eastern tip of San Marino, and pushed forward towards the high ground marked on the map as Point 153, which linked the Ceriano Ridge with the mass of San Fortunato. In the centre of the front, and across the river, Ward's 4th Division was held up in an awkwardly-exposed position at Aquilina, waiting for the Canadian Corps, on

* Baade was killed in an air attack on the last day of the war.

the right wing of Eighth Army, to take San Martino, which was the last German strongpoint south of the Ausa, and directly in front of San Fortunato.

Ironically, the Canadians, who had for so long had to fret impatiently while the British V Corps struggled fiercely in the difficult hills, were now themselves holding up V Corps by the difficulties they were experiencing at San Martino. The Canadian 3rd Brigade began well enough on 15 September, taking San Lorenzo, about a mile south of San Martino, and then, with the French Canadian Royal 22ᵉ Regiment – the Van Doos, as they are known in the Canadian Army, by a corruption of their French numeral – occupying the knoll of San Martino. That was the end of success. On the night of the 15th, faulty liaison between the Van Doos and the relieving Canadian battalion, the Seaforth Highlanders, led to San Martino being left temporarily ungarrisoned. This was not the kind of opportunity that Heidrich's 1st Parachute Division would ever miss. By dawn on the 16th, they had recaptured San Martino, and the Canadian offensive, dominated by fire from the knoll itself, and from San Fortunato a mile on the other side of the Ausa, came to a halt. The Canadian infantry were still half a mile short of the long straight embankment of the Rimini-San Marino railway line, which was intended to be the start-line for their assault across the Ausa towards San Fortunato.[2] *(Map 3.)*

Herr's 76th Panzer Corps had received considerable artillery reinforcements for this vital battle, and the 16th was a day of bloody chagrin for the Canadians. Only the Greek Mountain Brigade, which was now under command of the Canadian Corps, and the Royal Canadian Regiment of the 1st Brigade, managed to make difficult and expensive progress to the edge of the Rimini airfield on the right of the front, while the German guns smothered the exposed infantry in front of San Martino.

The Canadians were supported by the tanks of the British 21st Army Tank Brigade, which consisted of the 48th and 12th Royal Tank Regiment, and the 145th Royal Armoured Corps Regiment. This armour, too, was suffering heavy casualties – the 48th R.T.R. losing six tanks out of twelve when the 48th

Highlanders of Canada made another unsuccessful attempt to take San Martino during the day. The Germans were now adopting a not unfamiliar technique – it had been seen before at Cassino – of getting into dug-outs and cellars in the ruined houses around the village, and then calling down a great weight of German artillery fire on the area, so that the attacking Canadians were cut to pieces by shellfire even in the middle of the enemy position. Meanwhile the casualties, both Canadian infantry and British tank crews, mounted steadily. During 17 September, the Seaforth lost ninety men, the Royal Canadian Regiment seventy-four, the 48th Highlanders eighty-six.

'The ground up to the railway is still not clear, and we are unable to make any real progress,' Captain Stephen Owen, of the headquarters squadron of the 145th R.A.C. Regiment wrote in his diary. 'Bitter fighting continues. B Squadron had a bad day. Poor Jim was killed and four others. C Squadron lost Eddie Xavier killed. B Squadron badly depleted by the end of the day.'

The headquarters squadron of a tank regiment deals with its administration, and the diary goes on, in a reminder that war is a matter of indents and rations as well as of shooting:

'Men whose tanks have been brewed up come back to us for a rest. The question of rations is tricky and it is nonsense to say they can be reclaimed from the squadrons – they can't. And we try to be able to say we never refuse anyone. When a man loses his tank, the President of the Regimental Institute replaces free his soap and all necessaries for washing, etc. . . .'[3]

Meanwhile Eighth Army tried to counter the increased enemy artillery effort by a series of great air blows. The Desert Air Force flew 330 missions against San Fortunato and the San Martino area on 16 September, increasing their sorties next day to 486. These attacks, made by Kittyhawks and Spitfires screaming at treetop height across the German line, hurling bombs and rockets wherever infantry concentrated, and by Mitchells pounding the German gun positions with heavy and medium bombs, were frustrating to the German command as well as demoralizing to the German troops.

'If the reserves are kept near the front they are decimated by the preparatory (artillery) fire,' reported von Vietinghoff to Kesselring. 'If they are held farther back, they are dispersed by attacks from the air.'[4]

The British artillery supporting the Canadians was toiling day and night. On the 19th, for instance, the 5·5-inch guns of 6th/10th battery of the 3rd Medium Regiment fired more than 2,100 rounds. During the long day the paint on the guns melted and the oil in the gravity tanks boiled. Water poured into the muzzles to cool them boiled as it came out of the chambers, and one gunner died and four others were badly burned as the charges detonated in the heat.[5]

However, crouched in their dug-outs, and summoning up their considerable reserves of will, the German paratroopers at San Martino and San Fortunato held on, and any Canadian effort to move forward was bloodily repulsed.

During the 18th, two companies of Princess Patricia's Canadian Light Infantry pushed forward under heavy shelling and mortaring, but were finally pinned down about 200 yards from the railway, having been reduced to a total of about sixty men between them. On their left, the Carleton and York Regiment reached the embankment, only to be forced to scrabble what cover they could in the open flats between the railway and the Ausa, while the German artillery observers on San Fortunato deluged them with shells.

The commander of the Canadian 1st Division, General Vokes, now decided to try to by-pass San Martino by crossing the Ausa at night and striking direct for San Fortunato. He ordered that the 2nd Brigade should stay in its positions before San Martino, while the 3rd Brigade, supported by British tanks, attacked over the Ausa on the night of the 19th.

To Vokes's left, the 4th British Infantry Division would be ready to keep level with the Canadian flank as it crossed the river, while the 56th Infantry Division, farther still to the left, was to try to secure the whole of the Ceriano Ridge.

Whitfield's division had been engaged for two days in a stiff battle on the slopes of the ridge, but on 19 September the high ground was not yet captured. Enemy resistance was especially strong on the north-eastern portion of the ridge, and Whitfield on the 19th ordered the 7th Armoured Brigade, with the 7th Oxford and Bucks and 2nd/5th Queen's under command, to seize this ground to clear the way for 1st Armoured Division.

For once again, the key role had been allotted to Hull's division, the leading elements of which were just across the Ausa at Monte dell'Arboreta, between the 4th and 56th Divisions. Once again, too, and this time with more apparent justification, the word 'breakthrough' was being used in Eighth Army intelligence summaries. The Germans were believed to be desperately short of infantry, and it was thought that they were likely to crack under the renewed pressure of the Allied attack all along the line from Ceriano to Rimini. In these circumstances, Hull's division was to drive north across the Marecchia and into the plain. It must have been clear to the Eighth Army planners that this was the last chance for the breakthrough on which all their thinking and planning had been postulated. The weather would break any day, but with a little luck, and a quick push through the strained German front, von Vietinghoff's Tenth Army might yet be cut off and encircled as the tanks of the 10th Hussars, the 9th Lancers and the Queen's Bays swung out into the plain and raced for the River Po. One thing was certain, however. If it was to be done, it would have to be done quickly. Even more than before, one consideration now dominated Eighth Army thinking about the armour. That consideration was speed.

No one was more conscious of the need for speed than Goodbody, whose 2nd Armoured Brigade was now given the task of leading 1st Armoured Division over the high ground immediately ahead of it and through the German front. With the Canadians attacking San Fortunato on the right, and 7th Armoured Brigade moving on the north-eastern end of the Ceriano Ridge on the left, only a single feature lay between his tanks and the River Marecchia, with the plains beyond. This high ground was shown on the map as Point 153; it was, in fact, a small spur running off the eastern tip of the Ceriano Ridge.

Goodbody received his orders to capture Point 153 on 18 September, though at that time no time limit was set. The only stipulation was that the attack should take place as soon as possible. *(Map 3.)*

Goodbody's brigade had been considerably reduced in tank strength by the operations of the past fourteen days, and the three armoured regiments, which normally totalled 156 Shermans, were now down to 117 between them.[6] Goodbody's first thought was that the capture of Point 153 by the brigade would be possible only if a quick attack could be made, preferably at night, before the Germans had been able to settle into the positions which they had only just occupied. The success of his own operation would also obviously depend upon the progress made by the Canadians and the 4th Division on his right flank, and more especially by the 7th Armoured Brigade group in clearing the badly exposed high ground on his left.[7]

The ground, however, over which the brigade had to move was if anything even more difficult than that which had wrecked its chances near San Clemente on 4 September. Most of the armour was still well south of the Marano, and there was the usual difficult march at night before the tanks could get into position. Goodbody issued his orders at 7.30 p.m. on 18 September, and the war diary of one of the armoured regiments commented:

'The difficulty is for everyone to get where they ought to be by dawn, for there is no moon; the roads are inches deep in dust; bridges are blown and diversions frequent; and every formation seems to be using the same road. The events planned to take place from tomorrow morning onwards are based on the movements that are to be carried out in the next ten hours under conditions so unfavourable that the outcome cannot be foreseen with any degree of certainty.'[8]

Under Goodbody's plan, the task of taking Point 153 was given to the Bays, supported by the motor battalion, the 1st K.R.R.C., and the guns of the 11th H.A.C. The 9th Lancers were to move behind the Bays, to be used as the situation developed. The 1st K.R.R.C. would hold and clear the cross-roads between Point 153 and Ceriano after they had been seized by

7th Armoured Brigade, while another infantry battalion, the 9th K.O.Y.L.I., held the ground immediately north of the Ausa. Then the Bays would attack and capture Point 153.

This was clearly not an easy operation, since it involved a night march for the armour, and the attack itself would depend for its success on the progress made by a formation under the command of another division on the left flank. Moreover the need for speed made daylight reconnaissance impracticable. Goodbody had produced the best plan in the circumstances. All he could do was to hope that the Germans were not yet firmly established on Point 153.

The Bays were due to move just before midnight on the 18th, but congestion on the road cancelled this plan, and only one squadron got away on time to support the 9th K.O.Y.L.I., across the Ausa.

'A Squadron moved off leaving us all in bed,' wrote an officer.[9] 'They were lucky to stick to their programme, although they would miss their sleep, because false starts always increase the nervous tension everyone feels before battle. In the morning we rose before light and moved as dawn was breaking. We drove through small villages or the piles of rubble that once were villages, which, when we had last seen them, were in the hands of the Germans. Everywhere, we passed desolation. Dead cattle killed by shellfire stank nauseatingly as they lay swollen and rotting amongst the wreckage of farms. Sometimes we passed parts of the countryside that were left undamaged – usually in the low ground where the fighting had been less severe. The high places had been fiercely contested everywhere and the buildings were in ruins. A few dazed civilians pottered about the ruins of their houses trying to salvage what little remained to them in the world. We crossed a river by a ford as the bridge had been blown by the retreating Germans. We halted on the slope of a hill on the far side and dispersed among the fields. We had expected to go into action that morning, but once again we were put off. We spent most of the day in a maize field with the tanks under the trees by the edge of the maize. We waited a long time for something to happen and we couldn't settle down as we never knew when we should suddenly be told to move again. . . .'

It was now the morning of 19 September, and at 8.30 a.m. a report reached the Bays that the 7th Armoured Brigade on their left was only 200 yards from the road between Ceriano and point 153. The regiment waited in its maize field until 3 p.m., when orders came from Goodbody that the attack on Point 153 was to take place, if possible, that afternoon. The start-line for the attack was just beyond the cross-roads which was the 7th Armoured Brigade objective. This was more than three miles away from the Bays present position, along a narrow, difficult road, but there were four hours of daylight left, and the time-table did not seem impossible. The regiment moved at once. The Bays' officer takes up the story:

'The battle was closer now. On top of the crest we could see the bursts of shells, and Churchill tanks and a few fires on the skyline. Some of the fires burned with enormous clouds of black smoke which showed that a tank or petrol lorry had been hit. We went by several burned-out German tanks, which were an encouraging sight. In one place by a farm there were three of them together – two Panthers and a Tiger – with three or four of their crews lying dead beside them.

'Then we went down into another valley and crossed the railway and the main road from Rimini to San Marino. We hugged the protecting slope of the ridge that separated us from the enemy and moved westwards parallel to the road towards our start point. We had to cross the wadis that formed re-entrants in the hill to our right. Occasionally we were forced to come up to the crest in full view of the Germans. But mostly we kept to the low ground and moved slowly so that we shouldn't make dust and show the enemy plainly a large column of tanks moving into position. We passed by A Squadron headquarters hull-down on the ridge facing north. A little farther on, about 2,000 yards from the start-line, the column halted. We stayed there for a long time and we began to wish that we knew what was happening in front of us. Dusk was coming on and the attack had still not started. Soon it would be dark and too late to make the attack. We waited until it was properly dark, and then the Germans started sending over phosphorus shells which lit up the sky when they burst and then died down to a dull

glow. Once particles of burning phosphorus fired a haystack and
the shiny parts of the tank stood out orange in the light of the
flames. Then the Germans started dropping a few HE shells
round the area of the fire. . . .'

The going had been bad, and the 1st K.R.R.C. had been
heavily shelled on their way up towards the start-line, suffering
casualties.[10] At half-past seven in the evening, the tanks and
infantry were still halted on the crammed road in front of the
start-line, and it was clear that the attack as originally envisaged
could not take place that night. Still hoping that the ridge
would prove to be lightly occupied, Goodbody ordered 1st
K.R.R.C. to patrol forward to Point 153 and seize it if possible.
Two hours after midnight, this last hope was extinguished. The
infantry patrols had a sharp fight as they probed forward, losing
several men, and they reported that the position was strongly
held. Nevertheless, it was necessary to put this to the test. At
3.30 a.m. on the 29th the dozing tank crews were woken up and
given orders for the attack, which was now planned for first
light.

The information available was that the high ground
north and north-east of Ceriano was held by the infantry.
The Bays' account gives some idea of the ludicrously inadequate nature of the ground as a springboard for an armoured
attack.

'At 0400 hours we started to move forward to the start-line.
At first we had to follow small cart tracks. It was very difficult
to see where we were going in the dark, with tanks in front
churning up clouds of dust. Eventually we came out on a
narrow road which wound its way up towards our line of
advance. On each side of the road there was a deep ditch that
would bog any tank which got into it in the poor visibility. Such
a mishap would have effectively blocked the road and caused
untold (trouble). We had to squeeze past some infantry carriers
that were parked on the left of the road and everyone worried
like hell about getting ditched, but we managed somehow to
keep moving.

'By now the whole of the two squadrons were strung out along
the road and moving slowly in the dark, halting now and again
for no apparent reason. Soon it became obvious that something

had happened at the head of the column. A report came through that bazooka-men were about and that one of the leading tanks had been picked off in the dark. It was all very confusing as there was no definite information about the incident and one rather visualized German bazooka-men prowling about like ghosts in the dark. We learned eventually that the leading Honey had been knocked out a few yards over the start-line. B. Squadron started to deploy in front of us and we were ordered to pull off the road in the meantime. We remained scattered about the side of the road waiting for dawn to break. We wondered what we should see by the light of day; what the ground would look like; and how long it would be before the Germans spotted us and began to shell us. . . .

'As it got lighter we began to see more clearly the outline of houses and trees and the dark shapes of hills to our left and right and overlooking our positions. We did not know whether these features were held by our own infantry or the enemy – we hoped by the former. We could see our infantry, dug in the ploughed fields around us – rather thin on the ground and dispersed in battle groups in weapon pits. We began to sort ourselves out and get into some sort of fire positions by daylight. Everyone was milling around and the noise we made can have left no doubt in the enemy's mind that there was a large force of tanks in the vicinity. It was difficult to manœuvre as we found ourselves in a hole with steep sides, and if you went too far down the slope where it became steeper you were liable to turn over. There were two squadrons in the hollow – all jockeying for position. We had to avoid the slit trenches of the infantry, and the men in them gesticulated wildly so that we should see them. They looked tired and did not like us being there and hoped we would move on quickly. . . . Soon a German OP would enjoy shelling this little lot. Every now and then the sharp rip of a Spandau would come from the hill on the left, firing across the valley. Then enemy ranging shells started to come over. When they were satisfied with that they began to put down heavy artillery and mortar concentrations all round our tanks. . . . During the lulls in the shelling, stretcher bearers came out from a small grey house to our rear and picked up infantry casualties. Sometimes they would get caught carrying a casualty in another stonk, and the whole party, casualty and all, would go flat on the ground in the open. The infantry were having a bad time. . . .'

It was now daylight, and one unpleasant fact was clear. The Spandau fire which the Bays could hear on their left was coming from the high ground on the flank which had previously been reported as clear. This was the ground held by Baade's 90th Panzer Grenadier Division, and it was clear that these formidable opponents had infiltrated their way back into their positions. Soon after dawn it became increasingly obvious that this had happened, when British infantry came past the Bays' regimental headquarters and said they had been on the ridge but had been driven off during the night.

This area would obviously have to be cleared before the Bays could attack, and Asquith, the Bays' commanding officer, sent tanks from B Squadron to deal with the enemy infantry. The Bays' account describes what happened.

'Suddenly there was a tremendous crack and a noise like an express train going by. The German anti-tank guns had opened up at the B Squadron troops on the hill. Two or three tanks were hit, and the surviving members of the crews dashed like mad for the bottom of the hollow to get under cover. C Squadron were pushed forward to look over the crest to try to spot the anti-tank guns. There were at least two, firing from somewhere on our final objective, but we could not pin-point them. Every time our tanks came up hull-down, snipers opened up at the tank commanders' heads with rifles and machine-guns. The remaining tanks of B Squadron pulled back into the hollow to reorganize.'

It was now obvious that the ridge was an extremely difficult proposition, protected by high-quality infantry, with anti-tank guns on the flank. It was also being demonstrated just how helpless the crews in the formidable-looking thirty-ton Shermans were when the enemy remained in his positions to pick them off. Between the Bays and Point 153, the rolling, empty countryside dipped down in a long slope and then climbed slowly up to the Point itself. The distance over the ground was nearly two miles for the tanks to roll. There was no cover . . . hardly a tree or a fold in the ground. For once, the anxious officers and men of the cavalry regiments could find an almost exact parallel in their dashing past. If the order to advance was given, this would be an armoured Balaclava.

17
The Charge of the Bays

Goodbody was well aware of what would happen when the Bays moved forward over the crest. Not for the first time, however, he was having difficulties of communication. The roads were so jammed with casualties going back and troops and ammunition coming forward, that he could not get back quickly to Hull's divisional headquarters to explain the hazards of the attack, and it would be disastrous for the morale of the brigade – and a tremendous fillip for the Germans – if he explained his doubts in clear over the radio. The crowded roads, which hampered Goodbody's efforts to get back, also stopped any more senior commanders from easily getting forward. No one who had seen the ground could have ordered the Bays to attack. But no one senior to Goodbody had anything like such a clear idea of what the tanks were facing.

For the senior commanders of Eighth Army this was a climactic moment. The whole of the campaign of the Gothic Line had been planned with an armoured breakthrough in mind, and there had undoubtedly been considerable disappointment with the fiasco of the operations at San Clemente on 4 September. There was now a feeling of disenchantment about 2nd Armoured Brigade in Eighth Army, and a conviction that the regiments needed a spur if they were to roll forward and lead Eighth Army to the victory for which so many men had already died.

This meant little to Goodbody, however, who was facing the immediate prospect of the destruction of one of his armoured regiments. He could not understand why the brigade was being asked to perform what was virtually an impossible attack.

'I wanted to know,' he said later, 'to what extent 2nd Armoured Brigade was to be sacrificed to assist the operations of divisions on the flanks.'[1] Meanwhile he gave it as his opinion that Point 153 could not now be captured with the forces at his disposal. The brigade's History describes what happened:

'This opinion was represented through 1st British Armoured Division, but in order to fit in with the V Corps plan, it was ruled by V Corps that the attack must take place, and at 0945 hours the Bays were ordered to attack the original objective in fifteen minutes.'[2]

All that could be done to mitigate the effects of this order was now done. The divisional and brigade artillery put down concentrations on likely enemy sites for anti-tank guns, and smoke-screens were prepared to shield survivors. Owing to the need for 9th Lancers, who were now ordered to follow up the Bays, to get into position, the attack did not begin until 1050.

The Bays' account[3] continues:

'We were ordered to make the attack in the face of the anti-tank screen firing down the line of advance.

'We knew that we should not get far even if we could spot the guns that had already fired. There were probably more and after realizing what was coming the enemy had probably whipped up some more tanks to oppose us. While we waited for the word to go, we looked at the ground we had to advance over. There wasn't a stitch of cover anywhere that a tank could get hull-down behind and fire, not a single fire position between us and the objective. We could see the latter plainly about 2,000 yards ahead with a few trees and farms scattered about on it. We looked at likely places that might conceal enemy positions and started shooting with everything we had. Then we started to advance. . . .'

As the tanks sailed into view over the crest, the enemy anti-tank gunners must have rubbed their eyes with astonishment. Peering into the sights of their 88-mm. guns, they were roughly in the position of snipers with precision rifles firing at infantry trotting slowly forward in undeviating line across country where no cover was available.

The range was known to within a metre or two.

'. . . . The shelling in the hollow ceased, and the Germans

began to bring their attention to bear on the latest development.
. . . The express trains started up again with increased ferocity.
Armour-piercing shot seemed to come from all directions* –
some, the bad shots, passed overhead, others hitting the ground
with colossal force and kicking up earth and stones in front of
the tanks. As they halted to fire, to locate the opposition, the
tanks were knocked out one by one. Most of them burst into
flames immediately. A few were disabled, the turrets jammed or
the tank made immobile. As the survivors jumped out, some of
them made a dash across the open to get back over the crest
among our own infantry, but they were almost all mown down
by German machine-gun fire. The craftier men lay flat or dived
into small hollows in the ground and lay immobile, waiting until
they could get back under cover of darkness. All but three tanks
of the two squadrons that took part in the attack were destroyed,
and many gallant officers and men were killed in action that
morning. . . .'

The day, in fact, had cost the Bays twenty-four tanks, and the
loss of sixty-four men killed and wounded. In addition, the forward observation officer of the 11th H.A.C., who had accompanied the regiment down the slope in his Sherman, was killed
with all his crew. One of the Bays who died was Captain McVail,
whose account of an action at San Savino is given on an earlier
page.

The Bays were obviously not able to go farther, and 9th
Lancers were now ordered to pass through the burning Shermans of their sister regiment and continue to Point 153. Had
this order remained unchanged, the result could only have been
the destruction of another armoured regiment. However,
Colonel Price of the Lancers conferred with Asquith of the
Bays, and made a further representation to Brigade headquarters, saying that the attack could achieve nothing. The two
colonels waited anxiously in their tanks for an answer, while a
heavy German artillery concentration fell around them. After a
pause, the answer came: 'Hold on to the ground already won.'⁴
During the afternoon, divisional infantry, the 14th Foresters,
came up to take over the ground, and as darkness fell a few of

---

* In fact, the main weight of fire, from no more than six guns, came
from the Bays' left rear.

the tank crews who had lain out in the open all day came back into the British lines. The tanks began to move back to an assembly area, and then it began to rain, in drenching, cascading torrents, from the black night sky. Within ten minutes not a tank of the 9th Lancers was able to move. For the British armour, it set the seal on a bitter, bloody day.

★ ★ ★

Cheered, however, though the men of Baade's 90th Panzer Grenadier Division must have been by the sight of so many Shermans blazing in the valley in front of Point 153, for the German command 20 September appeared to take them to the brink of disaster. The Canadians, fighting forward after crossing the Ausa at night under Vokes's new plan, pushed on during 19 September through the vineyards and cornfields below San Fortunato. They were supported by air and artillery concentrations on a scale approaching those unleashed at Caen during the Normandy fighting, but the Germans also had many tanks and self-propelled guns in position, and the day was costly for the Canadian infantry and their supporting British tanks. Their advance, though checked in the late afternoon less than halfway up the San Fortunato Ridge, had at least made the German position in front of the Ausa at San Martino untenable, and the bitterly-contested hill village passed into Canadian hands during the day without further fighting.

The next day, the 20th, was decisive for San Fortunato. The San Fortunato Ridge was now held by four German regiments. The northern sector, under Heidrich's 1st Parachute Division, was held by a battalion of the 1st Parachute Regiment. The rest of the ridge was the responsibility of Major-General Fritz Polack's 29th Panzer Grenadier Division. He had a 2,000-yard front guarded by two battalions of the 71st Grenadier Regiment, a rifle battalion of the 20th Luftwaffe Field Division, two battalions from the 162nd Turcoman Division, and two from the 314th Grenadier Regiment of his own division.

The weak point in this impressive order of battle was the Turcoman contingent. These were troops recruited from ex-enemy sources on the Russian front, and their morale was not as good and their fighting ability considerably less than that of regular German troops. This thinner link in the German chain of defence buckled during the morning under the intense pressure of the new and resolute Canadian attack. By 11 a.m. von Vietinghoff was forced to report to Kesselring that the Canadian infantry had broken through the Turcoman sector, which did not now exist as a defended part of the line. General Herr, the 76th Panzer Corps commander, announced that some of his gun positions were under direct machine-gun fire, and it was abundantly clear soon after midday that Tenth Army could no longer hold south of the Marecchia. Kesselring, after a consultation with his staff, agreed to pull back behind the river. He was anxious and worried, and the Tenth Army war diary notes him as saying: 'I have the terrible feeling that the whole thing is beginning to slide.'[5]

On the night of the 20th, the crash of great explosions was heard from Rimini as the Germans destroyed their dumps, and the next morning the Greek Mountain Brigade, which had lost 314 men in the fighting round the airfield, hoisted the Greek and Canadian flags above Rimini town hall. By midday the Canadians were across the Marecchia, pushing on with infantry in the rain over sodden ground across which the armour could not follow them.

It appeared that Eighth Army had won a great and hard-earned triumph. The Allies were now on the edge of the Lombardy Plain, and one by one the divisions crossed the Marecchia, moving out of the hills which, over the past month, had cost them so many lives. The next day, the 22nd, Burns lunched with Alexander, Leese, and Mr Harold Macmillan, then Minister Resident at Allied Forces Headquarters, at an hotel in Rimini, and the party afterwards toured the battlefield. To most of them it must have seemed that all would yet be well, and that the great chase across the plain, so confidently anticipated during August, would now begin. Only Alexander could have had his doubts.

Eighth Army had advanced thirty miles in twenty-six days, and had lost 14,000 men in killed, wounded, and missing. More than 200 British tanks had also been destroyed, though, as

Alexander reported later, 'the tanks were easily replaceable, but the men were not'.[6] More than half the casualties had been suffered by British infantry battalions, and it was clear that considerable reorganization would be necessary.

To add to his worries in what outwardly appeared to be an hour of triumph, Alexander was well aware that Kesselring had received considerable replacements of troops in the past weeks. On the day before his luncheon party at Riccione, Alexander sent a grim signal to the C.I.G.S., General Brooke:

'To put it briefly, we shall have to continue the battle of Italy with about twenty divisions, almost all of which have had long periods of heavy fighting this year, and some for several years, against the twenty German divisions committed to the battle front, with the prospect of four more German divisions and probably two more Italian divisions, joining the battle at a later stage. We are inflicting very heavy losses on the enemy and are making slow but steady progress, but our losses are also heavy and we are fighting in country where, it is generally agreed, a superiority of at least three to one is required for successful offensive operations. It will be small wonder, therefore, if we fail to score a really decisive success when the opposing forces are so evenly matched.'[7]

There was little Alexander could hope for in the way of reinforcements. The British 78th Division, moving from the Middle East, would be available in about two weeks' time; and several Italian Gruppi di Combattimento, of approximately brigade strength, were being formed during the coming months. Meanwhile, however, there were unwelcome measures to be taken.

First of all, Hull's 1st Armoured Division was to be disbanded. Its 18th Infantry Brigade was reduced to nominal cadre strength, and its men were used as reinforcements for other divisions. Hull himself went to command an infantry division on the Western Front.

The 2nd Armoured Brigade remained intact, but Goodbody was replaced in its command by Brigadier John Combe. Both it and the 43rd Gurkha Lorried Brigade became independent brigades, for use in operations by any formation to which they were allotted.

Goodbody must be counted unfortunate to lose his command.

The armoured attack at Point 153 had failed, but the fault lay
deeper than the armoured brigadier. The responsibility for this
failure, and for the earlier frustration at San Clemente, belonged
to the initial incorrect thinking about the campaign which
allotted to the armour a role it was not capable of playing on the
unsuitable ground. In this sense, the responsibility rested with
the whole chain of command in Italy, and Goodbody's blame,
if he was to blame at all, was least of all.

The infantry divisions, too, felt the axe. In Whitfield's
battered 56th Division, 168th Brigade was reduced to cadre
strength, and its men split up among the other depleted infantry
battalions of the division. Finally, each British infantry battalion
was reorganized with three instead of four rifle companies,
making a total establishment for each battalion of thirty
officers and 700 men. This change would clearly have a sad
effect on the tactical efficiency of the battalions.

On the other side of the Marecchia, however, von Vietinghoff
was having similar problems, and the actual ratio of German to
Allied troops was not quite so equal as it appeared in the written
order of battle. The Germans had lost 8,000 men in prisoners
alone, and eleven German divisions had been badly cut about.
On 25 September, Tenth Army reported a total of ninety-two
infantry battalions, but only ten had more than 400 men. Of the
rest, thirty-eight battalions had fewer than 200 men each.[8]
Alexander was certainly justified in claiming that Eighth Army
had inflicted 'very heavy losses'.

Behind the Allied front, the dead were being buried, a task
which gave grim hours to their friends.

'Our cemetery is one organized by 2nd Canadian Brigade for
their own troops, and they invited us to share it,' Captain Owen
of the 145th Royal Armoured Corps Regiment wrote in his
diary. 'The crosses are made by the regimental carpenter and
painted by my driver. . . .

'Called to see Ted South at Brigade about our rum, but he
wouldn't play – said we could not have it. Went on to the
medical dressing station and saw Lieutenant-Colonel Clarke
who let me borrow three men to get bodies out of tanks. Picked
up the Padre from the casualty clearing post and we got
Sergeant Quinn and Trooper Hudson out of their tank, and

Trooper Whittaker out of Jim's, both of these being close together, and then Eddie Xavier and Lance-Corporal Hull out of
theirs. Padre buried the lads in the cemetery. Regiment moving
into billets at Riccione for a rest.'9

★ ★ ★

For the living, however, the Lombardy Plain for which the
others had died stretched ahead, and yet the idea of it as terrain
for an armoured breakthrough was soon to be proved a military
mirage. Eighth Army was now entering the Romagna, on the
south-east corner of the Plain; and the Romagna could hardly
have been more effective anti-tank country if it had been arti-
ficially constructed for the purpose. Eighth Army was out of the
hills. Now it faced the rivers.

'Water was now the main obstacle to Eighth Army's advance
rather than high ground,' Alexander reported later. 'The whole
area is nothing but a reclaimed swamp – and not wholly reclaimed in some parts – formed by the lower courses of numerous
rivers flowing down from the Apennines in their new north-
easterly direction. The principal rivers are, in order from east to
west, the Uso, the Savio, the Ronco, the Montone, the Lamone,
the Senio, the Santerno, the Sillaro, and the Idice; these are
only the principal rivers and there are hundreds of smaller
streams, canals, and irrigation ditches in between them. . . .
Even in the best drained areas the soil remembers its marshy
origin and when rained on forms the richest mud known to the
Italian theatre. It will be seen that under autumn conditions
we should have difficulty in making full use of our armoured
superiority.'10

And yet autumn conditions were exactly what Kesselring's
long, brave, stubborn defence had won him. As we have seen, it
had rained very heavily on the night of the 20th. The rain continued with heavy drizzle and drenching showers until the 29th,
when the skies opened fully and a violent rainstorm continued
for four days. Just in time for Kesselring, the brown torrents of
the growing rivers surged down the stony beds of summer;
bridges and roads disappeared; and infantry and armour

floundered in a desolate sea of mud. Each of the hundreds of farmhouses, floodbanks, lines of vines which stretched out across the Romagna could house a German Spandau or 88-mm. gun; the ground was cultivated in neat little olive groves and orchards which made excellent battle positions. Moving forward through the flat, vine-trellised countryside, the first that the Allied infantry could know about an enemy post was when a Spandau suddenly cut into them from the flank, or an 88-mm. picked off a struggling Bren carrier. The North Italian plain had been over-estimated from the start by the Eighth Army planners as suitable terrain for a swift advance. Even in the dust and heat of summer, the area would certainly have inhibited the Allied advance by reason of the local agricultural methods alone; under autumn and winter conditions it was passable only by a long, slogging advance which would cost many men and weeks and months of time. This was now what Eighth Army prepared to do, while the hopes of the high command centred on what was happening over to the west, where Mark Clark was assaulting the central defences in front of Bologna.

18

Mark Clark Attacks

'The assault with concentrated, and therefore very superior, forces upon a point of the front may certainly be met with a resistance which is very violent as regards that point, but which is very insignificant as regards the whole. After it is overcome, the line is pierced, and the object of the attack attained.'

Karl von Clausewitz,
The Defence of Mountains, 1832.

The great mountain mass of the central Apennines, sometimes blue in the autumn sunlight, sometimes obscured by dark clouds of driving rain, which lay before Clark's Fifth Army as it faced north from Florence towards Bologna, was about fifty miles deep, rising in places to peaks of more than 5,000 feet. The steepest side of the Apennine barrier was the one which faced the Allies; the slopes on the German side were longer and more moderate.

Behind the German front, the long, straight Route 9 ran diagonally north-west from the Eighth Army front at Rimini, successively through Forli, Faenza, Imola, and Bologna. Each of these towns was fed by one or more roads straggling down to it from the mountains. The cutting of Route 9 by Clark's forces at any point would make it impossible for Kesselring to move his forces to and fro across the front to reinforce positions of danger, and would, indeed, put his forces facing Eighth Army in the east into great peril.

Nature had provided one especially weak point in the central mountain rampart. This was the Futa Pass, twenty miles north of Florence on Route 65 to Bologna. The Todt Organization recognized this weakness when it built the Gothic Line, and the Futa defences were the most formidable of all. They consisted of an involved and intricate system of concrete emplacements, gun positions, and wire, with a three-mile anti-tank ditch covered by extensive minefields. The Futa defences extended seven miles to the east, to the Il Giogo Pass, on the road which ran from Florence to Firenzuola and thence to Imola on Route 9.

Through these two passes lay the shortest route to Bologna. With the chronic shortage of men which Operation Anvil had imposed upon him, it was clear that here, and here alone, could Clark make an effort with a good chance of success. Like Leese, he disposed of three army corps. Two were American – the II Corps, with the 34th, 85th, 88th, and 91st U.S. Infantry Divisions, supported by three tank battalions; and the IV Corps, with the 1st U.S. Armored Division, the 6th South African Armoured Division, and a regimental combat team (equivalent to a British brigade group) of the 92nd U.S. Negro Infantry Division.

The third corps under Clark's command was the British XIII Corps, commanded by Lieutenant-General Sidney Kirkman. It consisted of the 1st British Infantry Division, the 6th British Armoured Division, the 8th Indian Infantry Division, and the 1st Canadian Armoured Brigade. Thus, like Leese, Clark was strong in armour for country which was even less suitable for it, and weak in infantry in terrain which ate up foot soldiers.

Opposite Clark, however, General Joachim Lemelsen's Fourteenth Army was also short of men. At the end of August, seven German divisions had been disposed in front of Fifth Army. At the western end of the Gothic Line, near the seaside resort of Viareggio, was the 20th Luftwaffe Field Division – though this formation was under orders to move to the Adriatic. Then, as the line ran eastward, successively the 16th S.S. Panzer Grenadier Division, the 65th and 362nd Infantry Divisions, and the 4th Parachute Division. These were all in Fourteenth Army, and the German order of battle facing Clark was completed by the two right-hand divisions of von Vietinghoff's Tenth Army – the 356th and 715th Infantry.

By the end of the first week in September, however, the Eighth Army threat on the Adriatic had done a great deal to lessen German strength on the central front. The 29th Panzer Grenadier Division and the 356th Infantry Division, together with the armoured reserve of 26th Panzer Division, had been drawn east by the magnet of Coriano. Only a weak infantry division near Ravenna was available for immediate reserve in the central Apennines. Each division in the Fourteenth Army line held a front averaging ten miles. *(Map 4.)*

Clark's original plan, formulated in the middle of August, was to assault the powerful Futa defences with the U.S. II Corps and strike straight for Bologna; the method, though not the objective, was changed now by circumstances as the Germans began to withdraw voluntarily into the Gothic Line from the line of hills just north of Florence. Under the new plan, II Corps would attack along the road from Florence to Firenzuola, through the Il Giogo Pass – an attack which, if successful, would effectively outflank the Futa defences. Meanwhile the British XIII Corps would advance along the axis from Borgo San Lorenzo, about fifteen miles north-east of Florence, through the Gothic Line to cut Route 9 at Faenza. The remaining corps, the U.S. IVth, would hold the rest of the army line to the west, advancing whenever and wherever it was able.[1]

Clark's choice of the Il Giogo Pass as the battleground for his main effort could hardly have been bettered. In their obsession with the Futa Pass, the Germans had tended to discount the possibility of a major assault farther to the east, and, not for the first time, had under-estimated the ability of American soldiers to transform what was the most difficult country into viable ground for attack by the technical excellence of their logistic services, as well as by the fighting qualities of their soldiers.

Thus when the German 356th Infantry Division left for the Adriatic, the 4th Parachute and 715th Infantry Divisions were ordered to extend their fronts to absorb the gap, stretching them even thinner in face of the impending American blow. Of even more importance was the fact that the 4th Parachute Division was in Fourteenth Army and the 715th Infantry Division in Tenth Army, so that the German army boundary ran through this vital sector. Boundaries between units – and especially between armies – are always good ground over which to make an assault. It is only human for any commander who is short of men to try to get adjoining units to take over responsibility for as much of the edges of his area as possible, so that often boundary terrain is shared between two units, each of which is eager to leave as much as possible to the other. These units are, of course, also commanded by different headquarters, giving additional delay and confusion in the crisis of battle.

Although he did not reinforce the sector held by 4th Parachute and 715th Infantry Divisions, Kesselring *did*, in fact, make one move to strengthen the central front. He transferred the 334th Infantry Division, which had moved into Tenth Army reserve, into the Futa Pass where it replaced the troops of 29th Panzer Grenadier Division which had left for the Adriatic. Thus Kesselring continued until the last moment in the misappreciation of Clark's intentions which convinced him that the main American attack would still come in the Futa Sector.

Lemelsen's Fourteenth Army was not the equal in quality of von Vietinghoff's Tenth. It had been badly mauled in the retreat from Anzio to the Arno, and some of its reinforcements had been hastily and inadequately trained. Its 4th Parachute Division, for instance, which was to defend a vital part of the approaches to the Il Giogo Pass, was not – on paper at least – as formidable a proposition as a German parachute division usually seemed to those who had to fight it. It contained a core of Anzio veterans, but the mass of the division was composed of very young soldiers with only three months' training behind them. Some of the division's reserves had never fired live ammunition. These inexperienced boys, however, were expected to fight with the iron determination of battle-hardened troops. An order issued on 8 September to the division's 12th Parachute Regiment laid down that 'the position is to be held to the last man and the last bullet, even if the enemy breaks through on all sides, as well as against the strongest artillery or mortar fire. . . .'[2]

The U.S. II Corps which was now to be pitted against 4th Parachute Division in the Apennine gullies was commanded by Lieutenant-General Geoffrey Keyes, a tough and able soldier who had seen the corps through the fighting on the Rapido and later at Cassino. He knew the pressing need for numerical superiority in these mountains, and his attacking divisions had been strengthened as much as possible with extra armour and mortar units. He estimated that he would have a local superiority of three to one at the Il Giogo Pass,[3] and he must have been well aware that even this would be none too many.

His line-up of four infantry divisions to cover an area of only two or three miles was an impressive one on paper, but to those on the ground it meant much less. This could be no co-ordinated corps attack, with wave after wave of infantry leap-frogging on and on to seize more and more ground. In these rocky defiles, the issue would be decided by small groups of fighting men, often out of touch with and unsupported by their parent units, locked in a struggle of attrition aimed not so much at defending or seizing meaningless ground, as seeing who would crack first under the bloody pressure which each was exerting on the other.

Behind these small combat groups waited an army more than 200,000 strong, comprising an immense diversity of men and occupations – gunners, engineers, typists, carpenters, transport drivers, military police, mobile-bath units, medical services, hospitals, transport parks, leave camps, transit depots, store dumps, all in a vast, vital tail, stretching and spreading far back behind Florence, down to Naples in the south. Fewer than 1,000 men of this multitude were ever in contact with the enemy at one time. Upon these 1,000 men now fell the responsibility for breaking the Gothic Line, so that the rest of the army, busy about its own tasks, could advance through the gap that they would try to tear in the enemy defences.

★ ★ ★

On 10 September, Fifth Army launched its offensive. The II Corps began its advance astride Route 65, running north from Florence, with the 34th Division on the left of the road and the 91st on the right. Farther still to the right, the British XIII Corps also moved forward, with its 1st Infantry Division on the left of its line, nearest to the Americans, and positioned so as to assist Keyes' assault on the Il Giogo Pass. In the centre of the

British line was the 8th Indian Division, and on the right the 6th British Armoured Division, advancing up the road which led across the mountains to Forli, on Route 9.

There was only sporadic resistance as the Germans pulled back into the Gothic Line, and both corps moved swiftly on the line of the River Sieve, crossing it without difficulty on 11 September, and capturing the chain of little towns along the north bank – Barberino, Scarperia, Borgo San Lorenzo, and Dicomano. The two corps were now roughly twenty miles north of Florence, and almost beneath the looming ramparts of the Gothic Line. German resistance was increasing sharply, and Allied bombers tried to inhibit the movement of German reinforcements by attacking the mountain passes on 11 September, and then almost obliterating the little town of Firenzuola, the main communication centre for the sector, situated just behind the Line. More than 1,300 fighter-bomber and 550 medium-bomber sorties were flown during the next week, mostly concentrated on the Futa and Il Giogo Passes, until worsening weather stopped the air offensive.

Ahead of II Corps now rose the forbidding 3,000 foot peaks of Monticelli and Monte Altuzzo, which flanked the left and right of the Il Giogo Pass. From the south, these great heights, seamed with knife-edged ridges and deep rocky gullies, covered and searched with German Spandau and mortar fire, were a daunting military proposition. Yet they were the key to the breakthrough that Keyes hoped to make. Tremendous efforts had been made by the German planners to make them impregnable. Pillboxes and dug-outs, some of them blasted from the solid rock, were positioned so as to support each other up the sides of the mountains. The standard type held about six men. It was constructed of concrete, with a roof covered with three feet of logs and soil, and a firing slit six inches high and three feet long. In front of it was positioned barbed wire in row after row, with the gaps sown with anti-personnel mines. Larger dug-outs, like one found on Monticelli, were big enough to hold fifty men, and contained their own cooking and sleeping facilities.[4] These were used as holding positions for the immediate infantry reserves.

On 13 September, Keyes was ready to attack. He had already

had a demonstration of the determination of the Germans to defend the area, for during the previous day the 91st Infantry Division – the Powder River Division, as it is known in the U.S. Army – had made a bold attempt to secure both Monticelli and Altuzzo in one swift pounce. However, it had been sharply rebuffed and thrown back after a night of confused fighting. This can have been no more than Keyes expected, in view of the obvious strength of the German position, and during the 13th he reverted to a more methodical plan. He now committed the third of his four infantry divisions, the 85th, bringing it in to attack the east side of Il Giogo, with Altuzzo as its main objective. The west side of the pass, with Monticelli, was given to the 91st, while the 34th kept steady pressure on the left of the corps front, farther to the west. *(Map 4.)*

The 85th Infantry Division commanded by Major-General John B. Coulter, was a battle-experienced unit which had had heavy fighting in the Gustav Line in May. It bore a celebrated name in the United States Army, being known as the Custer Division, after the American general who was killed in an epic stand against the Sioux Indians at the Little Big Horn in Montana in 1876. The division was originally activated at Camp Custer in Michigan in 1917, and its nickname was embodied in the initials C D which formed its divisional sign.[5]

Coulter chose the three battalions of the 338th Infantry Regiment to make the main assault on Altuzzo, and the battalion commanders were left in no doubt as to the importance of the operation entrusted to them. General Clark himself, accompanied by Keyes, visited the 338th command post to discuss the attack, and told them: 'You'd better get on your hiking shoes. I'm going to throw you a long forward pass into the Po Valley and I want you to go get it.'[6]

The 338th was commanded by Colonel William H. Mikkelsen, and under his direction his officers had already made a detailed map reconnaissance of the position. The regiment also knew from Intelligence that its opponents on Altuzzo would be the 12th Parachute Regiment, whose members had received the 'death or glory' message quoted earlier. Under Mikkelsen's plan, the 1st Battalion of the 338th would seize the Altuzzo crest; the 2nd Battalion would attack the ground between

Altuzzo and Monticelli; and the 3rd would follow the first as an immediate reserve. There was plenty of artillery support – two field artillery battalions equipped with 105-mm. howitzers, another with 155s, and a couple of tank or tank destroyer battalions as well. Farther back, in general support, were two Field Artillery Groups, which included several 155-mm. battalions and two battalions of 240-mm. howitzers.

At midnight on the 12th, the men of the 1st Battalion reached their jumping off point at the foot of Altuzzo, after a twelve-mile march in the darkness across country. They dug in, and then slept for a little over three hours before the attack began at dawn. As light broke, the leading company moved up towards the mountain through the trees and thick underbrush which covered its lower slopes. They were under the impression – such is the confusion of mountain war – that they still had to pass through the forward outposts of the 91st Division, which had been rebuffed in its attempt to get farther during the previous day. But they were quickly disillusioned of this comfortable assumption when a Spandau caught them half-way across a cornfield. The battle of Altuzzo had begun. *(Map 5.)*

It was a frustrating day. Struggling into the rocky bowl of ground which lay below Altuzzo, the battalion suffered a steady dribble of casualties from Spandau and rifle positions on both flanks and in front. Because of the uncertainty of the whereabouts of the 91st Division outposts, there had been no preliminary artillery barrage and no supporting fire during the morning, and not until two hours after noon did the 91st finally give clearance for the guns to fire. Considerable artillery support was given in the afternoon, with machine-gun posts and pillboxes as the principal targets, though in the thick undergrowth it was almost impossible to observe the results of the shelling. Only one company of the battalion was committed during the day, and little was known at the end of it. Only one fact was clear. The battalion's previous easy optimism about Altuzzo was misplaced; 4th Parachute Division, waiting in excellent positions, was going to fight hard.

This opinion was reinforced by what happened during the day on the flanks of the 338th. On the right, an attack by the 339th Infantry was also at a standstill, held up by heavy fire from the eastern slopes of Monte Altuzzo, and from the high ground of Monte Verruca immediately ahead. Meanwhile, the left flank was faring no better. The 363rd Infantry of Major-General William Livesay's Powder River Division had been heavily counter-attacked on the lower slopes of Monticelli, and had progressed no farther than intermediate positions near the little, ominously-named village of L'Uomo Morto, the Dead Man.

On the morning of the 14th, the 338th Infantry renewed its attack on Altuzzo. But it was another day of confusion and exhaustion. Company B of the 1st Battalion struggled with mounting casualties to a secondary peak just west of the main Altuzzo summit. They received, on Keyes' orders, the 'absolute practicable maximum of artillery fire' for support, but observed fire was still difficult in the closed country, and much of the shelling was necessarily only harassing in nature, laid down on suspected enemy reserve positions and gun sites. The artillery fire did little to dislodge the German defenders who were already in position, but it did a good deal to inhibit enemy movement in the rear areas, and in fact, none of the German front-line positions was able to receive rations during the day.

Even had they known it, however, this would have been small consolation to the men of Company B. As they struggled along their rocky ridge, they were picked off one by one by accurate rifle and machine-gun fire, and when they finally scratched what desperate cover they could find in the stones and hard-packed topsoil, they were informed by battalion headquarters that this was not, as they had imagined, the main Altuzzo crest, but a secondary feature. They were on the wrong objective.

By the middle of the afternoon, the two leading platoons were reduced to about twenty-five men between them. They had little ammunition left, and when the senior platoon sergeant scrambled with difficulty down the ridge to outline the situation to the company commander, he was shot through the head and killed while making his report. Another sergeant was sent to command the battered platoons, but he was in turn killed by mortar fire as he reached their position. The Germans put in a sharp counter-attack, and more of the precious, shrinking supply of ammunition was expended in holding it off.

One unexpected act of enemy chivalry marked these hours. The American wounded were lying out on the exposed ground, until a group of nine or ten men, supporting and carrying each other as best they could, stripped to the waist to show they were no longer fighting, tied a white bandage to a stick, and stumbled behind this talisman to the relative safety of lower ground. The German riflemen and machine-gunners stopped firing while they went.

The remaining men were in a hopeless position. There exists an account, based on combat interviews taken immediately after the action, which reveals the terrifying predicament of the survivors, and the different ways in which they reacted to it. It describes an attempt by the men to withdraw from their untenable position:

'After moving west for approximately twenty-five yards along the upper side of the rock slab, the retreating men came to a place where the rock dropped off sharply. Since the rock at this point no longer shielded them from the south, the men stopped and bunched up at the opening, afraid to continue through it. As the machine-gun fire from the south sounded even closer, the Americans could see no way to get through the rock ledge without exposing themselves dangerously. The harsh sound of German voices floating up from the north-west added to the uneasiness. Having no idea that the 1st Platoon and their own company's machine guns were less than twenty-five yards away, the men were ready to believe that the Germans had surrounded them. Some took off their ammunition belts and began to cry 'Kamerad'.

'An assistant squad leader, Sergeant Seiverd, afraid that he would be captured and with him the 3rd Platoon's mail, stopped in the brush beside a tree near the ledge and covered the letters with dirt. Finding a few moments later that he had not buried them all, he covered the rest hastily with brush, hoping thereby to keep from the Germans any intelligence information the letters might contain.

'When the three squad leaders, Sergeants Lusk, Ford, and Spears, reached the opening in the rock slab, none of them tried to exercise firm control over the men, nor did they pause long at the opening. Braving the danger of fire from the south, they merely led the way, calling out that it was possible to get through and letting anyone follow who wished. No one knew how many men remained and were captured, but altogether there must have been about fifteen men in the group who went through the opening and withdrew safely.

'As fast as these men arrived at the 1st Platoon and Weapons Platoon positions, Sergeant Kelsey met them and began to place them in a new defence which Captain Peabody (the company commander) ordered to be set up at the north edge of the wooded area. But before they could form a new line, the German counter-attack hit them again. Many of the Company B riflemen could not return the fire because their ammunition was gone; others had only a clip or two left. The most effective fire came from Sergeant Mullins, Private Wilson, and Private Barrow, who had found several (Browning) magazines and kept the barrels of three automatic rifles hot with bullets.

'Despite the efforts of these men, the Germans, using hand grenades and rifle fire to good effect, overran a portion of the right flank. The other men heard cries of "Kamerad". Many thought at first the sound came from the Germans, but soon saw that Company B men were surrendering. As the men who continued to hold looked up the hill, they saw a column of about fifteen men file up the ridge through the rocks. In the lead was an American private holding a stick with a roll of white toilet tissue streaming from it. As the men surrendered, Private Wilson, an automatic rifleman, wanted to fire on them, but Sergeant Simmons, a 1st Platoon squad leader, forbade it. Some of those surrendering might be wounded men and, in any case, Sergeant Simmons thought the Germans would kill all the prisoners if the remaining Americans opened fire. Although someone yelled, "Put that g. . . d. . . flag down," the cry went unheeded. The prisoners continued to climb over the rock ledges towards the peak and finally disappeared from sight. . . .'[7]

When darkness came, the remains of Company B – about a score of men – were withdrawn to reserve positions farther down the mountainside. The Altuzzo crest was still in German hands, and the progress on the left flank of the 338th was little better. The 339th had spent the day in intensive shelling, supported by fighter bombers, of the enemy positions on Monte Verruca, while on the left the 363rd Infantry of Livesay's division did rather better, with one battalion ending the day only 100 yards below the Monticelli crest. But it was clear that only by superiority in weapons and firepower could the Americans hope to break the resistance of 4th Parachute Division along the crestline. Livesay, visiting the regimental command post of the 361st during the day, ordered its commander: 'Fire all the ammunition you can haul.'[8]

The American infantry were aware that during the coming days they must batter themselves yet again against the defences of Altuzzo. It was a grim thought, and there were those who wondered how long they would be able to do so without faltering. An American staff officer, discussing the next attack with a British colleague in XIII Corps, remarked wryly:

'I guess the next time the boys are told to go in, they'll just lean forward in their foxholes.'[9]

The German situation, however, was little better, and the German troops were stretched to their limit on the ground. Men from an anti-tank battalion were sent as riflemen to reinforce 12th Parachute Regiment's main line of resistance on Altuzzo, which American intelligence sources estimated as being manned by no more than 300 men. The regiment had all of its battalions in the line, and the only reserve available was a small group of engineers. If the American infantry of the 338th could break through, the road to Firenzuola was wide open. For the fundamental German misappreciation of the situation still persisted. Lemelsen continued under the delusion that Il Giogo was not the main point of American effort, but that this would come later, at the Futa Pass. Keyes was not yet at the point of breakthrough, but the pressure he was maintaining all along his front – and specially that of Livesay on the left – was leading the enemy into serious tactical error.

19
Breakthrough at Altuzzo

Clark was becoming increasingly impatient at the failure of the U.S. II Corps to break through at the Il Giogo Pass, and was already casting about in his mind for some alternative to battering the American infantry against the unyielding wall of Altuzzo and Monticelli. During 14 September, such an alternative was offered to him by the actions of the 1st British Infantry Division of Kirkman's XIII Corps, which was fighting in the hills a mile or so to the east of where the 338th Infantry struggled on the slopes of Altuzzo.

The 1st Division was commanded by Major-General Charles Loewen, a Canadian-born soldier who had begun his military career as a young gunner officer in 1918. His main axis of advance was along a secondary road running east of the American axis. This road – codenamed Arrow Route – climbed up from Borgo San Lorenzo, over the first rampart of the Apennines and the backbone of the Gothic Line, until it reached the village of Marradi. There it turned north-west through Palazzuolo, and then twisted down, a snaking white line through the jumbled contours of the map, to reach Route 9 at Castel Bolognese, between Imola and Faenza. At its best it was inadequate for the advance of an army corps; by the time it had been heavily shelled and blown by the Germans, with every bridge destroyed, it was a military nightmare.

By the evening of 12 September, the division's 3rd Brigade – consisting of the 1st Duke of Wellington's Regiment, the 2nd Foresters, and the 1st King's Shropshire Light Infantry – were a few miles north of Borgo San Lorenzo, moving astride Arrow Route. Ahead of them rose the 3,500-foot mass of Monte La

Faggeta, round the right flank of which Arrow Route wound its way north. This mountain, with the high ground of Poggio Prefetto on the left, and Poggio delle Travi on the right, must be the division's first objective. These were the forward positions of the Gothic Line.

Loewen's field for tactical decision was a small one, as must be any divisional commander's, whose approach to an enemy position is along only one road, with virtually trackless mountains on either side. The German line at this point was held by elements of 715th Infantry Division, which were occupying almost the exact divisional boundary between them and 4th Parachute Division. The German defences, however, had the weakness as well as the strength of a mountain position: they were hard to approach, but equally difficult to supply, and any attempt to cover each Spandau, rifle, and mortar, position with other posts in an interlocking series would eat up the scanty German units in the chaos of hills and ridges.

The best weapon in Loewen's hand was speed, and he decided to use it to the utmost. He planned to attack the position with his reserve brigade, the 66th, which was commanded by Brigadier Martin Redmayne. Redmayne had formed the brigade himself during the summer. Its infantry battalions were the 2nd Royal Scots, the 11th Lancashire Fusiliers, and the 1st Hertfordshire Regiment. This was the brigade's first major action, though it had a wearing struggle at Monte Calvana, just north of Florence, at the beginning of the month.

After only a few hours for preparation, during which every available lorry was commandeered to rush ammunition supplies up the crowded Arrow Route to the supporting artillery positions, Redmayne attacked during the late afternoon of the 14th. There had been heavy artillery bombardment of the general enemy line for the past forty-eight hours, but this gave little indication to the enemy of where and when the infantry attack would be made. The final support barrage was fired by the seventy-two 25-pounder guns of the divisional artillery – it amounted to 280 rounds per gun – for the two and a half hours immediately before the leading infantry crossed the start-line.[1]

It was clear very quickly that the speed of Redmayne's move

caught the German outposts by surprise. The leading battalion – the Hertfordshires – were carrying the maximum possible amount of ammunition in view of the tremendous difficulty there would be in supplying them later, and were also burdened for the same reason with digging tools and communication equipment. The signallers, for example, carried two miles of wire. They pushed on, often climbing on hands and knees, at a rate of progress estimated at 100 yards every ten minutes. During the fierce little fire fights in the dense, rock-strewn undergrowth, a German company was killed or captured, and as night came the Germans withdrew hastily from the forward slopes of Prefetto. This lapse was quickly exploited by the Lancashire Fusiliers, who were on the peak of Prefetto by midnight, and were joined at dawn by the Royal Scots. Only two half-hearted German counter-attacks were made during the morning, and both were dispersed by Fusilier bayonet charges. Speed and determination, with a resolute thrust at a weak spot in the German defences, had won the British infantry a strong toe-hold in the Gothic Line. *(Map 5.)*

Clark was characteristically quick to see the possibilities this raised for Fifth Army. He visited the British division during the day, and decided immediately to change Keyes' II Corps plan by putting the 85th Division reserve, the 337th Infantry, through the British positions to capture the adjoining height of Monte Pratone and exploit towards Firenzuola.[2] He asked that as a preliminary, a British infantry patrol should investigate Pratone. An officer and twelve men of the Hertfordshires set out, but by now, as so often happened, the Germans were recovering themselves. The little patrol was caught by fire from three sides and only two men returned alive.

On the same night, the Royal Scots attempted to seize Pratone by a swift attack, but they, too, found strong and determined German defenders. The leading company lost all its officers and its sergeant-major killed or wounded, and, commanded by a sergeant, dug in on an intermediate spur. During the next day the American infantry of the 337th Regimental Combat Team arrived, but uncertainty about the positions of the beleaguered Royal Scots company made it impossible to organise proper supporting artillery fire. Finally an order had to be given that the guns must open fire, whether the Royal Scots were in the area or not.

The Americans attacked on the 17th, supported by all the guns of the British 1st Division, as well as a great weight of II Corps artillery. After a slow and anxious start, the infantry fought their way on to Pratone peak. One of the main positions of the Gothic Line had fallen.

★   ★   ★

Meanwhile the German front opposite the 338th Infantry on Altuzzo was cracking even more dramatically. Keyes had raised no objection when Clark switched his reserves to the corps' right flank, but he still believed personally that Altuzzo was the key to Firenzuola. A new plan to attack the peak was now worked out by Brigadier Lee S. Gerow, the 85th Division's assistant commander, since Mikkelsen, the 338th commander, was ill with a high fever and nervous exhaustion.

Gerow had himself commanded the 338th during training in the United States, and he had particular confidence in the commanding officer of the 1st Battalion, Lieutenant-Colonel Willis O. Jackson, who had once been his adjutant. Thus the battered but indomitable 1st Battalion, which had been so cut about during the past three days, was again chosen to make the main effort in the new assault. The battalion was seriously depleted in numbers, averaging about seventy-five men in each of its A and C companies, instead of the normal 120. The third company, B, had been so mauled on 14 September that it was hardly now a fighting force.[3]

For an hour before the assault, the supporting guns rained shells along the Altuzzo crest. In the early evening of the 16th, the battalion moved forward, struggling through the wire of the enemy outposts while the sharp-shooters of each side picked off men as they emerged momentarily in gaps between the undergrowth and the rocks. The Germans had been combing the rear areas for new troops for Altuzzo for the past three days – twenty-five men from a battle school, for instance, were hurried into reserve positions on the 16th – but the American artillery had taken steady toll of the arriving reinforcements. The most important of these, the Grenadier Lehr Brigade, which was the Parachute Corps reserve, was moving into position on Verucca and Altuzzo even as the 338th Infantry began its attack. Some of the German infantry had to crawl the last kilometre on their hands and knees, so heavy and accurate was the fire of the American artillery and the supporting fighter-bombers.

Moreover, the Lehr Brigade was too late. Belatedly, Fourteenth Army was grasping the importance of the American attack on Il Giogo. But Jackson's battalion had learned a good deal in the last few days, and was now moving swiftly and firmly on the scattered groups of German defenders. These Germans had been subjected to murderous, pulverizing, artillery fire for several days. Some fought on bravely, but others were eager to surrender. Just after dawn on 17 September, an excited platoon commander, remembering that it was Jackson's birthday, reported over the wireless set: 'Colonel, I've got a birthday present for you. We've captured Altuzzo.'

The cost for 1st Battalion had been very high. Out of approximately 400 men in its rifle companies, 252 were killed or wounded in the five days of fighting for the peak – although the 338th Infantry as a whole lost only 290 men. The Germans, too, lost heavily. Apart from the unknown number it had killed and wounded, the 1st Battalion took 200 prisoners.[4]

Far more important, of course, was the effect of the 338th's victory when combined with the success of the 337th and the 1st British Infantry Division round Monte Pratone. Along the whole line from the Futa Pass for several miles to the east, the Germans fell back. On the 85th Division's right, the 339th Infantry took Monte Verruca, virtually destroying a battalion of the Lehr Brigade in the process, while the 91st Division on the left seized the crest of Monticelli. More important still, the elaborate defence works of the Futa Pass, with its dug-in tank turrets, wire, and terraced minefields, were completely outflanked as the German line pulled back to the heights behind Firenzuola. The great pass fell to the American infantry after only light rearguard fighting on 22 September.

Though the decisive break had been made in the centre, the left and right wings of Fifth Army also moved forward. The U.S.

IV Corps, edging forward in the west in its role of maintaining pressure on the Germans, occupied the coastal resort of Viareggio on the 15th and pushed on to Forte dei Marmi, just short of the western end of the Gothic Line. Here, too, the 6th Combat Team of the Brazilian Expeditionary Force entered the line, the first units from any South American country ever to fight on the soil of Europe.

These operations of IV Corps, gradual and undramatic though they seem beside the happenings in the centre, were not without loss. The U.S. 1st Armored Division alone, pushing into the valley of the Serchio, had almost 500 casualties among its own battalions and those of its supporting infantry while carrying out its 'secondary role'.[5]

On the army's right wing, the 8th Indian Division, under Major-General Dudley Russell, and the 6th British Armoured Division, under Major-General Horatius Murray, made steady gains. The Indians captured the considerable height of Femmina Morta on the 18th, after operating by night across mountains which contained scarcely a track, far less a road, over which to supply them. On their right, the 6th Armoured Division, on the boundary between Fifth and Eighth Armies, was advancing along Route 67, the Dicomano – Forli road. The divisional reconnaissance regiment, the Derbyshire Yeomanry, and the 16th/5th Lancers, the 17th/21st Lancers, and the 2nd Lothians and Border Horse – were having a frustrating time. The axis of advance, with great sections of road blown away or blocked, was hopelessly unsuitable for tanks, and the great column wound spasmodically along while the infantry assaulted the high ground, supported wherever possible by the guns of the Shermans firing at long range. The division's 1st Guards Brigade, profiting to some extent by what was now a general German withdrawal, captured the commanding heights of the San Godenzo Pass on the 18th. All along the line, Fifth Army was surging through the Gothic defences.

What had gone wrong for Kesselring and the German Fourteenth Army? Clark's attack on the Gothic Line, in fact, was an excellent illustration of Clausewitz's dictum, laid down more than a century before, that mountainous ground, especially when it is defended by a so-called 'wall of iron' composed of inter-connected positions like the Gothic Line, actually in the long run favours the attacker rather than the defender.

Clausewitz's argument was that the attacker is always able to choose a point at which to concentrate a superior force and break through, even though his losses at that point may be very considerable. The moment the breakthrough has been made, the mountainous country becomes a crippling liability for the defender. He cannot, by the nature of the country, quickly assemble and move up a mobile reserve. Moreover, he has to move quickly to abandon all the defensive works on the flanks of the breakthrough, because as the enemy comes through the gap the defending troops to left and right are in imminent danger of being cut off in their fixed mountain positions. Thus though the attacker may have lost heavily at the point of breakthrough, he will now gain the inestimable advantage of seizing great portions of the rest of the line with relatively light losses.

This is exactly what happened when Keyes attacked the Gothic Line at Altuzzo. He was able to bring to bear a superiority of infantry at the decisive point, and a considerable preponderance of artillery. The three American divisions at the Il Giogo Pass lost 500 men killed and more than 2,000 wounded.[6] These were heavy losses for Keyes' corps, but one cannot help feeling that the Todt engineers, when they lavished their care on the useless, outflanked concrete casemates of the Futa Pass, had hoped for a blood bath on a very much larger scale.

Yet perhaps the Futa defences had not been so useless, after all. For they had been one of the deciding factors in the Allied change of plan in mid-August, when Alexander decided to attack on the Adriatic instead of the centre. That attack had, of course, eventually helped Clark's operations by forcing Kesselring to draw off troops from the centre, but that had not been its principal intention. Eighth Army had been intended to break through on the Adriatic by itself, with Fifth Army adding a second punch in the mountains after Leese's victory. That victory had not been won, in the time and in the terms that the planners had hoped, and now the major role and the hopes of the campaign lay with Clark.

Military history abounds with 'ifs', but the student of the Gothic Line campaign must wonder if the whole picture would not have been very much more favourable to the Allies if the campaign had been fought as Alexander originally planned to fight it; that is, with a feint along the Adriatic and a massive blow in the centre. For above all, what Clark's delayed attack in the centre had lost was time. Instead of the end of August, it was now the end of September. Fifth Army was approaching the watershed of the mountains which looked down on Bologna, the Lombardy Plain, and the long diagonal highway of Route 9 which crossed it. Eighth Army was moving only slowly in the vast, flooded watery maze of the Romagna. One question now agitated the minds of both Alexander and Kesselring. Would Clark have time to cut Route 9 before the Italian winter closed down on the high Apennines?

20

Rain and Blood

The fall of the shattered ruins of Firenzuola to the U.S. 85th Division, and the crossing of the River Santerno on 21 September presented Clark with a choice of plans for further action. With both the Futa and Il Giogo Passes safely in his hands, he could push on down Route 65 to seize Bologna, cutting the great transverse highway of Route 9, and opening up a good supply route across the mountains.

A vital part of Alexander's army group plan, however, was the attempt to trap the German Tenth Army between the slowly converging wings of the Allied Fifth and Eighth Armies. It was originally intended that Clark would achieve his part of this plan by cutting Tenth Army's line of retreat at Bologna, while Eighth Army drove the Germans north along the Adriatic. But there were now elements of doubt about this plan.

Eighth Army was moving very slowly; Rimini, it will be remembered, did not fall until 21 September, three days after the breakthrough by Clark at Il Giogo. Ahead of Leese's army lay the Romagna, rapidly becoming a sea of mud which even the armoured optimists were beginning to see was hopelessly unsuitable for fast movement. Clark himself still had formidable difficulties of terrain in front of him. It seemed now, in fact, that since Leese, the right claw of the Allied pincers, was only making a few hundred yards a day, and since Clark, the left claw, had considerable mountains yet to cross, Bologna was too far along Route 9 to be a likely point to close the trap. Clark therefore decided to direct part of the U.S. II Corps across the mountains to Imola, twenty miles nearer to Eighth Army down Route 9 than Bologna, while his British XIII Corps continued to make its necessarily slow way across the exiguous roads towards Faenza, which was nearer still.

On 20 September, he ordered Brigadier-General Paul 'Bull' Kendall to attack with the reserve U.S. 88th Infantry Division down the Santerno valley towards Imola, only thirty miles away. Meanwhile the remaining three divisions of II Corps would continue along the axis of Route 65, through the Radicosa Pass to Bologna.[1]

Kendall's 88th – the Blue Devils, as its troops were known – was probably the best American division in Italy, and had won considerable respect from German commanders for its uninhibited zeal and drive during the Cassino campaign.[2] It moved quickly now, driving down the steep, rocky Santerno gorge and across the hills on either side. Its leading troops had captured Castel del Rio, a dozen miles down the Imola road, by the morning of the 27th, and were fiercely engaged in a group of three mountains, Pratolungo, Carnevale, and Battaglia, which were the last main heights between them and Imola.

The driving of this salient into the German mountain positions was countered by Fourteenth Army with desperate urgency as the gap between the German 4th Parachute and 715th Infantry Divisions was forced steadily wider. The 362nd Infantry Division was used to plug the defences north of Firenzuola, and an under-strength infantry Division, the 44th Infantry, which had lost heavily during Fourteenth Army's headlong retreat north of Rome in the summer, was hurried from opposite McCreery's Corps in the central mountains to the defence of the Santerno valley.[3]

Although they were through the Gothic Line, the advancing Fifth Army infantry, just like Eighth Army two or three weeks before, found the country beyond and its defenders an even more difficult proposition. And, again like Eighth Army, Fifth Army began to suffer from flank trouble. The ground along which the U.S. 88th Division was advancing was by no means easy, but the valley road itself was reasonably good. On the right of the 88th, however, the country became steadily more mountainous and difficult – and it was here that the British XIII Corps was trying to keep pace and supply flank support.

On the left of the British Corps – which was the immediate

right of the U.S. 88th Division – the British 1st Infantry Division was fighting to clear the road to Palazzuolo and then attack down the Senio valley, which ran more or less parallel with the Santerno towards the plain of the River Po. This, of course, was still Arrow Route, a precipitous road which had been easy for the Germans to demolish in great stretches.

As the U.S. 88th drove forward down the Santerno valley, a gap of about three miles opened up between it and the slower-moving British 1st Division. This was an opportunity which the Germans were not slow to exploit, and an enemy counter-attack across the open flank captured the headquarters of an American battalion on the night of 21 September.

Redmayne's 66th British Infantry Brigade captured Palazzuolo on 25 September, but by that time the 350th Infantry of the 88th Division were racing far ahead of the British troops on their right and the American 351st infantry on their left. They seized Carnevale on the morning of the 27th, and during the afternoon they advanced even farther, to Battaglia.

The American infantry were led to the peak of the mountain, which was crowned by a ruined castle, by partisans who announced that they were in possession of the area. The biggest single mountain obstacle on the road to Imola had fallen without a fight.

The German relinquishment of this vital bastion in such a way is a riddle, for the enemy certainly made prodigious and costly efforts to regain it in the next days. The Americans on the summit were Company C of the 350th's 2nd Battalion, and barely an hour after they had dug in during heavy rain, the first counter-attack came through the mountain mists. The company held on until dark, and then was steadily shelled all night until dawn, when a second counter-attack overran its outposts and reached within a few yards of the crest before the Germans were beaten back. Throughout the morning, small groups of German infantry, each of about platoon strength, tried to work into the American positions. In the afternoon a much stronger German attack was made by elements from four battalions of the 44th and 715th Infantry Divisions. Some of the Germans carried flame-throwing equipment. The Americans, however, were well placed, and although the attack almost reached the summit, it was beaten off. In the evening another American company, K, arrived with a mule train carrying ammunition and rations.

In the fog and rain of the morning of the 29th, the Germans once more swarmed up Battaglia, and this time got into the castle ruins, before being driven out with hand grenades. Between 7 and 10 a.m. more than 400 enemy shells fell round the American positions, but the Germans did not attack again until the 30th, when again they almost reached the crest before being driven back by the withering American fire. All next day, a steady drain of American casualties from German shelling continued, but when the Germans attacked again on 1 October, the besieged American companies were being supported by other battalions of the 350th Infantry, and the enemy attackers were driven headlong down the mountain in a costly repulse. By now British and American units were on the flanks, and Battaglia was, for the moment, secure.[4]

The struggle for the mountain, which illustrates so well the enterprise and the unyielding resolution of Kendall's magnificent division, has passed into the realms of legend, not only of the United States Army, but also of the partisans. The partisan unit which guided the 2nd Battalion to the peak on 27 September, was the 36th Garibaldi Brigade, which had been engaged in local fighting round Bologna earlier in the month. It later claimed a good deal of the credit for the successful defence. The most comprehensive history of the Italian resistance movement describes the struggle for Battaglia as 'the episode in which, more than in any other in the course of the Italian campaign, final victory was really a joint one, with equal sacrifice and will to fight'.[5]

How far this is true is difficult to discern in the romantic haze of partisan history. American accounts make little of the partisan role, though if Italians guided the Americans to the peak, it is reasonable to suppose that some may have stayed on while the Germans made their repeated attacks. This was one of the few occasions in the Gothic Line campaign that irregular units made operational contact with American troops, and it seems likely that the Italian part in the battle was based, not

on the shoulder-to-shoulder defiance of resistance legend, but
on the actions of comparatively few partisans.

One of the many ironies of the Gothic Line campaign, however, was that from the point of view of developing the operations down the Santerno valley the capture of Battaglia was in
vain. The Germans had not been able to recapture the mountain, but the forces they had brought up around it were too
much for the U.S. 88th Division to tackle alone, and yet the
American axis of advance was too narrow to permit of another
division being brought in to help Kendall's men. The enemy
troops opposite Battaglia now included units from the 44th,
305th, and 715th Infantry Divisions, and even a regiment of the
98th Infantry Division, which had been so badly battered
during the Eighth Army offensive on the Adriatic.

Moreover, the U.S. 88th Division had suffered heavily
during its spirited incursion into the Santerno valley. Between
21 September and 3 October, the division had 2,105 men killed
and wounded – not far from the total suffered by the whole of
the rest of the U.S. II Corps during the actual breaching of the
Gothic Line.[6]

Clark recognized quickly that his plan to reach Imola was not
likely to succeed, and he decided to switch his main effort back
to Route 65, the road to Bologna. The 1st Guards Brigade was
detached from the 6th British Armoured Division, far over on
the right, and was brought in to relieve the U.S. 88th Division
on Battaglia during the first three days of October. Once more,
Keyes had all four divisions of his U.S. II Corps available for a
new thrust.

The prospects for Fifth Army still looked good, despite the setback to Clark's original plan. For though the move of the 88th
on Imola had been frustrated, it had had important consequences in drawing German troops from the defence of Bologna
to the area of Battaglia. Keyes' corps pushed on steadily down
Route 65 and through the Radicosa Pass, and by 2 October
reached Monghidoro, less than twenty miles from Bologna. The
weather was rapidly becoming appalling. In the rain, low cloud,
and mist air support was scanty, and the aircraft were grounded
altogether on the last three days of September. Gradually the
roads became morasses, and each day the army had to drag its

supplies a little farther from its main dumps near Florence. Nevertheless, Bologna was getting nearer. On 3 October, Clark drove up Route 65 to Monghidoro, and from a high point in the little town looked out over the Po Valley in the distance to the faint snow-covered line of the Alps beyond.

'It seemed to me then,' he wrote later, 'that our goal was very close.'⁷

To Alexander, at once more detached from the immediacies of battle and with a better overall picture of events, the future did not look so good. He had reported to the Supreme Commander, Wilson, on 26 September:

'The trouble is that my forces are too weak relative to the enemy to force a breakthrough and so close the two pincers. The advance of both Armies is too slow to achieve decisive results unless the Germans break and there is no sign of that. . . .'⁸

On 2 October, after gloomy weather and casualty reports, he reinforced his warning to Wilson:

'. . . It is a slow and costly process and my fears are now that we may not be just quite strong enough to carry it through. I am reinforcing Fifth Army by giving them 78th Division for XIII Corps. It is my last remaining fully fresh division.'⁹

★ ★ ★

The British 78th Division, newly-arrived from the Middle East after resting and refitting following its heavy fighting round Lake Trasimene in June, was originally intended to reinforce Keightley's V Corps for the Eighth Army drive up Route 9 after the capture of Rimini. Its last-minute transfer to Fifth Army reflected a recognition that the hopes of the campaign now lay mainly with Clark in the centre, and also a sense of disillusion about the prospects and progress of Eighth Army on the right.

During the first three violent and bloody weeks of September, the line of the River Marecchia, flowing into the seaside resort of Rimini, had seemed to Eighth Army like the border of a promised land. On 22 September, the climactic moment of the campaign appeared to have arrived when the army reserve, the 2nd New Zealand Division, Alexander's *corps de chasse*, passed

through the 1st Canadian Division across the Marecchia and
began to roll north-west.

'Although the price had been heavy,' reported Alexander, 'no
one in Eighth Army doubted that a real victory had been gained,
for it was confidently expected that, after breaking into the flat
country of the Romagna, we should be able to exploit rapidly
to the Po. . . .'⁹

It was not, however, a broken or panicky German army which
pulled back over the Marecchia, but one which was withdrawing in good order, and which was considerably aided by the
weather. It had rained hard all night on 21 September, and the
movement of vehicles, and especially of armour, was made
highly difficult for the pursuit over the waterlogged ground.
The New Zealanders hit heavy opposition immediately they
crossed the Marecchia. A corporal of the leading 21st Battalion
wrote later:

'. . . We assembled and Major Hawkesby made an impas-
sioned address to the throng (going something like this):
"You've all got automatic weapons, well, give the bastards
hell." . . . The attack appeared to be a piece of cake at the start,
from our company point of view at least. After about a mile
things began to warm up and my platoon was pinned down
several times by Spandau fire and mortars. We had the tanks in
support and they drew fire like nobody's business. I remember a
Jerry Spandau expert bailed up in a near-by railway wagon on
our left. One of our tanks went to town on him. . . . By this time
things were getting really hot . . . his mortars were landing all
around. We also had taken quite a number of prisoners, almost
entirely Turcoman troops. Just like Japs. We began to wonder
if we were in the right country. Things began to get so hot we
took to houses for shelter and were shelled violently for several
hours.'¹⁰

These Turcoman troops were the battered and dispirited
remnant of the battalions of the German 162nd Division
recruited from captured Russian sources, which had been
broken by the Canadians at San Fortunato. The New Zealanders
noted that they had German paybooks with one page
entered in Russian, but that many of them were illiterate, and
that, as an official New Zealand account puts it, 'it was not

impossible that they even thought they were still fighting for Russia'.[11]

If the Turcomans had been the main element in the German rearguard, the New Zealand Division would have been swinging out towards the Po by evening. The main body opposite the New Zealanders was of a different calibre, however. This was Heidrich's 1st Parachute Division, and on 24 September its evening report stated proudly:

'During the last thirty-six hours the division has beaten off twenty-seven attacks in battalion strength. It is still holding a continuous line. . . .'[12]

Slightly to the west of Heidrich's men, between them and Route 9, the German line was held by the 20th Luftwaffe Field Division; and south of Route 9, in the Apennine foothills, by the badly-mauled 278th Division, stiffened, however, by 100th Mountain Regiment, the brave Austrian defenders of Gemmano. Farther still to the right was the 114th Jaeger Division. Behind the immediate front, Baade's 90th Panzer Grenadier Division was also being positioned to cover Route 9.

Against these opponents, the New Zealanders did not have the exhilarating pursuit which had been hoped for, but a slow and expensive progress. It was 26 September before the Staghound armoured cars of the New Zealand Divisional Cavalry reached the south bank of the Uso, a small river which flows into the Adriatic about six miles north of Rimini, and which disputes with the Fiumicino and the Pisciatello, a mile or so to the north, for the fame of being the ancient Rubicon stream, the crossing of which by Caesar in 49 B.C. signalled the beginning of his civil war with Pompey.*

Not only the New Zealanders were having trouble. Behind Eighth Army's advanced troops, the Marecchia was rising rapidly, making supply and reinforcement highly difficult. The stream was little more than ankle deep when it was first crossed on 21 September, but a week of rain had changed it to a wild brown torrent twelve feet deep, and the Royal Engineers were

* This echo of a classical past was not lost on Alexander, who pointed out later that he could not say when he himself crossed the Rubicon, until historians decided which river it was.[13]

facing tremendous problems as they struggled to bridge its greasy banks.

The Uso, by contrast, was narrow, and it was clear that von Vietinghoff would not try to stand long on this line. On the left of the New Zealanders, the Canadian armoured division, after four days of heavy fighting, seized a bridgehead over the river on 25 September. They had lost 350 men since the fall of Rimini.

Keightley's V Corps, on the left flank of the advance, made varying progress. The administratively-doomed 1st British Armoured Division took Santarcangelo and crossed the Uso just beyond on 25 September, while 56th Division pushed up Route 9 and reached Savignano, on the south bank of the Fiumicino, by the 27th. Farther over in the more difficult country of the foothills, however, the 4th Indian and 46th Infantry Divisions could not make such good progress, and had only a few leading troops over the river on the 26th. *(Map 3.)*

Meanwhile, the rain intensified, and from 29 September to 2 October it hardly stopped. Every ford over the Uso and the Marecchia was now impassable. Guns once in position took hours to haul out again in the road; tanks slithered, bellied, and stopped, impotently roaring their 500 horse-power engines; the two-wheel-drive British trucks stuck in the mud. A sodden weariness began to seep through the whole army, though men worked on grimly for a victory that was now receding. A battery commander of 56th Heavy Regiment, supporting the infantry forward near Rimini, wrote:

'It is really the gunners who need a rest. They are practically on their last legs. Have had very little sleep for the last month. All morning they were out in the rain for odd periods firing. There is something in their character which won't let them give in. They will go on indefinitely, grumbling a bit, but dogged. I feel an awful brute driving them sometimes. . . . Our chief trouble is that the German soldier proper is still the finest individual fighting soldier in the world, especially in defence, and there are still a hell of a lot of pure Germans to kill. . . .'[14]

Meanwhile, the Germans were winning time. On the line of the Fiumicino, three miles north of the Uso, the German Tenth Army turned again, and this time it held firm. Eighth Army dragged itself up through the mud and rain to the south bank of the river, but it was becoming more and more clear that it would need a major assault to cross it.

Confidently, Kesselring looked out across the soaked and desolate landscape to his south, and began to transfer vital units to meet the greater threat posed by Mark Clark in the centre. For Leese now, the Po looked very far away, and Vienna was no more than a dream.

At this moment, too, Leese ended his command of Eighth Army. In accordance with decisions taken some weeks before,[15] he was appointed to command the Allied Land Forces in South-East Asia. At the beginning of October, he was succeeded in command of Eighth Army by General Sir Richard McCreery, whose X Corps, sandwiched between the Fifth and Eighth Army, had so far played little active part in the campaign, acting merely as a holding force in the central hills, and also as a reinforcement pool for Eighth Army. McCreery was, however, an original and highly intelligent commander – 'a scientific soldier with a gift for the offensive,' Alexander called him – and he now tried to apply some of his direct and unorthodox thinking to break the impending stalemate.

The situation was not a good one to inherit. Courage and stubbornness there had been in plenty on both German and British sides during the past weeks, but the rain was a different matter. The rain fell on Kesselring's side, and it had come just in time. The grey, leaden skies of the Italian autumn changed every strategic and tactical calculation of the campaign.

And yet in spite of Kesselring's renewed and growing confidence, Leese and Clark had come nearer than anyone yet knew to beating him. The German commander had almost given up his struggle south of the Po. At the end of August, he had worked out a contingency plan to withdraw the German forces north of the great river if the Allied pressure became too great. This plan was codenamed *Herbstnebel*, and the codename itself became known to Allied Intelligence. *Herbstnebel* means Autumn Fog, and it was not difficult for the Allies to work out that it referred to a withdrawal in the notoriously misty Po valley – 'the danger,' Alexander said later, 'of having a secret codeword with a built-in clue to its meaning.'[16]

What the Allies did not know, although they had rumours

from German prisoners and deserters, was that this contingency plan was quickly proposed to Hitler as an actual basis for operations. Courageously, in view of his earlier promises to the Führer, Kesselring sent a senior staff officer on 23 September to ask Hitler's permission to put *Herbstnebel* into effect.

Hitler, however, had lost none of his inhibitions about yielding ground, and the request was immediately refused. Four days later Kesselring tried again, this time citing his own particular obsession about the possibility of a landing by Allied forces in his rear, as well as the difficulties he was in from both Fifth and Eighth Armies – especially as Clark at this time was still threatening Imola. Hitler did not yield an inch. Kesselring was informed that 'the Führer . . . has decided to defend the Apennine front and to hold upper Italy, not only until late autumn, but indefinitely'.[17]

In his memoirs, Kesselring glosses over this episode.

'When Hitler decided against Autumn Fog in October, I was not surprised,' he wrote. 'I had actually counted on this, and had merely put forward this first suggestion as a *ballon d'essai* to inform the OKW drastically in advance of the development of the situation and the possible consequences. To start it at once would indeed have been against my deepest conviction – so difficult an operation had had to be carefully and calmly thought out and put on paper with an exact time schedule. Thus I did not accept the refusal in October as a flat rejection of my proposal and I was confident of my ability to get it accepted if the situation became critical.'[18]

As to this, one can only note that for a field commander to put to Hitler – especially in the unpredictable mood which Hitler was in after the 20 July attempt on his life – an operational proposal which ran exactly counter to all the Führer's expressed thinking, was a very serious matter indeed. To have that request abruptly rejected, and then to renew it after only four days – this cannot reasonably be described as the launching of a trial balloon.

After the war Kesselring knew that he would be remembered in military history chiefly as the commander who fought a model delaying campaign, against crushing air superiority, in the Italian Apennines. It is not surprising that he should wish to pass quickly over the inevitable moments when it appeared to him that he had lost it, and when he was trying to act in that belief.

However, trial balloon or not, at the beginning of October he had his orders, and they were clear in intention, if not in method. Hitler expected him to fight on south of the Po. The German corps and divisional commanders were now instructed 'not to relinquish one foot of soil to the enemy without inflicting heavy casualties . . . . The enemy's reserves are not inexhaustible.'

★ ★ ★

Of the exhaustibility of reserves, the Allied commanders were well aware. The total of 14,000 men killed, wounded, and missing, in Eighth Army alone since 25 August was higher than the bill for Alamein, and Alexander, as we have seen, had already made drastic changes and reductions at the end of September. Now Clark and Fifth Army were in trouble, as casualties began to mount in the bitter fighting in the central Apennines. On 6 October, Clark signalled to Wilson's head-quarters at Caserta:

'Infantry replacement situation is so critical that current operation may be endangered. Supply of infantry replacements and infantry overstrength in divisions only sufficient to maintain divisions at authorized strength through 9th or 10th of October. Losses in my four infantry divisions during past five days have averaged 550 per day per division over and above returns to units. Heavy fighting continues, with enemy apparently rushing all available forces to halt our advance on Bologna. All divisions have been in heavy fighting twenty-three to twenty-six days under adverse weather conditions. Continuous supply of infantry replacements is imperative.'[19]

Three days later he followed this up with a message to Alexander, telling him that at the present casualty rate, Fifth Army would, by 1 November, be 8,000 infantry short for its United States divisions – a shortage of seventy-five men for each rifle company.

Alexander now made a personal plea for reinforcements to

General Eisenhower, asking him if he could give Fifth Army 3,000 men from the European Theatre of Operations. Eisenhower at once, with typical generosity, agreed, and Alexander was informed that the reinforcements were being sent by air. 'It was,' reported Alexander, 'a fine example of General Eisenhower's ready grasp of the big strategic picture and his willingness to cut through red tape to assist a friend in need.'[20]

Such a ready grasp of a vital issue was not so much in evidence at somewhat lower levels, however. Clark tried to persuade Lieutenant-General Jacob Devers, Wilson's American deputy at Allied Headquarters, to supply him with these replacements from the depots reinforcing the Anvil operation, and then to take Eisenhower's proffered 3,000 in their place. This would obviously save time and transport.

Devers, however, was not on good terms with Alexander or, for that matter, with Clark. In addition to being Wilson's deputy, he also commanded the Allied army group which was engaged in the Anvil operation in the South of France, and the clash of the French and Italian offensives no doubt exacerbated the mutual antipathy. Churchill, when he visited Italy in August, had noted the 'coolness' between Alexander and Devers, and wrote later, 'I was conscious of the tension between these high officers beneath an impeccable surface of politeness.'[21]

At any rate, whatever the reason, Devers did not accede to Clark's request. Instead, he sent to Clark on 19 October a message which said:

'I have just seen your reported daily casualty list. Suggest you rest a division or regiments within a division, as your casualty rate will break down any replacement system. Your problem is one of using available troops to best advantage.'

This somewhat complacent message, with its unnecessary final sentence, must have been peculiarly annoying to an army commander struggling with inadequate forces in very difficult country. Clark sent back to Devers a rebuke of a more stinging character than one general usually uses in writing to another:

'Your radio indicates a lack of appreciation of our tactical situation, the terrain, enemy resistance, and my mission. Unfortunately you have not been able to visit this front in approximately two months. I am keenly aware of my casualty rate, and have taken every possible opportunity to rest regiments within divisions consistent with the urgency of my mission . . .

'Our success now hangs in the balance, and our growing infantry shortage may prove the decisive handicap. General Alexander took up directly with General Eisenhower a request for 3,000 replacements. General Eisenhower has notified us that they are available, and arrangements are under way to fly all or part of them to this theatre. I regret that you did not see fit to release to Fifth Army the "Anvil" replacements in your depots as requested in my radio of 9 October. Had you done so, and arranged for the Seventh Army (Anvil) supply from SHAEF (General Eisenhower's headquarters) sources, it would have saved much time and obviated the necessity of shipping replacements from Italy to France and shipment back of an equivalent number to Italy.'[22]

Meanwhile, as Clark had warned, success hung in the balance. Fifth Army had a little less than twenty miles to go to reach Bologna, and unhinge the whole enemy position on the plain. Clark had estimated that by 1 November he would be disastrously short of infantry, and it was now clear that if the battle in the centre could not be won in the remaining three weeks of October, it would not be won at all. On 5 October, tired, muddy, and with steadily thinning ranks, the four American infantry divisions of Keyes' II Corps, and the British armoured division and British and Indian infantry divisions of Kirkman's XIII Corps, reinforced now by the fresh 78th Division, began a new push aimed at reaching the Po Valley before the autumn rain became winter snow.

21

The Race with Winter

The four American divisions of the U.S. II Corps attacked in line on 5 October, along a front which straggled through the mountains for approximately seven miles each side of Route 65. From west to east, the line of battle began with the 34th Division, then the 91st Division astride Route 65, and then the 85th and 88th Divisions. Thus the greatest weight of the attack fell to the east of the road, where the three American divisions were now supported on their right by the British 78th Division and the 1st Guards Brigade.

During the next four days, the Americans made gradual but relentless progress against stiffening enemy opposition, deployed in a series of temporary defence lines stretching across the front. The German Fourteenth Army was now moving troops from the quieter sector opposite the weak U.S. IV Corps; the 16th S.S. Panzer Grenadier Division was positioned opposite the U.S. 34th, while the 65th Infantry Division was brought in to face the U.S. 91st on Route 65.

It was along this road that the best American gain was made, when the 91st Division pushed on for three miles, capturing Loiano, the next town on from Monghidoro, on the afternoon of the first day. The division was then held up, however, by tenacious German defenders in the hills a mile or so to the north. Although the driving rain and mountain mist made observed fire difficult – and often impossible – a great weight of artillery support was given to the advancing American battalions. The divisional guns of the 91st fired a thousand shells into Loiano, ending the barrage less than half an hour before the infantry took the town.[1] The gap was slowly closing;

Loiano was about ten miles as the crow flies from the centre of Bologna.

On the flanks, the gains were smaller. The appalling weather, and the comparative freshness of German units from the newly-arrived divisions, slowed the 85th Division on the right of the road, and finally stopped it at the hill mass of Monterenzio. On the left, too, the 34th Division was entangled in the approaches to the Monterumici hills, and was making little progress.

In spite of the relative success of the advance down Route 65, little comfort could be taken from the prospect ahead. From the Monterumici hills in the west, through Livergnano on Route 65, to the Monterenzio mountains in the east, the Americans were now faced with the most formidable of the German holding positions in front of Bologna. It was christened the 'Caesar Line' by the Germans, and its centrepiece was the gigantic Livergnano escarpment which straddled Route 65 at the little town of the same name. This daunting, southward-facing barrier consisted of a virtually sheer rock wall nearly three miles long, and in places more than 1,500 feet high. Behind it stretched a row of hills, from the peaks of which any troops who finally stormed the escarpment would immediately come under the fire of well-sited German guns. There were two small breaks in the great wall – one where the road cut through it at Livergnano itself, and another through a footpath two miles to the east.

Livesay's 91st Division did not pause, however. It began its attempt to tackle the escarpment on 9 October, sending the 1st Battalion of its 361st Infantry Regiment into the town itself, and the 2nd Battalion to the east, where the footpath broke the line of rock near Bigallo. The Americans were given a rapid demonstration of the near-impossibility of assaulting the escarpment under the existing conditions of rain and fog. The 1st Battalion got a company into Livergnano, but the enemy machine-gun and rifle fire was so intense that movement became impossible. The company's survivors scrambled desperately to the cover of a large four-storey building in the centre of the town. Here they were repeatedly attacked by German infantry, but managed to beat off each attack until the Germans brought up two tanks and methodically blew the building to pieces. Almost the whole American company was killed or captured; only ten men, crouched unnoticed in a near-by pigsty, were able to get back to the American lines.

The 2nd Battalion was also in grave difficulty. Above the Bigallo footpath, the rock wall soared high into the mist, and it was not possible to climb it in battle order. The riflemen slung their rifles across their shoulders, and scaled it finger-and-toe, while German rifles and machine-guns picked off men in small groups as they neared the rim of the escarpment. The American machine-gunners were in even greater difficulty. They had to take their weapons to pieces, distributing the parts amongst each other's pockets to leave hands and shoulders clear for climbing.[2]

After an afternoon of tremendous endurance and courage, the leading company actually reached the rim, but found that it had to use almost all its remaining strength to man-haul ammunition up the escarpment and protect the footpath from the pockets of enemy infantry who, it was now all too clear, completely surrounded it. The evacuation of the American wounded was proving an almost insuperable task, for it took almost twelve hours to carry a wounded man down the escarpment. The night of 9 October, with one American company sitting sullenly in German prison cages, and another pinned on the escarpment, was an anxious one for General Livesay.

The next morning, however, the German defenders crouched in the Livergnano rock gullies looked apprehensively for the first time for many days at clear blue skies. The weather improved rapidly, and the American artillery, free of the mantle of mist which had hampered it for so long, turned eagerly to its task. Farther south, on the air-strips near Florence, fighter and medium bombers roared down the runways. Within a few hours, the German infantry once more felt the flail of air power.

Fighter-bombers began to support the American infantry along the escarpment with attacks no more than 350 yards in front of them, while the 91st Divisional artillery alone fired 24,000 shells between 12 October and 14.[3] A great deal of this artillery support was fired in the nerve-shattering technique known as TOT – Time on Target, a method by which all the shells fired by a group of guns, sometimes more than a hundred, hit the target area at exactly the same second.

The American infantry clung on to its hold on top of the escarpment, and gradually, along the line, other American units began to join them, fighting bitterly against Germans ensconced in caves, who dropped hand-grenades almost vertically on the sweating attackers as they swarmed up the rocks. The steady, sustained pounding of the American artillery, supported now by self-propelled tank destroyer guns firing directly into caves and embrasures, was now, however, beginning to batter many Germans into submission.

A new American effort began all along the escarpment line on 13 October, preceded by a tremendous artillery bombardment of 2,120 rounds in sixteen minutes. Gradually, the American infantry pushed on. The Germans pulled out of Livergnano on the 14th, and by the end of the next day the Americans held the escarpment and the heart of the Caesar Line.

On the left of the 91st Division, progress had not been so good, and the Monterumici hills were still holding up the U.S. 34th Division, which was now being reinforced by armoured infantry battalions hurried over from 1st U.S. Armoured Division on the IV Corps front.

The bill had been heavy. The four American divisions lost 2,491 men in killed, wounded, and missing between 10 and 15 October, making a total of about 5,700 since 1 October. The striking power of Keyes' Corps was growing less and less. The rifle companies – the heart of these mountain attacks – were especially badly hit. Sometimes a company would be led into the assault by only two officers, and platoons were at less than half-strength. So many officers were being killed and wounded that an increasing number of enlisted men was offered battle-field commissions, though this only partly solved the problem, since it removed an equal number of experienced N.C.O.s.[4]

Moreover, after four days, the fine weather ended, and the troops were back in the familiar rain, mud, and fog. Men stumbling and crawling up the muddy mountain slopes were often wet to the skin for days on end. For some, a mild kind of dysentery or diarrhoea developed – caused, many thought, by eating handfuls of the grapes that were beginning to rot on the neglected vines, or by the rough vermouth 'liberated' from the ruins of shattered hamlets. Thus to the danger of battle, men added the sordid discomfort of squatting amongst the wet rocks. Even fit, strong young men have a limit of physical endurance; for some in Fifth Army that limit was now being reached.

The number of non-battle casualties was already worrying Clark. On 6 October, he wrote to Marshall, the U.S. Chief of Staff:

'The incidence of manpower loss from psychiatric causes began to be felt in January, when the combat forces available to the Fifth Army were so limited that it was necessary to keep infantry units in the line for very extended periods. . . . Our assaults against fortifications were made with divisions which became materially under strength and could be given little respite as we pressed forward.

'A similar situation confronts us today in the Apennines. My troops have been negotiating the most difficult mountain terrain we have had to face in Italy, involving the bitterest fighting since Salerno. . . . The decision which has faced me is one of halting our attack in order to rest or of pushing on in an all-out effort to gain our objectives before winter catches us in the Apennines. Fifth Army troops have made significant advances every day for more than two weeks.

'I do not yet know the answer to the psychiatric problem. It appears clear from the report, based largely on Fifth Army experience, that susceptibility to psychiatric breakdown is directly related to the length of time in combat. I shall continue to take every practical measure to give my troops the opportunity for rest.'[5]

★ ★ ★

Though the operations of the British divisions on the right of II Corps did not have the immediate drama of the American thrust at Bologna, they were fought with equal determination through country quite as difficult.

The German command, of course, knew nothing of Clark's decision to switch the main American drive from Imola to Bologna, and the substitution of the British 78th Division and the Guards Brigade on the Imola axis kept the enemy anxious about this sector. In particular, the Guards Brigade on Battaglia, which it had taken over from the Americans early in October, was given no respite by the Germans. Shelling was so heavy that the Guards' positions could be approached only by night, and in the mist and darkness small raiding parties of German infantry constantly infiltrated into the British lines. The confusion of this shadowy warfare was described by a Welsh Guards subaltern:

'. . . Three of us were going back in the half-light before dawn when, fifty feet after being challenged by our own sentries, we were opened on by six Germans with a machine-gun and some machine-carbines. The captain was in front, only seven yards from the guns, then five feet behind him was a corporal, and five yards behind him myself. We flung ourselves over the bank in a jiffy. Quickly we found that none of us was hit. It was wonderful. The captain later found bullet marks on his clothes.'

There were gruesome moments, too, particularly in the Battaglia castle where the American 350th Infantry had made their magnificent stand:

'The castle, a ruin, is under virtually continuous shelling. It is littered with American bodies in all stages of decomposition. We even have one hanging in through a high window of our stronghold. Movement is only by night and one continually treads on severed heads, limbs, bodies, etc. . . .'[6]

While the Guards Brigade, in the face of repeated German attacks, held firmly on to Battaglia, the 78th Division, commanded by a former Black Watch officer, Major-General Robert Keith Arbuthnott, was brought in between the Guards and the U.S. 88th Division, to the right of the Imola road. Like all other units on this axis, it immediately faced severe supply problems, since the division itself, the Guards Brigade, and the U.S. 88th were all being maintained along a single road which was barely wide enough for two-lane traffic. An added difficulty was the technical inadequacy of the British Army trucks, whose two-wheel drive proved frequently incapable of negotiating the mud on the roads. This problem was partly solved for some British units in XIII Corps when the Americans lent them the far-superior U.S. Army four-wheel-drive transport, with Negro drivers.

Typical of the obstacles to the movement of infantry on this front was the Bailey bridge which had been built high over the destroyed viaduct south of Castel del Rio. Even when the toiling engineers had constructed the bridge, it proved possible to pass only one battalion a day across it, because of the delay imposed by the need for every vehicle to remove its chains when crossing. The engineers had warned that otherwise the vibration might destroy the bridge.[7]

The role of the division was to act as a flank guard to the American advance on its left, and to do this it was, in fact, continuing the line of advance originally followed by the U.S. 88th Division down the Imola road. This had already been abandoned by Clark as a practical proposition, as we have seen, and it seems that the main role of the British troops was envisaged as engaging the attention of the 334th, 715th, and 305th German Infantry Divisions to allow the main Fifth Army drive to continue in the centre.[8]

The first principal objectives for Arbuthnott's division were Monte Spaduro, a commanding height between the Santerno and Sillaro rivers, and Monte dell'Acqua Salata, a little to the south-east. Between them these two great features barred the way to Route 9 and the plains of Lombardy.

On the night of 13 October, the division's 11th Brigade attacked Monte Pieve, an intermediate height on the way to Monte Spaduro, but received a costly rebuff. The 2nd Lancashire Fusiliers lost fifty-nine men to heavy German mortaring and machine-gunning during the night and next morning. When the 5th Northamptons took up the attack, supported by Canadian tanks – of the Three Rivers Regiment from the 1st Canadian Armoured Brigade – they had nearly 100 casualties, while the armoured support failed after one tank stuck on a narrow track and blocked the way for the others. Three Canadian tanks were knocked out, but their crews stayed in the motionless hulks, firing every round of their ammunition to support the withdrawing British infantry.[9] The third and last battalion of the brigade made a new assault at midnight on 15 October. This was the 1st East Surreys, and although they were able to fight their way on to the lower slopes, they were finally stopped at a sheer cliff, down which the German defenders rolled scores of hand-grenades on to the exhausted infantry. One small party actually fought its way to the top of the cliff, but its losses were so heavy that it could not remain. On 16 October, with 78th Division not yet in possession of Monte Pieve, Monte Spaduro still barred the way, and was also beginning to hamper the American operations on the left.

Meanwhile, down on the right of the XIII Corps front the 1st British Infantry Division, which was advancing slowly through very difficult country, had been engaged between 3 and 9 October in a savage struggle with the German 715th Infantry Division for Monte Ceco, a forbidding 1,500-foot height which commanded Arrow Route at Castagno. This small village was in yet another of the interminable river valleys – in this case the Senio – north of Palazzuolo.

No British or American division during the Second World War operated over more heart-breaking country than that over which 1st Division was now advancing. The rain and the immense amount of traffic had in effect destroyed Arrow Route as a recognizable road, and yet the moment troops began to operate out on its flanks, they were reduced to being supplied by jeep at the best, and more often by mule. For wounded men, this sometimes meant that an injury which in better country would have meant no more than a long time in hospital, now meant death. A man shot on the steep, shaly slope of an Apennine crest first had to be reached by his companions, often climbing hand and toe, and then lowered down for as much as a mile before he could be brought to relatively open ground. Here he would be loaded on to a mule which carried two stretchers as it swayed and lurched down the mountain trails. Sometimes a mule would throw a wounded man down the steep slopes on either side. It often took six hours to get a man from the point where he was shot down to the necessarily cursory attention of the Regimental Aid Post, and perhaps a further eight hours before he finally reached a vehicle waiting at the roadhead on Arrow Route. Then it would be a further hour or more, as the ambulance splashed through the quagmire of the road, before he could reach a surgeon. Thus a man often died from loss of blood or exhaustion before he reached proper aid.

To meet this situation, the division established advanced

surgical centres – mobile operating theatres – each carried by twenty mules and forty volunteer porters and maintained as far forward as brigade headquarters, so that a wounded man could have a major operation at least ten hours before he would have received attention had he gone back to hospital down Arrow Route.[10]

Not only the medical services found the gradually lengthening distance between the leading troops and the main army services to be an almost insuperable problem. The Royal Electrical and Mechanical Engineers, charged with the recovery of ditched, damaged, and stranded vehicles, was now facing a situation in which the nearest major workshops were forty miles away, a distance which on crowded Arrow Route took between four and six hours to cover. The workshops could not be moved forward, for there simply was no site on Arrow Route where they could be re-established. Even a small recovery post of two or three vehicles was hard to accommodate in the sea of mud, where the divisional artillery, too, was competing for the few possible pieces of open ground at the sides of the road. The only consolation was that German shells, plunging deep into the semi-liquid ground, often failed to explode or had their blast effectively muffled, so that it took a direct hit to do real damage. Under these circumstances of nearly-impossible endeavour, the R.E.M.E. units, working prodigious hours in the driving rain, through slipping, crawling columns of men and lorries, carried out 339 vehicle recoveries in the first week of October alone.

For the troops in the line, the most difficult problem was that of handing over a section of the front to another unit. This was an operation which had received scant attention at army training establishments, but in the central Apennines the movement of one battalion forward and another back, at virtually the same time and along the same stretch of inadequate road, could result in chaos. The problem here was solved in a way quite revolutionary in the British Army, where a unit's list of supplies and equipment had always been as jealously guarded as its mess silver or its battle trophies. A scheme was evolved by which the unit moving out of the line left its stores, weapons, and ammunition behind for the relieving battalion to take over, and in turn picked up the same equipment left by the relieving battalion farther back.[11]

Both the British and Indian infantry divisions were using mules on a considerable scale. A Mule Corps of 30,000 animals had been raised in Italy, with mules coming from Sicily, Cyprus, and even some from South America. The organization of so many animals under modern battle conditions required a flexible extension of old military techniques, if the troops in the line were to be properly supplied. In 8th Indian Division, operating in the even more trackless and desolate country to the right of the British 1st Division, mule transport was brought to a fine art.

To lift one day's supplies and ammunition for a brigade group in the line required three-and-a-quarter mule companies – a total of about 1,000 mules. A fair average daily march for a mule was sixteen miles, so that any force operating solely on a pack basis could not cover more than eight miles in a day.[12]

Mules, like men, fell sick from time to time, and to the rear of the division a central mule camp was established, with an extensive veterinary section near by. To those looking out across the mud where thousands of animals were penned, and where columns of mules arrived and departed beside the lines of tents, the scene seemed to have gone back in time to the Crimea of almost a century before. Only the roar of an aircraft or the buzzing of the ubiquitous jeeps were a reminder that this was war in 1944.

This was the general logistic background against which Loewen's 1st Division launched its assault against Monte Ceco early in October. The attack began on 3 October, when the Sherwood Foresters of Brigadier Peter St Clair-Ford's 3rd Infantry Brigade got a footing on the mountain by an attack in drenching rain, but were driven off by a sharp German counter-attack after only a few hours. The Foresters attacked again next day, but were again stopped on the slopes. An attempt by another battalion of the brigade, the 1st King's Shropshire Light Infantry, supported by the medium machine guns of the 2nd/7th Middlesex, reached to within 300 yards of the summit, but could get no farther.

St Clair-Ford's hopes now rested with his remaining battalion,

the 1st Duke of Wellington's Regiment. Their first attempt
ended in bloody frustration. A heavy covering barrage was
fired, timed to end just before the leading troops ran into the
assault. However, climbing desperately upwards through thick
mist and heavy rain, the battalion took longer than estimated
to get into position. Exactly on time, the barrage stopped. A
few minutes later, the tired infantry reached the crest, but by
then the Germans, swarming back into their positions, cut them
down with withering fire. Protected by artillery fire brought as
near to their positions as possible, the remainder of the battalion
dug in a bare fifty yards from the crest.

The commanding officer of the Duke's, Lieutenant-Colonel
Shiel, decided to make another attempt on 8 October, not this
time by night, when he felt that the Germans would expect it,
but in the early afternoon when after long observation of their
positions, he had decided that they rested.[13] There was furious
hand-to-hand fighting when he took his battalion into the
attack, helped by the ferocious courage of a single private,
Richard Burton, who personally killed or wounded the crews of
three Spandau positions until the leading platoons had a firm
hold along the crest. After five days of bitter fighting, Monte
Ceco was captured. The weary British infantry moved north to
the next ridge, shuffling and reshuffling battalions and brigades
to give men the greatest possible amount of rest.

For his bravery, Private Burton was awarded the Victoria
Cross. Lieutenant-Colonel Shiel did not know, however, of the
honour won by his battalion. He was killed by a final burst of
Spandau fire as his men mopped up the last Germans on the
Ceco summit.

22

Time Runs Out

In spite of the determination and courage of the American and British infantry in the streaming, sodden mountains and water-logged Romagna, by the last half of October, Alexander was running out of time. The autumn was now well advanced, and it was becoming increasingly clear that far from reaching Vienna, or even the Venice–Padua–Verona–Brescia line laid down in Wilson's directive of 5 July, the Allied armies would be lucky to get as far as the Po. Alexander's prediction to Wilson that 'we may not be just quite strong enough to carry it through' was coming bitterly true.

Yet early in October, the dream of a British Army advancing into Austria, which was always at the background of Wilson's and Alexander's strategy, received one more genuflexion from the planners. This time it involved a landing on Yugoslavia, and an advance up the Yugoslav Adriatic coast.

'Ever since the fall of Rome,' reported Alexander, 'I had borne in mind the possibility of forcing an entry into Austria through the Ljubljana Gap, a stroke which might even lead us to Vienna. Before the withdrawal of troops for the invasion of southern France it had seemed likely that this could be achieved by an overland advance through north-eastern Italy, possibly assisted by an amphibious operation against Austria or Trieste. With our present reduced strength, and especially after the losses and exhaustion incurred in the battles for the Apennines, it would be impossible, after breaking through into the Po Valley, to be certain of destroying the enemy south of the river and I should have to face a succession of hard-fought frontal attacks against a still-powerful enemy on the many river lines of

Venetia: the Adige, the Brenta, the Piave, the Tagliamento, and the Isonzo.'[1]

If this happened, of course, Alexander would see the ruin of both his short-term object of the campaign – the destruction of the German armies – and his long-term object – Vienna. He would also be failing to play even his thankless role of containing the maximum number of German troops, since he himself now calculated that the Germans would need only eleven divisions to hold the shortened Adige line.

'Rather than accept this,' he wrote, 'it would be better to make a two-handed attack up the two opposite coasts (he means the Adriatic coasts of both Italy and Yugoslavia), designed to meet at the head of the Adriatic. This would undoubtedly tie down more German forces than a frontal attack on the Adige and would give more scope for a flexible strategy and a greater chance for a decisive success. . . . It is interesting to speculate on what the results might have been if the plan had been carried into effect. The terrain of Dalmatia is rugged and unpromising for operations, and the maintenance of the force would have met serious difficulties. On the other hand, the relatively weak and inexperienced German troops would probably have offered only an ineffectual resistance to six veteran divisions of Eighth Army, assisted by strongly reinforced Partisan formations, and an entry into Austria might have been possible before the general capitulation.'

However, like all the other plans which, even implicitly, embraced the word 'Vienna', it was not to be. Alexander met Wilson on 2 October, and the plan was discussed between them there, and at later conferences. Briefly, it envisaged that Clark's Fifth Army, reinforced by the Polish Corps, which would have been unsuitable for political reasons to be employed in the Balkans, would remain in Italy, to contain the Germans on the Adige line. Meanwhile Eighth Army would seize ports in Yugoslavia – Split, Sibenik and Zadar were named – and use them as a springboard for an advance early in 1945 to Ljubljana and Fiume.

The planning went on, but the circumstances changed. Even as it was being discussed, Alexander's weakened armies received another blow, when the crisis in Greece meant that he had hurriedly to transfer the 4th Indian Division and the Greek Mountain Brigade from Italy to Athens. This was a bad blow for McCreery's Eighth Army, and indirectly a bad one for Clark's Fifth, too, for during October the roles of the two armies had become reversed.

One limited objective was now immediately attainable as a reward for all the blood that had been spent in the past two months. That objective was Bologna, and it was clear that Clark, only eight miles away in the mountains, had a much better chance of reaching it than McCreery, nearly sixty miles away down Route 9, with a series of rivers to cross. Thus, in effect, the role of Eighth Army at this point was necessarily secondary, and McCreery, however hopefully and vigorously he might plan, would really be confined to holding the attention of the maximum number of German troops while the U.S. II Corps led the last desperate Fifth Army bid to reach Bologna. If the Americans were to succeed, McCreery must try to stop Kesselring from moving more troops from the plains to the central Apennines.

Kesselring himself was clear about where the main danger lay.

'From the middle of October,' he said later, 'the situation south of Bologna gave matter for grave concern. If one or another sector of the Po plain between Bologna and the Adriatic were lost, it might be of secondary importance, but if the front south of Bologna could not be held, then all our positions in the Po plain east of Bologna were automatically gone – in which event they must be evacuated in good time so as at least to save the troops and material.'[2]

This was an anxious time for the German command, and yet it soon became clear that circumstances were working for them, for in spite of McCreery's new ideas and less orthodox approach, Eighth Army simply could not hold the attention of all the Germans in front of it.

As soon as he assumed command, McCreery had cancelled earlier orders by Leese which had been intended to bring the now-reinforced Polish Corps forward along the coast. Instead, less inhibited by the idea of mountain warfare than was Leese, and more conscious of the hill-fighting qualities of his Indian divisions, he switched the Poles to the mountains on the left of the Eighth Army front, eventually directing them towards Forli on Route 9.

Meanwhile, the almost complete destruction by the October rain of the army communications in the Romagna had halted the Canadians at the Fiumicino for the first ten days of October. McCreery therefore decided that the best line of attack was through the foothills where Keightley's V Corps was advancing. The 10th Indian Division was brought under Keightley's command, relieving 4th Indian. On 5 October, the Indians, moving dexterously through the kind of country where they had been specially trained to fight, seized two crossings high up the swollen Fiumicino, crossed the river, and two days later stormed Monte Farneto, the main German position covering Cesena on Route 9.

The line of the Fiumicino was now turned and the Germans – Baade's 90th Panzer Grenadiers – pulled back hastily along Route 9, abandoning Savignano to the 56th British Infantry Division. Eighth Army had advanced twenty miles up Route 9 towards Bologna, and yet, paradoxically, the German situation was rapidly improving. As Kesselring had correctly appreciated, it did him little harm to lose positions between Bologna and the Adriatic. Indeed, the farther Eighth Army advanced, the more his own front shortened and the nearer and more compact it became in relation to the defences opposing Clark in front of Bologna. In contrast, across the flooded wastes of the Romagna, Eighth Army's line lengthened, and the problems of supply along sodden roads became more and more difficult.

Armour was at a discount. The Divisional Cavalry of the New Zealand Division, which had been envisaged as flying across the Lombardy Plain in pursuit of a disorganized foe, was now, despairingly, taken out of its armoured cars and converted into much more vital infantry. On the day before its cavalry career was ended, a trooper wrote:

'It was our day in the country we had dreamed of as ideal for armoured cars. How different proved the reality. We hacked down trees to fill ditches. Axle deep, we just got up the very slight inclines beyond, and ahead was another ditch to

cross. . . .'[3] On 21 October, McCreery reached the line of the
Savio at Cesena, and the Germans stood firm again. Eighth
Army was still forty-seven miles from Bologna.

★ ★ ★

Clark, however, could almost see the city, and the four weary
infantry divisions of the U.S. II Corps, forming the spearhead of
Fifth Army, gathered themselves on 16 October for a last effort
to take it.

'We were so close to the Po Valley,' Clark remembered later,
'that every day we would tell ourselves: "Now if we can just
push on a little farther today, then we'll make it. We are right at
the edge of success." It is difficult now to explain the agonizing
hope we then felt that "just another mile", or "just a few miles",
would do the job. . . .'[4]

The shrinking of the German front as the right wing of
Tenth Army and the left wing of Fourteenth Army slowly withdrew towards Bologna, however, gave von Vietinghoff the
means of reinforcing danger points more quickly than when the
armies had been farther apart. He now drew from the Romagna
the three best divisions in either German Army – the 29th
Panzer Grenadier, the 90th Panzer Grenadier, and the 1st
Parachute. Stationed on Tenth Army's right wing, these
divisions stood between Clark and the plains. (Map 6.)

At this point, too, the great Allied advantage in artillery,
which was sometimes the decisive factor in supporting infantry
forward through the maze of enemy mountain positions, was
suddenly lost, while the German command was scraping up
every gun it could find, and the volume of German fire was increasing day by day. The ponderous logistics of global war had
apparently at this point demanded, in view of the inexorable
approach of eventual German defeat, a world-wide reduction in
ammunition production.[5] The Italian front was not the only one
to feel the blow, but it was the only one in which the loss
of ammunition was almost certainly decisive. A glance at
the ammunition expenditure figures for the U.S. 91st Infantry Division, attacking at this time just north of Livergnano,

reveals just what the shortage meant for the troops on the ground.

During the last week of October, the division was given an allowance of 7,000 rounds of high explosive and 700 of white phosphorus, giving its ordinary artillery battalions an average of a little over 360 rounds each a day. This was a derisory allowance compared with the scale of fire support previously given; indeed, the entire firing for the last week of October did not equal the amount fired during one eight-hour period on 2 October, when the division was fighting in front of Loiano.

By contrast, the Germans were pouring shells on the American infantry. During the last fortnight of October, there were only four days in which the American positions were not struck by more than 1,000 shells, and on the 20th, in the middle of the last desperate effort to get to Bologna, the Germans fired 4,700 rounds.[6] In the rain and mist, air support could not even begin to redress the balance. The one unquestioned Allied advantage was gone.

For eleven days more, with the odds against them growing taller and taller, the American infantry struggled towards Bologna and Route 9. Both the 34th and the 91st Divisions were unable to make real progress – the 91st, in particular, was facing tremendous difficulties in bringing forward anti-tank guns and tank destroyers to support the infantry. Where the powerful prime movers and bull-dozers failed to haul and nudge the guns into position in the mud, the desperate artillerymen finally tried oxen, but even so it took the entire night of 16 October to get one anti-tank gun into position north of Livergnano.[7]

Better progress was made on the right, where Kendall's 88th Division seized Monte Grande on 20 October after a heavy bombardment from the division's carefully hoarded ammunition. Monte Grande was only four-and-a-half miles from Route 9, and when this American success was followed three days later by the storming of Monte Spaduro by the British 78th Division, it seemed for a moment as though Fifth Army might yet win through.

Yet though the arrows on the map showing the Allied advance

were reaching nearer and nearer to Route 9, they were mislead-
ing. The four-and-a-half miles between the Americans and
success were of broken, difficult country, and they were now
packed with first-class German troops. Fifth Army was beating
impotently on a door which it no longer had the strength to push
open.

Since the II Corps offensive began on 10 September, the four
American divisions alone had lost 15,716 men in killed and
wounded. More than 5,000 had fallen in the 88th Division
alone. Kendall was now more than 1,200 men below strength,
and there was no chance of Eisenhower's promised reinforcements reaching him in time.[8] In the mud and the rain, the
hollow-eyed, exhausted infantry gradually stopped moving forward. Almost tacitly, the offensive was abandoned. By 28
October, Keyes issued written orders to all his divisions to go
over to the defensive, but in reality the main drive of the corps
had virtually stopped two days before then. Clark wrote later:
'The Fifth Army's offensive did not stop with any definite
setback or on any specific date. It merely ground slowly to a
halt because men could not fight any longer against the steadily
increasing enemy reinforcements on our front. In other words,
our drive died out, slowly and painfully, and only one long
stride from success, like a runner who collapses reaching for, but
not quite touching, the tape at the finishing line. At the time I
felt that with a month of rest we might yet be able to break into
the Po Valley before winter clamped down on the Apennines.
After all the effort that had been expended, after all the
casualties we had suffered, it seemed almost impossible to give
up the idea of completing the breakthrough that autumn . . . at
the end of October, a definite date was set for renewal of both
the Fifth and Eighth Army attacks towards Bologna, but we
never kept the date. . . .'[9]

Sixty-four days had passed since Leese's three army corps had
rumbled across the River Metauro to open the Gothic Line
campaign; and after all the blood and toil, the two armies were
stopped at the very frontier of victory. Ahead of them now lay
what they had fought so hard to avoid – winter in the mountains, and a long wait until the spring sunshine hardened the
roads so that the big grey Shermans and Churchills of the

armoured formations could emerge from their camouflage nets and begin once more to seek a break in the German front.

This was not realized at once. Plans for new offensives were made over the next few weeks, and Eighth Army continued what was basically a subsidiary drive up the Adriatic, capturing Ravenna on 5 December. The ammunition shortage alone, however, made any lengthy operation impossible; on 13 November Alexander estimated to Wilson that Eighth Army would have enough shells for only a fifteen-day offensive in December, and Fifth Army for a bare ten days.[10]

As the Germans established themselves along the floodbanks of the Senio for the rest of the winter, even the prospect of an immediate, face-saving success by the capture of Bologna receded from any realistic calculations. The city, which had been expected to be reached by Hull's division in early September, did not fall until 21 April, at the climax of the Allies' triumphant spring offensive, and only eleven days before the German armies in Italy surrendered.

Alexander himself had virtually admitted failure by a broadcast to the partisans on 13 November. They were ordered to call off large-scale operations, and go on the defensive. This was a clear indication that Alexander had little hope of further success in the immediate future, and although the message was clearly sent with humanitarian motives, it caused fury and consternation among the partisan bands. The German-Italian offensive against them was able to deploy more troops now that the situation in the Apennines had quietened down; it was impossible for thousands of men to return to their homes as though nothing had happened; and their supplies were now threatened by a rapid rise in prices which swept through the ramshackle economy of Mussolini's Salo Republic.[11]

They also fiercely resented the fact that the announcement was made in a broadcast which the Germans, too, could hear. Among the Communists, there were wild theories that the Allies had deliberately broken off the offensive to allow the Germans to exterminate the Communist resistance which might later be an embarrassment to the victorious Western powers.[12]

For both Allied troops and partisans, a bitter winter waited. Kesselring and his armies had put up one of the sternest struggles in German military history. He had kept his promise to Hitler: he had halted the Allies and helped to give the Führer time. What the Führer did with the time was outside the scope of Kesselring's command.

A last irony remained. Kesselring was not in a position to enjoy his success. On 25 October, just as Clark was making up his mind to call off the Fifth Army offensive, the German commander, driving down Route 9 past a column of troops, collided with a gun coming out of a side-road. He received severe head injuries, and was in hospital for three months, during which von Vietinghoff took over the army group. While Kesselring waited for his injuries to heal, he could reflect that, as he claimed after the war, 'to hold the Italian front under the circumstances described, when the enemy had complete air supremacy, will be seen as the maximum attainable result by any objective student of history'.

Epilogue

There is a military cemetery on the slopes of the Coriano Ridge, where hundreds of soldiers lie, who fell in the battle for this quiet countryside. To stand there in the dusk is, inevitably, to wonder about the campaign in which they died. The rows of white crosses stretch away into the shadows, each with a unit crest, a name, and an inscription chosen by someone who cared for the man who lies below. There are other cemeteries in northern Italy – American, British, Polish, Greek – but this burial ground has a special significance, for it was here that the autumn campaign was decided.

These are the men who tried their best, and did not live to know whether they had won or lost. Most of those here are British, Canadian, or New Zealanders, though there must also be some of the Germans who defended the ridge, for every so often in the neat rows is the grave of an unknown man with above it the words:

'A soldier of the Second World War, known unto God.'

The thoughts one has in such a place seem trite beside the fact of what happened to these young men. For them, the world stopped at Coriano. The decisive autumn victory which they sought was not won, and so it would be easy to decide that they died in vain.

Well, why *did* they die? A cynic might say that they died for Vienna, and their army did not get there. That would be a foolish over-simplification, but not without an element of truth. There remains the other justification, more often advanced, that the whole of the Italian campaign was a vast holding operation, engaging the attention of considerable enemy forces which might have been invaluable elsewhere. Alexander himself holds firmly to this view, as do many other Allied generals. Disconcertingly, Kesselring held it, too. He said after the war that he had played his part by pinning down Allied troops. He won time for Hitler – and Hitler used it to gas countless thousands of people in his insane race-war.

The questions raised by the Italian campaign in general, and perhaps most of all by the battles for the Gothic Line, cannot be answered while the war itself is still close to the lives of those who write and read about it. A campaign has four dimensions: the casualties, the ground gained or lost, the immediate effect upon the opposing forces, and the long-term effect upon history. The mysterious fourth dimension may not be measured for many years.

The men who led the formations which clashed in the autumn battles are almost without exception passing from the active scene. Alexander, after becoming Governor-General of Canada and later Churchill's Minister of Defence, still takes some part in public affairs; Leese grows cacti at his home in Shropshire; Mark Clark runs a military academy in South Carolina. Harding became Governor of Cyprus during the emergency, and also Chief of the Imperial General Staff. Hull also became C.G.S., and went on to the peak of his profession, being promoted Field-Marshal in 1965 on appointment as Chief of the Defence Staff.

Death has hit at both sides, but more often on the German than the British. Two of the staunchest opponents died on the very edge of peace: Hawkesworth of 46th Division as he sailed home on a troopship, and Baade of 90th Panzer Grenadiers, killed in an air attack on the last day of the war while on the way to his estate in Holstein. Kesselring, found guilty of responsibility for the shooting of Italian hostages, was sentenced to death in 1947 by a military court. Both Alexander and Leese spoke out for him. Evidence was given at his trial that Alexander said that he had fought fairly, and Leese said afterwards that he was 'very sad' at the verdict and that Kesselring was a 'very gallant fighter . . . controlled his men well and fought a chivalrous battle'. Harding was commanding in Italy when the sentence was laid before him for confirmation, and he commuted it to life imprisonment. Kesselring was released in

1952, and died in 1960. Von Vietinghoff died in 1952, and von Senger in 1963.

Soon the war will recede over the immediate horizon of history, and there will be new judgements on those who fought it, high and low. For those who served and died in the polyglot armies in Italy, there is a poem by T. S. Eliot which says all that can yet be said:

> This was not your land or ours: but a village in the
>   Midlands
> And one in the Five Rivers, may have the same
>   memories.
> Let those who go home tell the same story of you –
> Of action with a common purpose, action
> None the less fruitful if neither you nor I
> Know until the judgement after death,
> What is the fruit of action.

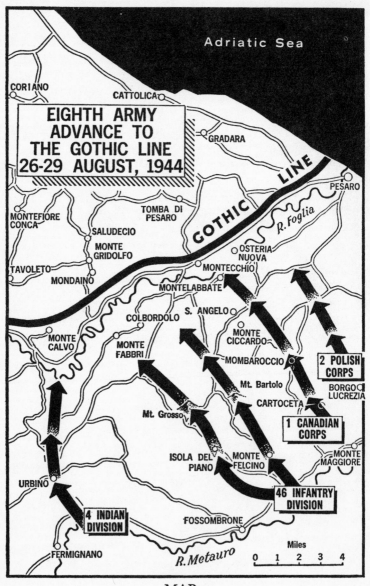

Adriatic Sea

CORIANO

CATTOLICA

GRADARA

GOTHIC LINE

PESARO

EIGHTH ARMY
ADVANCE TO
THE GOTHIC LINE
26-29 AUGUST, 1944

MONTEFIORE
CONCA

TOMBA DI
PESARO

SALUDECIO

MONTE
GRIDOLFO

TAVOLETO

MONDAINO

MONTE
CALVO

R. Foglia

OSTERIA
NUOVA

MONTECCHIO

MONTELABBATE

COLBORDOLO

S. ANGELO

MONTE FABBRI

MONTE
CICCARDO

MOMBAROCCIO

Mt. Bartolo

CARTOCETA

2 POLISH
CORPS

BORGO
LUCREZIA

Mt. Grosso

1 CANADIAN
CORPS

ISOLA DEL
PIANO

MONTE
FELCINO

MONTE
MAGGIORE

URBINO

46 INFANTRY
DIVISION

4 INDIAN
DIVISION

FOSSOMBRONE

FERMIGNANO

R. Metauro

Miles

0   1   2   3   4

MAP 1

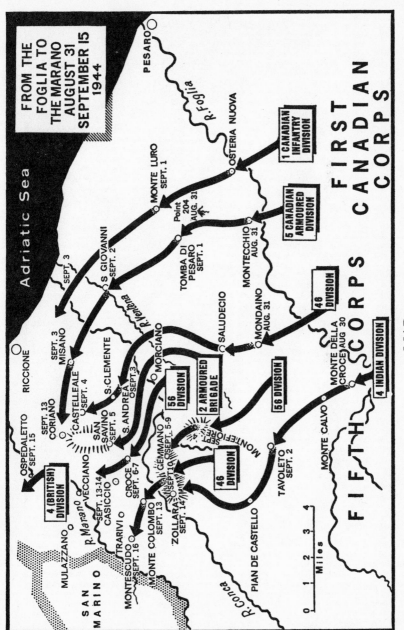

FROM THE
FOGLIA TO
THE MARANO
AUGUST 31
SEPTEMBER 15
1944

Adriatic Sea

PESARO

R. Foglia

OSTERIA NUOVA

MONTE LURO
SEPT. 1

Point
204
AUG. 31

TOMBA DI
PESARO
SEPT. 1

S. GIOVANNI
SEPT. 2

SEPT. 3

MONTECCHIO
AUG. 31

R. Ventena

SEPT. 3
MISANO

MONDAINO
AUG. 31

SALUDECIO

RICCIONE

SEPT. 3

SEPT. 4
CASTELLEALE
SEPT. 4

S. CLEMENTE

S. ANDREA
SEPT. 3

MORCIANO

MONTE DELLA
CROCE) AUG. 30

1 CANADIAN
INFANTRY
DIVISION

5 CANADIAN
ARMOURED
DIVISION

46
DIVISION

4 INDIAN DIVISION

FIRST
CANADIAN
CORPS

SEPT. 13
CORIANO

SAN
SAVINO
SEPT. 5

56
DIVISION

2 ARMOURED
BRIGADE

56 DIVISION

MONTE CALVO

OSPEDALETTO
SEPT. 15

4 (BRITISH)
DIVISION

VECCIANO

SEPT. 13-14
CASICCIO

CROCE
SEPT. 6-7

SAN GEMMANO
SEPT. 5-9

ZOLLARA
SEPT. 14

SEPT. 10

MONTEFIORE
SEPT.

46
DIVISION

TAVOLETO
SEPT. 2

FIFTH
CORPS

SAN
MARINO

MULAZZANO

R. Marano

TRARIVI

MONTESCUDO
SEPT. 16

MONTE COLOMBO
SEPT. 13

PIAN DE CASTELLO

R. Conca

0   1   2   3   4
Miles

MAP 2

RIMINI AND
THE ROMAGNA
SEPT 17 –
OCT 1 1944

Adriatic Sea

MAP 2

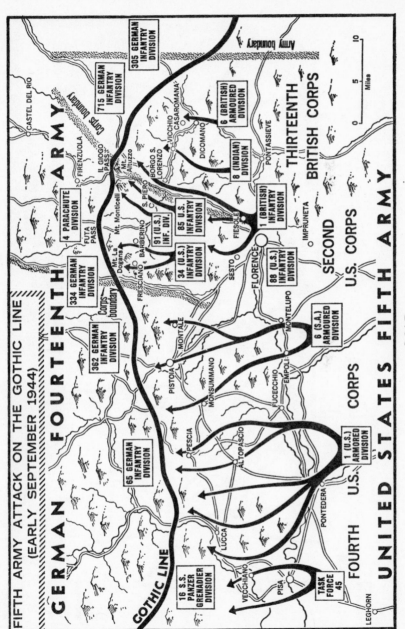

FIFTH ARMY ATTACK ON THE GOTHIC LINE
(EARLY SEPTEMBER 1944)

MAP 4

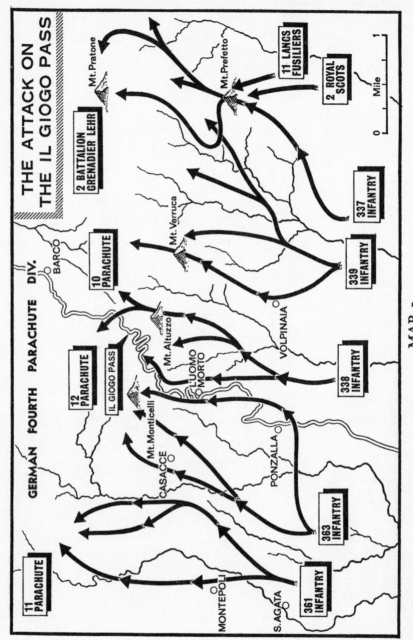

THE ATTACK ON
THE IL GIOGO PASS

GERMAN FOURTH PARACHUTE DIV.

11 PARACHUTE

12 PARACHUTE

IL GIOGO PASS

10 PARACHUTE

2 BATTALION GRENADIER LEHR

11 LANCS FUSILIERS

2 ROYAL SCOTS

337 INFANTRY

339 INFANTRY

338 INFANTRY

363 INFANTRY

361 INFANTRY

Mt. Pratone

Mt. Prefetto

Mt. Verruca

Mt. Altuzzo

L'UOMO MORTO

Mt. Monticelli

BARCO

VOLPINAIA

PONZALLA

CASACCE

MONTEPOLI

S. AGATA

0   Mile   1

MAP 5

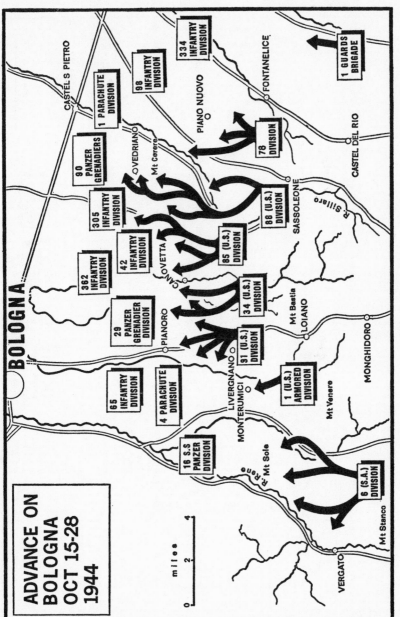

ADVANCE ON BOLOGNA OCT 15-28 1944

miles
0 2 4

MAP 6

BOLOGNA

CASTEL S PIETRO

1 PARACHUTE DIVISION

90 PANZER GRENADIERS

98 INFANTRY DIVISION

334 INFANTRY DIVISION

1 GUARDS BRIGADE

FONTANELICE

CASTEL DEL RIO

PIANO NUOVO

OVEDRIANO

Mt Cerere

305 INFANTRY DIVISION

42 INFANTRY DIVISION

362 INFANTRY DIVISION

29 PANZER GRENADIER DIVISION

78 DIVISION

88 (U.S.) DIVISION

SASSOLEONE

R Sillaro

85 (U.S.) DIVISION

CANOVETTA

PIANORO

34 (U.S.) DIVISION

Mt Bastia

LOIANO

65 INFANTRY DIVISION

4 PARACHUTE DIVISION

91 (U.S.) DIVISION

LIVERGNANO

MONTERUMICI

1 (U.S.) ARMORED DIVISION

Mt Venere

MONGHIDORO

16 S.S PANZER DIVISION

Mt Sole

R Reno

6 (S.A.) DIVISION

Mt Stanco

VERGATO

APPENDIX A

Order of Battle Allied Armies in Italy on 25th August 1944 down to and including divisions

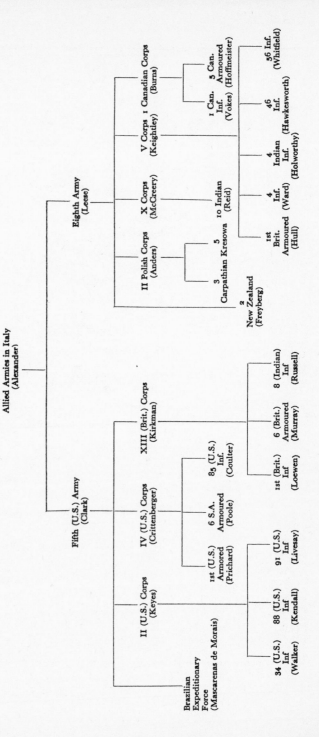

APPENDIX B

ARMY GROUP C

Order of Battle as at 25th August 1944 down to and including divisions

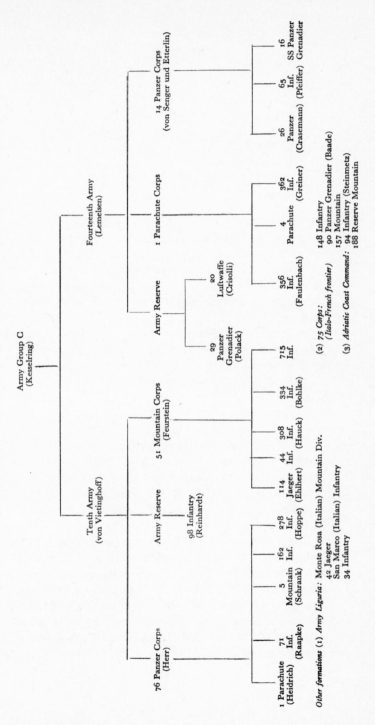

Army Group C (Kesselring)

Tenth Army (von Vietinghoff) — Fourteenth Army (Lemelsen)

Tenth Army (von Vietinghoff)

76 Panzer Corps (Herr)
- 1 Parachute (Heidrich)
- 71 Inf. (Raapke)
- 5 Mountain (Schrank)
- 162 Inf.
- 278 Inf. (Hoppe)

Army Reserve
- 98 Infantry (Reinhardt)

51 Mountain Corps (Feurstein)
- 114 Jaeger (Ehlhert)
- 44 Inf.
- 308 Inf. (Hauck)
- 334 Inf. (Bohlke)
- 715 Inf.

Fourteenth Army (Lemelsen)

Army Reserve
- 29 Panzer Grenadier (Polack)
- 20 Luftwaffe (Crisolli)

1 Parachute Corps
- 356 Inf. (Faulenbach)
- 4 Parachute
- 362 Inf. (Greiner)

14 Panzer Corps (von Senger und Etterlin)
- 26 Panzer (Crasemann)
- 65 Inf. (Pfeiffer)
- 16 SS Panzer Grenadier

Other formations (1) *Army Liguria:* Monte Rosa (Italian) Mountain Div.
42 Jaeger
San Marco (Italian) Infantry
34 Infantry

(2) *75 Corps:*
(Italo-French frontier)
148 Infantry
90 Panzer Grenadier (Baade)
157 Mountain

(3) *Adriatic Coast Command:* 94 Infantry (Steinmetz)
188 Reserve Mountain

Appendix C
Churchill and Vienna

Churchill's reasons for desiring a British advance upon Vienna have been the subject of a great deal of controversy. Churchill-orientated commentators of the immediate post-war years, particularly British ones, saw his motives as generated by a far-sighted realization of the Soviet threat in Eastern Europe, and the pressing need to counter it as far as possible. Of latter years, doubt has crept in.

'The policy of forestalling Soviet Russia in the Balkans was an invention of the post-war years, partly encouraged by Churchill himself when he became anti-Russian in 1946,' writes Professor A. J. P. Taylor. 'There is no contemporary evidence for it. On the contrary, all the strategies – Soviet, British, and American – were designed with the sole object of defeating Germany, however much they differed on the way to do it. . . .'[1]

This view has American support. Stimson, the U.S. War Secretary, said after the war that never at any point of his long, fierce dispute with Churchill over the question of a Mediterranean strategy did the British Prime Minister advance as an argument the need to block Russia in Central or Eastern Europe.[2]

It is true that there is no documentary evidence that such a consideration was urged by Churchill upon Roosevelt, but this is not surprising. Churchill could hardly bring this up for discussion at any Big Three meeting at which Stalin was present, and he was soon made aware that Roosevelt preferred to sit in the middle of the trio, and was unwilling to adopt any posture which might make Stalin think that America was siding with Britain against Russia. In view of the extent of Russian distrust of Britain, Churchill would have been unlikely to commit to paper such a thought about an ally, especially if that paper was going to the United States. Even Churchill's old companion Smuts, writing to him at the end of August 1944, was very circumspect in warning him that 'from now on, it would be wise to keep a very sharp eye on all matters bearing on the future settlement of Europe. This is the crucial issue on which the future of the world for generations will depend. . . .' Vague though this injunction was, it was answered next day by Churchill's own letter about 'a dash with armoured cars' to Vienna[3] (see Chapter 5). Both men must surely have had the Russians in mind.

It would be natural, then, if Churchill stuck to purely military arguments in urging the case of Alexander and his armies. However, he was aware of the Communist threat in the Balkans long before 'he became anti-Russian in 1946'. He showed this late in 1944, when he moved swiftly and ruthlessly, against mounting opposition at home and in the United States, to crush the pro-Communist insurrection which threatened to take over Greece. To do this, in fact, he ignored purely military considerations, and withdrew vital divisions from his cherished offensive in Italy (see Chapter 22). For although Stalin made no overt move to help the Greek Communists, and seemed to be sticking to the 'spheres of influence' agreement* reached in Moscow that October,[4] Churchill thought he saw clearly what would happen if the Greek Communists succeeded. He wrote to Smuts on 22 December 1944:

'. . . if the powers of evil prevail in Greece, as is quite likely, we must be prepared for a quasi-Bolshevised Balkans peninsula, and this may spread to Italy and Hungary. I therefore see great perils to the world in these quarters. . . .'[5]

No doubt, however, there was another consideration. The Italian theatre of war had a British Supreme Commander. When the Allies eventually reached Berlin, the Americans or the Russians would take the lion's share of the credit. But if Churchill's favourite general, Alexander, took Vienna, that

---

* Under this, Britain and Russia were to share out the 'say' in Europe as: Rumania 90% Russian; Greece 90% British; Bulgaria 75% Russian; Hungary and Yugoslavia 50-50.

would be a tremendous fillip to British prestige. It would be wrong to dismiss this as a dream of empty glory. No one was better aware than the British Prime Minister of how prestige might be used as a lever to arrange the world to better advantage.

References:

1. A. J. P. Taylor: *English History 1914–45*, O.U.P., 1966, pp. 576–7
2. Henry L. Stimson: *On Active Service in Peace and War*, Hutchinson, 1949, pp. 236–7
3. Churchill, *The Second World War*, Cassell, 1948–54, VI, pp. 90–91.
4. Churchill, VI, p. 198.
5. Churchill, VI, p. 270.

NOTES TO CHAPTER ONE

1. Joseph Goebbels: *The Goebbels Diaries*, Hamish Hamilton, 1948, pp. 343-4
2. Albert Kesselring: *The Memoirs of Field-Marshal Kesselring*, William Kimber, 1953, p. 182
3. *Command Decisions*, ed. Greenfield, Methuen, 1960, p. 228
4. Goebbels, p. 341
5. Goebbels, pp. 344-5
6. Siegfried Westphal: *The German Army in The West*, Cassell, 1951, p. 153
7. Kesselring, p. 184
8. Walter Warlimont: *Inside Hitler's Headquarters*, Weidenfeld and Nicolson, 1964, p. 382
9. Warlimont, pp. 383-4
10. *The Rommel Papers*, ed. Liddell Hart, Collins, 1953, p. 446
11. Westphal, pp. 154, 164
12. Hitler briefing conference, 31 August 1944, quoted Warlimont, pp. 450-51
13. Winston Churchill: *Second World War*, IV, Cassell, 1948-54, p. 586
14. Alanbrooke Diaries: quoted Arthur Bryant, *Triumph in the West*, Collins, 1959, p. 555
15. Henry L. Stimson: *On Active Service in War and Peace*, Hutchinson, 1949, p. 218
16. Stimson, p. 228
17. Ernest J. King: 'Joint Chiefs of Staff Organization World War II' (Navy Department pamphlet quoted Hanson Baldwin's *Great Mistakes of the War*)
18. Alanbrooke Diaries: *Triumph in the West*, p. 27
19. Field-Marshal Montgomery: *Memoirs*, Collins, 1958, p. 195

NOTES TO CHAPTER TWO

1. Churchill, V, p. 74
2. Kesselring, p. 15
3. Westphal, p. 168

4. B. H. Liddell Hart: *The Other Side of the Hill*, Cassell, 1948 (interview with Westphal), p. 375

5. Alanbrooke Diaries: quoted *Turn of the Tide 1939–43*, Collins, 1957, pp. 107–8

6. Dwight D. Eisenhower: *Crusade in Europe*, Heinemann, 1949, p. 534, footnote 15 (see also p. 231)

7. Churchill, IV, p. 147

8. Churchill, V, pp. 430–31

9. Field-Marshal Alexander's Dispatch: 'The Allied Armies in Italy'; Appendix A (Order of Battle as at 25 August 1944)

10. Alexander Dispatch, Appendix B

11. Montgomery, p. 113

12. General Leese, conversation with the author

13. Alanbrooke Diaries: *Triumph in the West*, p. 216

14. Alanbrooke Diaries: *Triumph in the West*, pp. 221-2

15. Churchill, VI, p. 55

16. This exchange is fully quoted in Churchill, VI, Appendix C

17. Churchill, VI, p. 57

18. Alexander Dispatch, 2934

19. Alexander Dispatch, 2936 footnote

20. Alanbrooke Diaries: *Triumph in the West*, p. 222

21. Alexander Dispatch, 2936

22. Wynford Vaughan-Thomas: *Anzio*, Longmans, Green, 1961, Chapter 2

23. Kesselring, p. 223

24. Alexander Dispatch, 2936

NOTES TO CHAPTER THREE

1. Alexander Dispatch, 2390, footnote

2. Warlimont, pp. 430–31

3. Rommel Papers, p. 428

4. Frido von Senger und Etterlin: *Neither Fear nor Hope*, Macdonald, 1963, p. 241

5. Warlimont, p. 431

6. Kesselring, p. 207

7. G. W. L. Nicholson: '*The Canadians in Italy 1943–5*': *Official History of the Canadian Army Vol. II*, p. 495, quoting Appendix 801c to 51 Mountain Corps War Diary, 18 June 1944

8. Summarized Nicholson, pp. 494–7

9. Alexander Dispatch, 2941

10. Kesselring, p. 209

11. Alexander Dispatch, 2943
12. Nicholson, p. 491
13. General Leese, conversation with the author, and also Alexander Dispatch, 2943
14. Eric Linklater: *The Campaign in Italy*, H.M.S.O., 1951, p. 348
15. Field-Marshal Lord Harding, conversation with the author
16. Linklater, p. 349
17. Alexander Dispatch, 2943
18. Nicholson, p. 490
19. Martha Gellhorn: *The Face of War*, Rupert Hart-Davies, 1959, p. 168
20. R. F. H. Nalder: *The Royal Corps of Signals*, Royal Signals Institution, 1958, p. 402
21. Nicholson, p. 493, quoting telephone conversation 17 August 1944. Appendix 374b to Tenth Army War Diary 8
22. Alexander Dispatch, 2945
23. F. W. Deakin: *The Brutal Friendship: Mussolini, Hitler and the Fall of Italian Fascism*, Weidenfeld and Nicolson, 1962, p. 687
24. Deakin, p. 724
25. Kesselring, pp. 227–8
26. Von Senger, p. 277

NOTES TO CHAPTER FOUR

1. Alexander Dispatch, 2944
2. Alexander Dispatch, 2946
3. Nicholson, pp. 498–9
4. *Official History of New Zealand in the Second World War: '25th Battalion'*, by Sir Edward Puttick, pp. 485–6
5. *Swift and Bold: The Story of the King's Royal Rifle Corps in the Second World War*: account by Capt. J. P. Waterfield, Gale and Polden, 1949, pp. 204–5
6. Hugh Williamson: *The Fourth Division 1939–45*, Newman Neame, 1951, pp. 218–20
7. V Corps Planning Instruction: Operation Olive: 16 August 1944
8. Westphal, p. 155
9. Captured letter, quoted in *The Times*, 1 September 1944
10. Alexander Dispatch, 2946, and Nicholson, p. 504
11. *The Story of 46th Division* (printed in Austria), pp. 7–8
12. Squadron Leader J. F. Wallace, M.C., account given to the author

13. Lieut.-Col. G. R. Stevens: *Fourth Indian Division*, McLaren and Sons, Toronto, pp. 341–3, and D. Pal: *Indian Armed Forces in World War II: 'The Campaign in Italy 1943–45'*, p. 367
14. Churchill, VI, p. 107
15. North Irish Horse Battle Report: North Africa–Italy, p. 59
16. Nicholson, pp. 510–11
17. Appendix, p. 617 to Tenth Army War Diary 8, quoted Nicholson, p. 612

NOTES TO CHAPTER FIVE

1. John Ehrman: *Grand Strategy*, Vol. V, H.M.S.O., 1956, p. 391
2. Churchill, VI, p. 108
3. Churchill, VI, p. 91
4. Churchill, VI, p. 110
5. Alanbrooke Diaries, 4 July 1944, quoted *Triumph in the West*, p. 227
6. *Triumph in the West*, p. 256
7. Field-Marshal Lord Harding, conversation with the author
8. Nicholson, p. 513
9. *Fourth Indian Division*, p. 345
10. *The Royal Leicestershire Regiment*, 1928–56, p. 151
11. *History of the Sherwood Foresters*, 1919–57, p. 129
12. *The Royal Hampshire Regiment*, Vol. 3, p. 189

NOTES TO CHAPTER SIX

1. *Fourth Indian Division*, p. 341
2. *Fourth Indian Division*, p. 343
3. General Holworthy; unpublished diary supplied to the author
4. *Fourth Indian Division*, p. 346
5. Col. J. N. Mackay: *History of 7th Duke of Edinburgh's Own Gurkha Rifles*, William Blackwood and Sons Ltd., 1962, pp. 259–61; and *Fourth Indian Division*, p. 348
6. Nicholson, p. 515
7. Lieut.-Col. J. M. McAvity: *Lord Strathcona's Horse* (Royal Canadians), Toronto, 1947, p. 125
8. Nicholson, p. 523
9. Alexander Dispatch, 2946–2947
10. Nicholson, p. 525

NOTES TO CHAPTER SEVEN

1. *46th Division,* p. 77
2. General Whitfield, conversation with the author
3. General Keightley, conversation with the author
4. History of the 2nd/6th Battalion The Queen's Royal Regiment in the Italian Campaign, pamphlet, p. 33
5. General Whitfield, conversation with the author
6. 56th Division Operation Order No. 2, 3 September 1944
7. 56th Division Operation Order No. 3, 4 September 1944
8. General Whitfield, conversation with the author

NOTES TO CHAPTER EIGHT

1. Field-Marshal Hull, conversation with the author
2. *The 9th Queen's Royal Lancers 1936–45,* ed. Joan Bright, pp. 168–9
3. George F. Howe: *Battle History of the 1st (U.S.) Armored Division,* Compact Forces Press, Washington, 1954, Appendix III (figures from a paper prepared in the Office of the Chief of Military History)
4. Von Senger, p. 263

NOTES TO CHAPTER NINE

1. *9th Lancers,* pp. 180–81
2. Maj.-Gen. W. R. Beddington, *History of the Queen's Bays 1929–45,* Warren and Sons Ltd., The Wykeham Press, Winchester, p. 164
3. History of the 2nd Armoured Brigade: typescript, Imperial War Museum: tank state appendix
4. David Scott Daniell: *Fourth Hussar,* Gale and Polden, 1959, pp. 355–60
5. *Fourth Hussar,* p. 357

NOTES TO CHAPTER TEN

1. *Bays,* p. 165
2. 2nd Armoured Brigade typescript, 3
3. *The 10th Royal Hussars in the Second World War,* Gale and Polden, 1948, p. 140
4. *Bays,* p. 166

5. *10th Hussars*, pp. 140–41
6. 2nd Armoured Brigade typescript, 4
7. *Bays*, p. 168
8. *Bays:* Appendix E: Account of C Squadron's action at the San Clemente Ridge, 4 September 1944, written by Capt. J. C. McVail
9. *10th Hussars*, p. 141
10. *9th Lancers*, p. 184
11. 2nd Armoured Brigade typescript, 4 (tank state at last light, 4 September 1944)
12. Field-Marshal Hull, conversation with the author.
13. Nicholson, pp. 527–8

NOTES TO CHAPTER ELEVEN

1. 2nd Armoured Brigade typescript, 4
2. *9th Lancers*, p. 186
3. *9th Lancers*, p. 185
4. *Regimental Fire: The H.A.C. in World War II*, by Brig. R. F. Johnston, p. 149
5. *9th Lancers*, p. 187
6. Nicholson, p. 530
7. Lieut.-Col. S. J. Linden Kelly, conversation with the author
8. Nicholson, p. 530

NOTES TO CHAPTER TWELVE

1. General Whitfield, conversation with the author.
2. *The London Scottish in the Second World War*, ed. Brig. C. N. Barclay, William Clowes and Sons, p .134
3. C. Northcote Parkinson: *Always a Fusilier*, Sampson Low, 1949, pp. 212–13
4. Northcote Parkinson, p. 216
5. *London Scottish*, pp. 135–6
6. *The Oxfordshire and Buckinghamshire Light Infantry War Chronicle, Vol. IV*, p. 222, et seq.
7. General Whitfield, conversation with the author
8. *Oxford and Bucks IV*, p. 222, et seq.
9. General Whitfield, conversation with the author
10. *History of The Queen's Royal Regiment, Vol. VIII, 1924–48*
11. Roy E. Bullen: *History of the 2nd/7th Battalion The Queen's Royal Regiment*, p. 120

12. The 2nd/6th Battalion The Queen's Royal Regiment in the Italian Campaign, pamphlet, p. 34
13. *Queen's Royal Regiment*, Vol. VIII, pp. 430–33
14. *2nd/7th Queen's*, p. 120

NOTES TO CHAPTER THIRTEEN

1. Linklater, p. 363
2. Alexander Dispatch, 2947
3. Churchill, VI, p. 131
4. Ehrman, V, p. 510
5. Alanbrooke Diaries: *Triumph in the West*, p. 272
6. Churchill, VI, p. 137
7. Field-Marshal Wilson's Dispatch: Report by the Supreme Allied Commander Mediterranean to the Combined Chiefs of Staff on the Italian Campaign: Part III, p. 64

NOTES TO CHAPTER FOURTEEN

1. Nicholson, p. 533
2. *46th Division*, p. 79
3. General Whitfield, conversation with the author
4. *46th Division*, p. 80
5. 2nd/6th Queen's, p. 36
6. *Queen's Royal Regiment*, VIII, p. 433
7. *2nd/7th Queen's*, p. 122
8. Account by Capt. S. R. F. Elmslie, quoted in *The Tanks*, by B. H. Liddell Hart, Vol II, pp. 281–2
9. *2nd/7th Queen's*, pp. 122–3
10. Nicholson, p. 535
11. Nicholson, quoting Appendix 1015 to Tenth Army War Diary 8
12. Information from General Whitfield
13. Williamson, p. 224
14. *The Second Battalion The Royal Fusiliers: 1943–45*, Gale and Polden, p. 60
15. *Fourth Indian Division*, p. 224
16. *Fourth Indian Division*, p. 353
17. The 79th News; journal of the Queen's Own Cameron Highlanders: letter dated 12 November 1944: issue dated April 1945
18. Dr James Speer, conversation with the author

NOTES TO CHAPTER FIFTEEN

1. *46th Division*, p. 81
2. Northcote Parkinson, p. 226
3. *Fourth Indian Division*, pp. 225–6
4. *Official History of New Zealand in the Second World War: '25th Battalion'*, by Sir Edward Puttick: conversation quoted, pp. 483–4
5. *Fourth Indian Division*, p. 354
6. Holworthy diary entry, 18/19 September 1944
7. Pal, pp. 401–2

NOTES TO CHAPTER SIXTEEN

1. Von Senger, pp. 207–8
2. Nicholson, pp. 540–42
3. Diary of Capt. Stephen Owen, 145th Royal Armoured Corps Regiment, unpublished, supplied to the author
4. Telephone conversation 13 September 1944, quoted Nicholson, p. 548
5. *History of the 3rd Medium Regiment Royal Artillery 1939–45*, pp. 210–11
6. 2nd Armoured Brigade typescript
7. General Goodbody, conversation with the author
8. *9th Lancers*, p. 192
9. Account of the action at Point 153, by an officer of the Queen's Bays: included in 2nd Armoured Brigade typescript
10. *Swift and Bold*, p. 207

NOTES TO CHAPTER SEVENTEEN

1. General Goodbody, conversation with the author
2. 2nd Armoured Brigade typescript
3. Account by Bays' officer, already quoted.
4. *9th Lancers*, pp. 193–4
5. Appendix p. 1187 to Tenth Army War Diary 8, quoted Nicholson, p. 558
6. Alexander Dispatch, 2949
7. Alexander Dispatch, 2950
8. Appendix 1319 to Tenth Army War Diary 8, quoted Nicholson, p. 563

9. Owen diary, already quoted
10. Alexander Dispatch, 2950

NOTES TO CHAPTER EIGHTEEN

1. Lieut.-Col. Chester G. Starr: *From Salerno to the Alps; A History of the Fifth Army 1943–5*, Infantry Journal Press, Washington, 1948, p. 310
2. Charles B. MacDonald and Sidney B. Mathews: *U.S. Army in World War II: 'Three Battles: Arnaville, Altuzzo, and Schmidt'*, Office of the Chief of Military History, Washington, 1952, p. 106, quoting Fourteenth Army War Diary
3. *Fifth Army History*, p. 314
4. Major Robert A. Robbins: *The 91st Infantry Division in World War II*, Infantry Journal Press, Washington, 1947, p. 99
5. Paul L. Schultz: *The 85th Infantry Division in World War II*, Infantry Journal Press, Washington, 1948
6. Mathews: *Altuzzo*, p. 109
7. For a detailed description of the Company B action, see Mathews, *Altuzzo*, pp. 133–75
8. *91st Division*, p. 113
9. General Kirkman, conversation with the author

NOTES TO CHAPTER NINETEEN

1. *History of the 1st Division: Florence to Monte Grande: August 1944–January 1945*, printed in Cairo, p. 35
2. General Kirkman, conversation with the author, and also *1st Division*, p. 36
3. Mathews: *Altuzzo*, pp. 203–7
4. Mathews: *Altuzzo*, p. 239
5. George F. Howe: *Battle History of the 1st Armored Division*, Combat Forces Press, Washington, 1954, p. 383
6. Linklater, 378

NOTES TO CHAPTER TWENTY

1. *Fifth Army History*, p. 332
2. Rudolf Bohmler: *Monte Cassino: A German View*, Cassell, 1964, p. 286
3. *Fifth Army History*, p. 333
4. *Fifth Army History*, pp. 336–7

5. Roberto Battaglia: *Storia della Resistenza italiana*, Einaudi, Turin, 1953, p. 406
6. *Fifth Army History*, p. 338
7. Mark Clark: *Calculated Risk*, Harrap, 1951, p. 373
8. Wilson Dispatch, Part III, p. 75
9. Alexander Dispatch, 2949
10. *Official History of New Zealand in the Second World War: '21st Battalion'*, by J. F. Cody, pp. 375–6 (account by Lance-Corporal L. B. Crews)
11. *Official History of New Zealand in the Second World War: 'Divisional Cavalry'*, by R. J. M. Loughnan, p. 375
12. Cody, p. 496
13. Alexander Dispatch, 2951
14. Major P. L. Neild, letter written 29 September 1944, supplied to the author
15. See Alanbrooke diary entry for 14 September 1944 (*Triumph in the West*, p. 274)
16. Field-Marshal Earl Alexander: *Memoirs*, p. 137
17. Nicholson, pp. 570–71
18. Kesselring: *Memoirs*, p. 217
19. Clark, p. 373
20. Alexander Dispatch, 2952
21. Churchill, VI, p. 105
22. Clark, p. 376

NOTES TO CHAPTER TWENTY-ONE

1. *91st Division*, p. 152
2. *91st Division*, p. 163
3. *Fifth Army History*, pp. 351–2
4. *Fifth Army History*, p. 353
5. Clark, p. 374
6. From a letter written home by Lieut. Paul Carr, 3rd Battalion, Welsh Guards, October 1944, supplied to the author
7. Cyril Ray: *Algiers to Austria: A History of 78th Division in the Second World War*, Eyre and Spottiswoode, 1952, p. 161
8. *Fifth Army History*, p. 362
9. Ray, pp. 166–7, and Nicholson, p. 604
10. *1st Division*, pp. 54–5
11. From notes supplied to the author by Major-General Sir Peter St Clair-Ford

12. From a paper prepared by Lieut.-Col. O. R. C. Carey, D.A.Q.M.G., 8th Indian Division
13. *1st Division*, p. 60

NOTES TO CHAPTER TWENTY-TWO

1. Alexander Dispatch, 2955
2. Kesselring, p. 213
3. Loughnan: p. 379, account by Trooper R. Pinney
4. Clark, p. 375
5. Alexander Dispatch, 2954
6. *91st Division*, p. 187
7. *91st Division*, p. 183
8. *Fifth Army History*, p. 360
9. Clark, pp. 378–79
10. Alexander Dispatch, 2954
11. Deakin: *The Brutal Friendship*, p. 734, and Roberto Battaglia: *Storia della Resistenza italiana:* chapters headed *La crisi invernale* and *La crisi e superata, passim.*
12. Roberto Battaglia, p. 402

Bibliography

Alexander, Field-Marshal Earl: 'The Allied Armies in Italy', dispatch published as supplement to the *London Gazette*, 6 June 1950

Alexander, Field-Marshal Earl: *The Alexander Memoirs 1940–45*, Cassell, 1962

Barclay, Brig. C. N. (ed.): *The London Scottish in the Second World War*, William Clowes and Sons

Battaglia, Roberto: *Storia della Resistenza italiana*, Einaudi, Turin, 1953

Beddington, Maj.-Gen. W. R.: *A History of the Queen's Bays 1929–35*, Warren and Sons Ltd., The Wykeham Press, Winchester

Bohmler, Col. Rudolf: *Monte Cassino*, Cassell, 1964

Bright, Joan (ed.): *The Ninth Queen's Royal Lancers 1936–45: The Story of an Armoured Regiment in Battle*, Gale and Polden, 1951

Bryant, Arthur: *The Turn of the Tide 1939–43*, Collins 1957

Bryant, Arthur: *Triumph in the West 1943–46*, Collins, 1959

Bullen, Roy E.: *History of the 2nd/7th Battalion The Queen's Royal Regiment 1939–46*, printed by Besley and Copp, Exeter

Churchill, Winston: *The Second World War*: Volumes IV, V, and VI, Cassell, 1948–54

Clark, General Mark: *Calculated Risk*, Harrap, 1951

Cody, J. F.: '*21 Battalion*' (*Official History of New Zealand in the Second World War*), War History Branch, Department of Internal Affairs, Wellington, 1953

Deakin, F. W.: *The Brutal Friendship: Mussolini, Hitler, and the Fall of Italian Fascism*, Weidenfeld and Nicolson, 1962

Ehrman, John: *Grand Strategy*, Volumes V and VI. *History of the Second World War: United Kingdom Military Series*. H.M.S.O., 1956

Foster, Maj. R. C. G. (compiler): *History of The Queen's Royal Regiment: Volume VIII 1924–48*, printed for the Regimental History Committee by Gale and Polden

Gellhorn, Martha: *The Face of War*, Rupert Hart-Davies, 1959

Gilbert, Felix (ed.): *Hitler Directs His War: The Secret Records of his Daily Military Conferences*, Oxford University Press, New York

Goebbels, Joseph: *The Goebbels Diaries*, Hamish Hamilton, 1948

Greenfield, Kent Roberts (ed.): *Command Decisions*, Methuen, 1960

Heymann, Ludwig: *Geschichte des Grenadier-Regiments 992*, Pohl-Drückerei und Verlagsanstalt, Celle

Howe, George F.: *The Battle History of the 1st Armored Division*, Combat Forces Press, Washington, 1954

Johnston, Brig. R. F.: *Regimental Fire: The Honourable Artillery Company in World War II*, printed by Williams, Lea and Co., London

Keilig, Wolf: *Das Deutsche Heer*, Podzun-Verlag, Bad Nauheim

Kesselring, Albert: *The Memoirs of Field-Marshal Kesselring*, William Kimber, 1953

Knight, Col. C. R. B.: *Historical Records of the Buffs* (Royal East Kent Regiment), The Medici Society, 1951

Liddell Hart, Captain B. H. (ed.): *The Rommel Papers*, Collins, 1953

Liddell Hart, Captain B. H.: *The Tanks*, Cassell, 1959

Liddell Hart, Captain B. H.: *The Other Side of the Hill*, Cassell, 1948

Linklater, Eric: *The Campaign in Italy*, H.M.S.O. 1951

Loughnan, R. J. M.: *'Divisional Cavalry' (Official History of New Zealand in the Second World War)*, 1963

McAvity, Lieut.-Col. J. M.: *Lord Strathcona's Horse (Royal Canadians)*, Toronto, 1947

Macdonald, Charles B. and Mathews, Sidney B.: *'Three Battles: Arnaville, Altuzzo, and Schmidt' (U.S. Army in World War II)*, Office of the Chief of Military History, Washington, 1952

Mackay, Col. J. N.: *History of the 7th Duke of Edinburgh's Own Gurkha Rifles*, William Blackwood and Sons, Ltd, 1962

Martineau, G. D.: *History of the Royal Sussex Regiment 1701–1953*

Montgomery, Field-Marshal Earl: *Memoirs*, Collins, 1958

Muir, Augustus: *The First of Foot: The History of the Royal Scots* (The Royal Scots History Committee, printed by Blackwood, 1961)

Masters, Capt. J. W. A.: *The 2nd Battalion The Sherwood Foresters 1939–45*, Gale and Polden, 1946

Nalder, Maj.-Gen. R. F. H.: *The Royal Corps of Signals* (Royal Signals Institution), 1959

Neville, Lieut.-Col. Sir J. E. H. (ed.): *The Oxford and Buckinghamshire Light Infantry War Chronicle, Vol. IV*, Gale and Polden, 1954

Nicholson, Lieut.-Col. G. W. L.: '*The Canadians in Italy 1943–5*' (*Official History of the Canadian Army, Vol. II*), published Edmond Cloutier, Queen's Printer and Controller of Stationery, Ottawa, 1957

Pal, Dr Dharm: '*The Campaign in Italy 1943–5*' (*Official History of the Indian Armed Forces in the Second World War*), Combined Inter-Services Historical Section, India and Pakistan, 1960

Parkinson, C. Northcote: *Always a Fusilier: The War History of the Royal Fusiliers*, Sampson Low, 1949

Puttick, Sir Edward: '*25th Battalion*' (*Official History of New Zealand in the Second World War*), 1960

Ray, Cyril: *Algiers to Austria: A History of 78 Division in the Second World War*, Eyre and Spottiswoode, 1952

Rissik, David: *The D.L.I. at War*, Durham Light Infantry Depot, 1953

Robbins, Maj. Robert A.: *The 91st Infantry Division in World War II*, Infantry Journal Press, Washington, 1947

Schultz, Paul L.: *The 85th Infantry Division in World War II*, Infantry Journal Press, Washington, 1949

Scott Daniell, David: *Fourth Hussar: The Story of the Fourth Queen's Own Hussars 1685–1953*, Gale and Polden, 1959

Scott Daniell, David: *Regimental History of the Royal Hampshire Regiment: Vol. 3, 1918–54*, Gale and Polden, 1955

Senger und Etterlin, Frido von: *Neither Fear nor Hope*, Macdonald, 1963

Starr, Lieut.-Col. Chester G.: *From Salerno to the Alps: A History of the Fifth Army*, Infantry Journal Press, Washington, 1948

Stevens, Lieut.-Col. G. R.: *Fourth Indian Division*, published by McLaren and Sons, printed in Toronto

Taylor, A. J. P.: *English History 1914–1945*, Oxford University Press, 1965

Trevor-Roper, H. R. (ed.): *Hitler's War Directives 1939–45*, Sidgwick and Jackson, 1964

Vaughan-Thomas, Wynford: *Anzio*, Longmans, Green, 1961

Warlimont, Walter: *Inside Hitler's Headquarters*, Weidenfeld and Nicolson, 1964

Westphal, General Siegfried: *The German Army in the West*, Cassell, 1952

Williams, David: *The Black Cats at War: the 56th (London) Division 1939–45*, typescript, Imperial War Museum and Ministry of Defence Library

Williamson, Hugh: *The Fourth Division 1939–45*, Newman Neame, 1951

Wilson, Field-Marshal Lord: *Report by the Supreme Commander Mediterranean to the Combined Chiefs of Staff on the Italian Campaign:* Part II May 1944 to August 1944, and Part III August 1944 to December 1944, H.M.S.O. 1948

UNIT HISTORIES NOT ATTRIBUTED TO ANY AUTHOR

The Story of 46 Division: printed in Austria at the end of the war

North Irish Horse Battle Report: North Africa-Italy 1943–5

The 2nd Battalion The Royal Fusiliers 1943–5, Gale and Polden

History of the 1st Battalion The King's Shropshire Light Infantry 1943–5. Typescript

History of the 3rd Medium Regiment R.A. 1939–45, Northern Publishing Co., Liverpool

History of the First Division: Florence to Monte Grande, printed in Cairo

The War History of 337, 338 and 461 Mountain Batteries, R.A.

The 10th Royal Hussars in the Second World War, Gale and Polden, 1948

History of the 2nd Armoured Brigade, Typescript, Imperial War Museum

Swift and Bold: The Story of the King's Royal Rifle Corps in the Second World War, Gale and Polden, 1949

The 2nd/6th Battalion The Queen's Royal Regiment in the Italian Campaign. Pamphlet

The Tiger Triumphs: The Story of Three Great Divisions in Italy, H.M.S.O., 1946

General Index

Alexander, Gen. Sir Harold: background and temperament, 13–14; warns on effect of Operation Anvil, 20; estimate of forces needed for Gothic Line assault, 21; receives Gothic Line directive, 22–3; accepts Leese's change of plan, 30–31; new plan, 36–8; desires advance on Vienna, 51; visits front, 113; asks for Polish reinforcements, 117; signal to Brooke about reinforcements, 159; assessment of Romagna as anti-tank country, 161; warns Wilson on difficulties, 188; assessment of McCreery, 192; asks Eisenhower for reinforcements, 194–5; coolness with Devers, 195; discusses landing in Yugoslavia, 208–10; other references: 29, 48, 52, 116, 158, 182, 183, 189, 192, 215, 218

Ancona: 11, 33, 82

Anvil, Operation: 18–20, 22, 29, 164, 195, 196

Anzio: 11, 12, 14

Arbuthnott, Maj.-Gen. Robert Keith: 202–3

Asquith, Lieut.-Col. D. V. H.: 87, 92, 152

Autumn Fog, Operation: see Herbstnebel, Operation

Baade, Lieut.-Gen. Ernst Gunter: 142, 152, 157, 190, 218

Block, Brig. Allen: 55, 56, 133

Bologna: 22, 33, 37, 38, 52, 70, 93, 112, 163, 165, 183, 186–8, 194, 201, 210, 212–15

Brooke, Gen. Sir Alan: assessment of Marshall, 7; and of Alexander, 13; in Rome, 49; criticism of Alexander, 51; at Second Quebec Conference, 115; signal from Alexander about reinforcements, 159 other references: 8, 9

Burns, Maj.-Gen. Eedson: 40, 47, 62, 100

Burton, Private Richard: wins Victoria Cross, 207

Caesar Line: 198

Cassino: 11, 42, 128

Casualties: Kesselring's estimate of losses caused by partisans, 35–6; Eighth Army and German by first week September, 112; estimated German at Gemmano Ridge, 128; estimated Eighth Army daily loss for middle September, 131;

Index of Military Formations

Brigades – *continued*
10th British Infantry: 137
11th Canadian Infantry: 124
11th Indian Infantry: 127
12th British Infantry: 126, 136
18th British Infantry: 74-5, 96, 99, 124, 159
21st British Tank: 40, 143
25th British Tank: 41, 100
28th British Infantry: 136
43rd Gurkha Lorried: 74, 75, 159
128th British Infantry: 55, 56, 67
138th British Infantry: 68, 119
139th British Infantry: 55, 133
167th British Infantry: 70, 71, 102, 103, 108
168th British Infantry: 70, 71, 102, 103, 104
169th British Infantry: 68, 69, 106, 108, 120

Units (Royal Armoured Corps)
Queen's Bays: 74, 83, 84, 90-2, 96, 146, 147-53, 155-7
4th Hussars: 74, 84-6, 87, 94
7th Hussars: 121
9th Lancers: 74, 82, 84, 87, 93, 96-8, 102, 124, 146, 147, 156-7
10th Hussars: 74, 84, 87, 88-9, 93, 146
2nd Royal Tank Regiment: 70, 122-3
8th Royal Tank Regiment: 108
12th Royal Tank Regiment: 65
48th Royal Tank Regiment: 64, 143
145th Royal Armoured Corps Regiment: 143-4, 160
North Irish Horse: 46, 137

Units (Reconnaissance Corps)
44th Reconnaissance: 70, 105, 107, 108

Units (Canadian Armoured)
British Columbia Dragoons: 64
Lord Strathcona's Horse: 64

Units (New Zealand Armoured)
Divisional Cavalry: 189, 211-12

Units (British Infantry)
2nd Bedford: 137
6th Black Watch: 126, 135
1st Buffs: 74, 93, 96
2nd Camerons: 62, 127-8, 139-40
6th Cheshire: 108
16th D.L.I.: 119
5th Foresters: 56-7
14th Foresters, 74
1st/4th Hampshire: 57-8
2nd Hampshire: 56, 134
2nd/4th Hampshire: 136
5th Hampshire: 44, 67, 134
1st K.R.R.C.: 39, 88-9, 97, 147
2nd King's: 136
2nd/4th K.O.Y.L.I.: 119
9th K.O.Y.L.I.: 74, 100, 148
6th Lincoln: 119-20
2nd/5th Leicester: 55-6, 57-8, 133-4
1st London Irish: 103
1st London Scottish: 103, 105-6
7th Ox and Bucks: 71, 107-8, 146
2nd/5th Queen's: 108-10, 146
2nd/6th Queen's: 69, 108-10, 121
2nd/7th Queen's: 108-11, 121-3
2nd Royal Fusiliers: 126, 135
8th Royal Fusiliers: 71, 104-5